THE SHAAR PRESS

THE JUDAICA IMPRINT
FOR THOUGHTFUL PEOPLE

Encounters

THE
SHAAR
PRESS

RABBI NACHMAN SELTZER

With Greatness

Rabbi Daniel Yaakov Travis reflects
on his interactions with outstanding Torah personalities
of our generation

Published by **SHAAR PRESS**
Distributed by MESORAH PUBLICATIONS, LTD.
4401 Second Avenue / Brooklyn, N.Y 11232 / (718) 921-9000

Distributed in Israel by SIFRIATI / A. GITLER
POB 2351 / Bnei Brak 51122

Distributed in Europe by LEHMANNS
Unit E, Viking Business Park, Rolling Mill Road / Jarrow, Tyne and Wear, NE32 3DP/ England

Distributed in Australia and New Zealand by GOLDS WORLD OF JUDAICA
3-13 William Street / Balaclava, Melbourne 3183 / Victoria Australia

Distributed in South Africa by KOLLEL BOOKSHOP
Northfield Centre / 17 Northfield Avenue / Glenhazel 2192, Johannesburg, South Africa

ISBN 10: 1-4226-2049-2 / ISBN 13: 978-1-4226-2049-6

Printed in the United States of America
Custom bound by Sefercraft, Inc. / 4401 Second Avenue / Brooklyn N.Y. 11232

~Kollel Toras Chaim

BUILDING FUTURE POSKIM TO SERVE KLAL YISRAEL

Harav Daniel Yaakov Travis
FOUNDER & ROSH KOLLEL

Senior Faculty

Rabbi Yonason Harris
DIRECTOR OF WRITING TESHUVOS

Rabbi Shlomo Menschel
DIRECTOR OF TORAS CHAIM

Rabbi Menachem Veiner
DIRECTOR OF NISHMAS KEDOSHIM

Rabbi Avraham Peron
DIRECTOR OF TIME MANAGEMENT

Dedications

Mr. Naftali Leshkowitz
SHAYLOS & TESHUVOS PROGRAM

Mr. Kalman Oppenheimer
WALL STREET TORAH PROGRAM

Mr. and Mrs. Philip Travis
ROSH KOLLEL'S SHIURIM

Mrs. Doris Travis
WOMENS DIVISION

Yachad Kollel - LA, California
YARCHEI KALLA PROGRAM

Mr. Meir Weinraub
HARAV SHLOMO BREVDA
MUSSAR PROGRAM

Mr. Aryeh Michelson
NVC PROGRAM

Kollel Toras Chaim Dedicates "Encounters With Greatness" To the Rabbanim HaGaonim Who Guided the Kollel in the Past

Rav Shlomo Zalman Auerbach *zt"l*
Rav Yisroel Belsky *zt"l*
Rav Shlomo Brevda *zt"l*
Rav Nachman Bulman *zt"l*
Rav Aryeh Finkel *zt"l*
Rav Shimshon Pincus *zt"l*
Rav Moshe Shapira *zt"l*
Rav Shlomo Wolbe *zt"l*

Kollel Toras Chaim Dedicates "Encounters With Greatness" To the Rabbanim HaGaonim Who Guide the Kollel Today

HaGavad Rav Moshe Sternbuch *shlit"a*

Rav Asher Arieli *shlit"a*
Rav Ezriel Auerbach *shlit"a*
Rav Yitzchak Berkowitz *shlit"a*
Rav Dovid Cohen *shlit"a*
Rav Shlomo Fisher *shlit"a*
Rav Yaakov Hillel *shlit"a*
Rav Yehoshua Kalish *shlit"a*
Rav Yitzchak Kaufman *shlit"a*
Rav Ben Tzion Kermaier *shlit"a*
Rav Tzvi Kushelevsky *shlit"a*
Rav Moshe Meiselman *shlit"a*
Rav Baruch Moskowitz *shlit"a*
Rav Shlomo Yedid Zafrani *shlit"a*

JERUSALEM LOCATION 10 Michal Street, Sanhedria, Jerusalem ▪ DSL: 718-337-8531 ▪ dytravis@actcom.com
USA OFFICE c/o Travis Family, 67-66 108th Street, Apt. D6, Forest Hills, NY 11375 ▪ 347-808-8380

Contents

Preface

There are many halachos in the *Shulchan Aruch*, and each of them play an integral part in leading a Torah life. But there is one halachah that I have personally built my life on: "A person should accustom himself to say, '*Kol man d'avid Rachmana l'tav avid* — Everything that the Merciful One does is for the best'" (*Orach Chaim* 230:5, based on *Berachos* 60b).

While this halachah sounds great in theory, when a person is under fire with the most intense *nisyonos* he can imagine, it becomes much more difficult to follow. How does a person put into practice these words of our Sages? How can one come to a true recognition that what looks bad is in truth good in disguise?

Chazal teach us, "A person cannot free himself from prison" (*Sanhedrin* 95a). Rashi explains that a person who is suffering doesn't have the clarity of mind to extricate himself from his own difficulties. Often, when someone is suffering, he needs other people to help get him out of his crisis. He needs people from the outside who can look at his life objectively and advise him.

Turning to Gedolei Yisrael

From the time my wife and I got engaged, we were bombarded with a plethora of trying circumstances. The situation became so dire that my wife and I weren't sure how we would muster the strength to go on. It was during that period of intense darkness that Hashem showed me the powerful light of *gedolei Yisrael*.

After being saved miraculously from near death in a mugging, a car accident, and many other tribulations, I decided to express my thanks to Hashem by publishing a *sefer* on giving thanks titled *Mizmor L'Sodah*, after the psalm of thanks (*Tehillim* 100) that we say in our daily *tefillos*. Before publishing the *sefer*, I went to many *gedolim* seeking *divrei Torah* on the topic, and I took the opportunity to ask them what we could do to get out of our formidable situation.

Each of the *gedolim* shed new light on our circumstances with their advice, and I established a relationship with many of them. It was then that I truly realized the great gift we have in our *gedolei Yisrael* and wanted to grow as much as possible from their wisdom.

Diamonds Caked in Mud

One of the most significant relationships I forged was with Rav Shlomo Brevda, *zt"l*. He taught me that in times of *tzaros*, Hashem wants our heartfelt *tefillos*. These times of darkness are in truth Hashem calling out to us to come closer and closer to Him.

Rav Brevda wrote a special *tefillah* just for me and promised me almost prophetically that if I recited this *tefillah* with all my heart, in time the *tzaros* would subside. I saw Rav Brevda's words come true, and for the next eighteen years consulted with the *rav* at every major juncture in my life.

Rav Brevda instilled within me that *tefillah* is not a periodic experience; it is a constant mitzvah, as David HaMelech expressed, "I am prayer" (*Tehillim* 109:4).

When the smoke from these tribulations started to clear, I came to the realization that all the struggles that my wife and I had gone through had led to tremendous growth. As Rav Moshe Shapiro, *zt"l*, remarked to me, "We do not ask for *yissurim*, but we are not *mevater* even one of them." I realized that hidden by the darkness of these difficulties was the beautiful light of Hashem.

Since I have come to this recognition, I have tried constantly to live by the directive of the *Shulchan Aruch* to constantly say and believe that everything the Merciful One does is good. I have seen with my own eyes how it changed my life completely. Besides experiencing a life of much greater serenity, I have seen how the situations that appear the worst are in truth a beautiful diamond cloaked in cakes of mud.

My Personal Megillah

Rav Shlomo Wolbe, *zt"l*, taught me that each person writes his own *Megillas Esther*. In order to see the light of Hashem in one's difficulties, one needs to write down all of his experiences and then view them in the totality — as one "megillah." Following Rav Wolbe's directive, over the past years I have written down incidents of great *hashgachah pratis* that I have witnessed myself. It seemed to me that after experiencing so many incidents of Divine Providence, it was incumbent on me to put them together into one work and publicize the great kindness Hashem has shown me.

But, as I mentioned, it's difficult for a person to see his life objectively enough to produce such a work. Although I've published numerous *sefarim*, I searched for the *mechaber* of my personal megillah.

I learn in a *beis midrash* located in Sanhedria, in Yerushalayim, and many *talmidei chachamim* come from outside the city to study there. One of them is Rabbi Nachman Seltzer, who learned *daf yomi* there with his father for many years. Very impressed with Rabbi Seltzer's renowned and vibrant writing skills, I approached him to help me write my megillah.

Rabbi Seltzer agreed on one condition. He showed me that in truth my megillah was not merely my personal story, but it included a tapestry of experiences, insights, and inspiration that I had gained from *gedolei Yisrael*.

It was from this recognition that *Encounters With Greatness* was born.

"HaPa'am Odeh Es Hashem"

(Bereishis 29:35)

Leah was the first individual to properly thank Hashem *(Berachos* 7b). Although there had been many before her who had also expressed gratitude, she innovated thanking Hashem for things that appear to be bad: Her children were born as a result of her "being hated," and she thanked Hashem not only for the children, but for the entire experience. I humbly follow in her footsteps and try to emulate her, expressing my thanks to the Almighty for both that which looks good and that which looks bad.

The number of individuals I must thank is countless, and each one knows how much love and appreciation I have to them for helping me. I can't thank Rabbi Seltzer enough for helping me write my megillah and gaining a clearer picture of how much my life has been shaped by the guidance of *gedolei Yisrael*. May he continue to bring merit to the public with his inspirational works.

I am obligated to express thanks to my parents and in-laws, who have given my wife and me life in this world, and to all of my *rebbeim*, who have given me life in the next world.

My children and son-in-law have stood by my side at all times, and I have inexpressible gratitude to all of them.

My wife and I have gone through many experiences together,

and words could not do justice to her great *mesirus nefesh*. The only thing I can put into words is that everything I have is hers. May we be *zocheh* together to see Hashem's light in this world and the next, and may we have continued *nachas* from our wonderful children and grandchildren. May Hashem shower His great kindness on them all and on the rest of the Jewish nation. Most importantly, may He give us the peace of mind to recognize that buried within the deepest darkness is infinite light, and may He help us access this light by opening our eyes and our hearts to turn to Him at all times.

If we accustom ourselves to following the ruling of the *Shulchan Aruch* and say, "*Kol man d'avid Rachmana l'tav avid,* Everything the Merciful One does is for the best," I believe every person will come to the recognition that "It's All Good!" *Amen, kein yehi ratzon.*

Rabbi Daniel Yaakov Travis

"HaPa'am Odeh es Hashem"
Adar 5778, Yerushalayim

Prologue

riday morning. Rabbi Daniel Yaakov Travis has just left Yeshivas Heichal HaTorah to purchase things he will need for his baby daughter's kiddush.

The Yerushalayim air is fresh and cool on his skin, and he is in an excited frame of mind. The trip to the nearby shop shouldn't take long at all.

But as he steps out onto Givat Shaul Street, the unexpected and the tragic happens: he is hit by a car and thrown a devastating ten feet into the air. When he lands, it is squarely on his head.

This is how the real story begins.

Encounters With

Rav
Shlomo Brevda
זצ"ל

Artist of Prayer

"If you're sitting next to someone in shul," he said to me once, "and you don't say hello to him, that's sinas chinam. You are not allowed to be caught up with yourself to the point where you don't pay attention to the Yid next door. And you have to fargin people. You don't get extra credit for that. These are the basics of being a Jew!"

Chapter One

I was hit by a car on an *erev Shabbos*, four weeks after my daughter was born. I had just left my yeshivah building — I was learning in Heichal HaTorah, Rav Tzvi Kushelevsky's yeshivah, at the time — and was descending the stairs alongside the Zupnick *shtiebel* to purchase food for a *kiddush* when my entire life changed from one second to the next.

The yeshivah was located on Givat Shaul Street, an extremely busy artery that merged with the Tel Aviv–Jerusalem highway as it entered the city. Buses were constantly coming and going in both directions, and the sounds of traffic were an integral component of life on that street at all hours of the day and night.

A bus had pulled up to a nearby bus stop to allow passengers to get off and on. It blocked my vision from seeing oncoming traffic but didn't stop a speeding car, driven by a seventeen-year-old, from trying to save half a minute by detouring around it. He swerved back into the proper lane just in time to hit me head-on, the force of the collision throwing me ten feet into the air.

The trauma of being hit so forcefully was horrific, but nothing compared to the way I landed — which was headfirst on the concrete. One onlooker would later tell me that he had been on the bus and seen the accident from the window. "You went flying up into the air," he said, showing me the angle at which I'd flown, "and then you came down like this," and he made a straight line with his hand, indicating the near fatal angle at which I had hit the pavement.

"I couldn't sleep for a long time after I saw what happened to you" was how he put it.

As I lay in the street, blood gushing from my battered head, a watermelon truck came screeching to a stop, literally resting on my legs and barely managing to avoid running me over. The driver jumped out of the truck, ripped his own shirt off his body to staunch the blood, and Rav Aharon Fisher, who "happened" to volunteer for Hatzolah and "happened" to be there at the right time, bandaged my injuries himself.

Everyone on the street thought I was dead. It was impossible to think otherwise. I had been flung through the air like a rag doll and came down on my head. The trauma to my skull was immense. It was clear to every one of the witnesses that the only thing left to do was call the *chevrah kaddisha*.

My dear friend Rav Ben Zion Kermaier arrived at the scene, frantic with worry, to be told by those who had seen the whole thing, "He's dead."

The ambulance driver who transported me to Hadassah Hospital (another friend of mine) would later tell me, "We delivered you with every expectation that you were dead. There was no way anyone could have survived that accident — the free throw and the landing."

I opened my eyes as they were wheeling the stretcher through the hospital doors and noticed a doctor staring down at me, a serious expression on his face.

"Don't worry," he said, "you've just arrived at the best hospital in Israel."

That's when I really started to worry.

Which I did for about a second, before losing consciousness yet again.

◆　◆　◆

My wife, of course, had rushed to the hospital — not simple for a woman who had given birth just a few weeks earlier. But her worry changed to wonder when the hospital performed a CT scan: there was no sign of any damage to the brain whatsoever. The professor who was handling my case, one of the top neurology specialists countrywide, couldn't get over what he was seeing.

"I don't believe in G-d," he said to my wife, "but this is a miracle!"

◆ ◆ ◆

I went on to recover. My recovery challenged all logic and common sense, and there was no way to explain it from a purely medical perspective. When I left the hospital and returned to everyday life, one of my first stops was the Gra Shul in Shaarei Chesed where I knew that I'd find Rav Shlomo Zalman Auerbach, *zt"l*, in the minutes before it was time to daven Minchah. I was intent on asking him two questions that were weighing on my mind.

The first question I had imagined was open and shut, but I decided to ask him anyway. Both *Maseches Berachos* (*daf* 54a) and the *Shulchan Aruch, Orach Chaim* (*siman* 218), discuss the concept of making a blessing in a place where one experienced a miracle (the *berachah* is "*she'asah li neis bamakom hazeh* — Who did a miracle for me in this place"), and I wanted to know whether it was incumbent on me to recite this *berachah* at the scene of the accident.

I asked the question, describing the scene to the best of my abilities. Rav Shlomo Zalman heard me out in silence, looked me in the eye, and replied with an unequivocal no. I did not have to recite the *berachah*.

I was shocked.

"But, Rebbi," I protested, "I was hit by a car and thrown ten feet in the air. Then I landed directly on my head, which sustained the full brunt of the trauma. My wife was told there was no way I'd survive!"

"Even so," Rav Shlomo Zalman reiterated, "this is not called a miracle."

"But, Rebbi, if what happened to me isn't considered a miracle, then what is?"

Rav Shlomo Zalman, who was in his eighties at the time, jumped vigorously out of his chair in my direction and pronounced, "If a lion jumps on top of you and you manage to survive, that's called a miracle!"

To be honest, I still couldn't understand how he didn't think my survival of the accident was a miracle, when in my mind there was no question at all that it was a huge *neis*. But I wasn't going to argue with him further; he had answered my question. And yet, I found the answer hard to accept. Really, how could it be that he didn't consider my being thrown ten feet up in the air and landing on my head and living to tell about it, a miracle?

Then I asked him my second question.

"My life was saved. Everyone agrees that the chances of my ever being able to walk, talk, or even think again were close to zero. I can't help thinking that Hashem probably wants me to change my life in some way."

"You're right," Rav Shlomo Zalman said, this time agreeing with me.

"So what should I do?"

"I can't answer that for you. You need to figure out for yourself what it is that you need to do."

So ended our conversation.

◆　◆　◆

I left Rav Shlomo Zalman, at a loss. Here I had imagined that my question was open and shut and found to my great surprise that he didn't agree with my halachic assessment. I truly felt that what had happened to me was an outright miracle and wanted to celebrate my wondrous survival with a *seudas hoda'ah* and the recitation of the *berachah* of *she'asah li neis* with intense *kavannah* right at the spot where I had been hit and sent airborne.

The *she'eilah*, and Rav Shlomo Zalman's subsequent reply, gave me no rest. I was puzzled by his reasoning, and in an effort to clarify it I discussed the question with numerous *talmidei chachamim*, among them Rav Yosef Shalom Elyashiv, *zt"l*, who *paskened* that being thrown ten feet into the air and living to tell the tale most certainly did enter the category of miracle. Virtually every one of those I conferred with differed with Rav Shlomo Zalman's *psak*, a ruling that followed one particularly stringent opinion.

I had unaccountably found myself in the middle of a complex *machlokes* in halachah between Rav Shlomo Zalman Auerbach on one side and his son Rav Ezriel Auerbach, Rav Yosef Shalom Elyashiv, and numerous other *poskim* on the other side. After a few weeks of serious halachic research, I returned to Rav Shlomo Zalman and asked him again.

"No, no," he said to me. "It's not a miracle and you don't make the *berachah*."

Until then I had never learned halachah in a serious way and had certainly never written anything on halachic matters. Yet having found myself embroiled in a *machlokes* that directly pertained to my life, I began researching the issue and writing down what each *posek* had to say on the matter, as well as my own halachic conclusions. It took time, but the pages began adding up, and one day I took a look at everything I had written down and found to my surprise that I was holding a *kuntres* in my hand. It was personal, well researched, and, at about seventy pages, fairly comprehensive.

I hadn't planned on writing a *sefer* on the topic, but Rav Shlomo Zalman's *psak* had given me no rest. It had sent me to the homes and yeshivos of many *gedolim*, the majority of whom differed with Rav Shlomo Zalman's *psak*. In the end, I was convinced to sit down and study the *sugya* myself until I arrived at a clear understanding of all the opinions involved. My research was as extensive as could possibly be in the days before the era of downloading computer programs containing the entire Torah. This was over twenty years ago, and back then there were no shortcuts. If you wanted to know a *sugya*, you had to open the *sefarim* yourself and delve inside for the answers.

As part of my research, I visited the library at Hebrew University in Jerusalem and took out over three hundred *sefarim* pertaining to the *Orach Chaim* section of *Shulchan Aruch*. I checked out every single *sefer* and *kuntres* ever written on the topic of making the *berachah* in question and finally achieved a certain degree of peace of mind on the subject.

◆ ◆ ◆

One day I was discussing the idea of publishing the *sefer* with a friend who had actually been outside the yeshivah when it happened and witnessed my accident.

"It's a very nice *kuntres*," he said to me, "but who's going to buy a *kuntres* on such an obscure topic?"

"What do you suggest I do, then?"

"How about if you turn the *kuntres* into a *sefer* on giving thanks to the Ribbono shel Olam for the millions of kindnesses that He does for us every single day? It should be a *sefer* on the topic of thanking Hashem."

I considered his idea. The more I thought about it, the more I liked it.

The subsequent *sefer* would completely change my life in every way. Now that I was compiling a comprehensive *sefer* on the topic of giving thanks — the first seventy pages devoted to the original *she'eilah*, the rest to the concept of giving praise — I began retracing my steps to the homes of every single one of the twenty-five *gedolim* whom I had consulted regarding my earlier question. I requested that they contribute a Torah thought on the subject of giving thanks to Hashem, to be included in my forthcoming *sefer*, titled *Mizmor L'Sodah* — "Song of Thanks."

Of course, I went to Rav Shlomo Zalman Auerbach and asked him for a Torah thought for the *sefer*. I asked Rav Asher Arieli, the renowned *maggid shiur* at the Mir, for a *shtickel* Torah as well. Rav Asher had never published anything until that point, but a friend of mine who was in his *shiur* had written up one of his *shiurim* on the topic of Chanukah and *hoda'ah*, and Rav Asher agreed to have it be printed.

Rav Yitzchok Ezrachi, a *rosh yeshivah* at the Mir, had delivered a *shiur* on the exact topic of giving praise a few days before I approached him, and he graciously allowed me to use it. Rav Elyashiv was also gracious enough to give me something to include, and many other *gedolim* participated in my newfound project of thankfulness, either with a short piece on the halachic aspect of thanks or a *vort* from a hashkafic angle.

I even went so far as to contact Rav Moshe Feinstein's family in America, requesting a Torah thought from the *gadol hador* on the topic of thanking Hashem (Rav Moshe had passed on by that time), and they, too, agreed.

With many *gedolim*, the process went smoothly and I didn't have to return more than once or twice. With others it wasn't that simple, and I found myself returning to see them time and again. I had to see Rav Wolbe quite a few times before I received the actual piece in hand. This, however, would prove to be a tremendous opportunity and afforded me a chance to initiate a relationship with one of *Klal Yisrael's* masters of *mussar*.

Rav Moshe Shapiro was another *gadol* who contributed a Torah thought to my *sefer*. When we met, I told Rav Moshe the entire story from beginning to end. He gave me a lot of time and *chizuk*, but one thing in particular made a very big impression.

"*Anachnu lo mevakshim nisyonos*," he said in his beautifully poetic style of speaking. We don't ask Hashem for challenges. "*Aval al tevater al af echad meihem*." But do not forgo any one of them.

In retrospect, the terrible accident that came extremely close to ending my life served both as a catalyst for me to begin a career writing over twenty *sefarim* in many areas of halachah, *mussar*, and *hashkafah* and as an introduction to many of *Klal Yisrael's* greatest *poskim* and *ba'alei mussar*, who opened their homes to me, offered me advice and wise counsel, and were there for me in my many hours of need.

Everyone was enthusiastic and everyone was on board.

And then there was Rav Shlomo Brevda.

Chapter Two

"**W**ould the Mashgiach possibly be able to contribute a Torah thought on the topic of blessing Hashem for the *sefer* that I'm compiling?"

I had gone to see Rav Shlomo Brevda, who was on one of his frequent visits to Eretz Yisrael, with the same request I'd made of twenty other *chashuve talmidei chachamim*. He considered my petition for a while, and though he didn't explicitly promise that he would contribute, he also didn't turn me down. I understood that there was a good chance of my receiving a Torah thought from Rav Brevda for the *sefer*.

But the days passed, and I didn't hear any follow-up from Rav Brevda. So I went back to see him again. And again he agreed in somewhat noncommittal fashion to give me something to include in the *sefer*. Time went by, and still I hadn't received any Torah thought. I thought it was very possible that he wanted to help me out, but he hadn't found the right piece for the *sefer*.

By nature I'm extremely persistent (this is a theme that will come up throughout this book) and don't give up easily on matters I feel are important. I was willing to return to Rav Brevda five hundred times if that was necessary to make this happen, and since we were seeing each other so often, it wasn't long before I'd begun to open up to him. I began to tell him about my trials and challenges and share with him the many problems that kept coming our way. It was as if a dam had burst, and I couldn't hold it in any longer. Suddenly I had to share the pain in my heart, and nothing could stop me from talking.

On one visit I told him how my father-in-law had passed away in July of 1991, just before our wedding, and how it was only due to the brilliance of Rav Shlomo Zalman Auerbach that the wedding took place on the designated date. I told Rav Brevda all about our visit to Brazil to be with my mother-in-law after the *shivah*, and about wanting to daven to Hashem on a beautiful Brazilian beach near my in-laws' home in Rio. How I'd gone down there early in the morning at a time when the beach should have been completely deserted and I was almost choked to death by members of the Brazilian mafia (more on this later).

I told Rav Brevda all about the tiny apartment my wife and I had rented during our *shanah rishonah* and how I'd worked for hours to construct a succah. In the end, after putting my heart and soul into the job, I managed to build a succah I was proud of.

"What happened?" he asked me.

"Three hours before Yom Tov began I heard noises coming from outside and the sound of people breaking something. I went to investigate to find my neighbors knocking down the succah walls because they mistakenly claimed it was *pasul!*"

I told Rav Brevda how I'd been learning at Yeshivas Chofetz Chaim one evening when a neighborhood boy came rushing over to me.

"There's a fire in your apartment," he said urgently.

Though it didn't decimate our apartment completely, the fire caused considerable damage before being extinguished.

On another visit, I told Rav Brevda how we had finally purchased an apartment, only to run into legal questions of ownership, which meant we couldn't even move and we were forced to find other places to live. That winter was one of the coldest winters in Yerushalayim history. Our heat didn't work properly, the apartment was terribly drafty, there were large snowdrifts outside the front door, and nothing was going right despite our best efforts to find our footing. We were really trying our best to make things work, to no avail. No matter what we did to help ourselves, something went drastically wrong. Quite honestly, I felt like I was going out of my mind!

I poured out my heart to Rav Brevda, telling him how I had arrived home from yeshivah one evening with a pounding headache that stubbornly persisted no matter how many painkillers I took.

"It was so bad I couldn't sleep the entire night. By the time morning arrived, I felt as if a jackhammer was slamming against the side of my head. Against all odds, I managed to drag myself to shul (I attribute this to my innate stubbornness), and after davening, I all but crawled to the office of our family doctor on Pardes Street, literally collapsing on the doorstep from the awesome pain."

The doctor took one look at the hapless creature lying on his floor and diagnosed me with meningitis. He asked me a few questions about how I'd spent the night and the early morning hours before arriving at his door, and when I told him that I'd dragged myself out to daven *neitz*, he was shocked. He wouldn't have thought it humanly possible to daven Shacharis in such a physical condition.

The doctor called an ambulance, which took an hour to arrive. When the paramedics finally showed up, they seemed skeptical about the diagnosis; too many people with nothing more than a bad headache called them claiming to have meningitis. Even the doctors at the hospital didn't believe me at first and wanted to send me home, ignoring the symptoms that had sent me there in the first place and my local doctor's firm diagnosis. *Baruch Hashem*, in the end they agreed to treat me, but it was a close call.

Then, I related, our daughter was born and needed to spend time in an incubator. Israel was experiencing a heat wave, and she became dehydrated several times. On top of that she was underweight. Eventually her health stabilized, and it seemed that life was finally beginning to calm down. All this brought me to the morning of the accident and how traumatic that had been and how I had survived — just barely.

I poured out my heart to this *adam gadol*, telling him about all my troubles and about my feeling that it was too much and becoming more and more unbearable. Rav Brevda listened closely to my story, and I knew that he felt my pain in the deepest part of his heart.

◆ ◆ ◆

One day I went to see Rav Brevda, and I was feeling particularly agitated. By now I had already shared all my troubles with him, and I looked him in the eye and said, "Rebbi, I can't take it anymore! I can't go on living this way!"

Plain and simple. I wasn't being dramatic. I was at the end of my rope and facing rock bottom, financially, physically, emotionally.

Rav Brevda returned my gaze, mine despairing, his empathetic. Then he said the following:

"I hear what you're saying. Come back tomorrow and I'll have the answer to all of your problems."

No one had ever given me an answer like that before, and I was filled with a burst of cautious optimism.

Having me return the following day was a brilliant move on Rav Brevda's part. The anticipation of receiving his solution made me even more receptive to it than I would have been otherwise.

Needless to say, the next twenty-four hours were spent in a state of high anticipation as I waited to hear the answer to all my challenges. I spent much of that time wondering what he was going to say. Would he suggest a kabbalistic approach? Read to me from an ancient, secret *sefer* with brittle, yellowed pages that only he had access to?

Finally I sat before him, tapping my foot on the floor, waiting with bated breath.

"The answer to your problems," Rav Brevda declared, as if he were announcing the winner of the Powerball lottery, "is *tefillah*. Prayer!"

Then he quoted a midrash (*Shemos Rabbah* 21:5) about *Klal Yis-rael*'s state of mind in the final moments before the Splitting of the Sea.

"With scorpions and snakes on all sides, the Egyptians just behind them and the sea blocking them from continuing further, the Jews had no choice but to daven. Hashem desired their *tefillos*, so He placed them in an untenable position.

"When a person has so many problems, it means that Hashem wants his prayers! I will write a special *tefillah* just for you, and I promise you that things are going to improve in your life. I can't guarantee that this *tefillah* will work for anyone else, but I promise that it will work for you."

I sat with him for forty-five minutes as he dictated a *tefillah* to me. The *tefillah* was based on a *Gra*, and the basic idea was that we need to realize that we don't deserve anything and that everything we receive from above is an outright gift from Hashem.

He put tremendous thought into every single word that he told me to write, closing his eyes and appearing to search deep within his *neshamah* for the proper phrasing and words to use. It was obvious that Rav Brevda was treating this *tefillah* with the utmost seriousness.

When I left his presence that day, I was holding a *tefillah* in my hand that had been composed just for me, and I felt a heavy weight slipping from my shoulders.

I began saying his *tefillah* every single day, and within a short time, our life had begun to stabilize. It never became completely normal (until today we have a fascinating life with many unique challenges), but it reverted from out of control to manageable.

So began my relationship with one of the most phenomenal *ba'alei mussar* of our generation. Many people were close to him, and many people sought his advice, yet the relationship that developed between us was something few achieved.

To me this is not a surprise, since I credit Rav Brevda with saving my life.

This is part of the special *tefillah* that Rav Brevda wrote.

Recite your own personal request at the very end of *Shemoneh Esrei*, before taking three steps back, and then add the following:

אַף עַל פִּי שֶׁאֵינִי כְּדַאי לְבַקֵּשׁ בַּקָּשׁוֹת כָּאֵלּוּ, מִכָּל מָקוֹם נָא אַל תְּשִׁיבֵנִי רֵיקָם מִלְּפָנֶיךָ, כִּי בְּלֵב נִשְׁבָּר הִנְנִי מִתְחַנֵּן מִלְּפָנֶיךָ, וְעַל גְּדֶל טוּבְךָ וְרַחֲמֶיךָ הָעֲצוּמִים הִנְנִי בּוֹטֵחַ וְנִשְׁעָן, יָגֵן לִבִּי בִּישׁוּעָתֶךָ.

Even though I am not worthy to ask for such requests, nonetheless please do not return me empty-handed from before You, for I am pleading to You with a broken heart, and on Your tremendous kindness and Your incredible mercy I put all of my trust. May my heart rejoice in Your salvation.

Chapter Three

Although my situation definitely improved, there were still many challenges that arose and I sought Rav Brevda's advice time and again. Usually we met in the United States where he lived, but we also saw each other during his numerous visits to Eretz Yisrael. Or I'd call him on the phone and share whatever it was we were experiencing at the time. His ever-present answer to me was "*Tefillah* — prayer."

He made a point of stressing that ninety percent of the Chafetz Chaim's *eitzos* revolved around *tefillah*. When I was finally ready to print *Mizmor L'Sodah*, I asked Rav Brevda for permission to include the special prayer he had written for me.

"You know that it's patented," he said with a twinkle in his eye, then relented and gave me his permission.

All in all, Rav Brevda penned quite a few personal *tefillos* for me over the years. And every time we sat together, with me unburdening my heart and him listening, I wondered how he'd respond this time. But the answer and the advice was perennially the same — always focused on prayer!

◆ ◆ ◆

In 1991, when the first Gulf War was about to break out, there was overwhelming tension throughout Eretz Yisrael, as everyone wondered what the next few months would bring and whether Saddam Hussein would carry out his threats to attack the country with chemical warfare. The entire population was provided with gas masks, and there was a genuine feeling of anxiety in the air and on every face. A number of years later there was another threat of a gas attack and I called Rav Brevda.

"Rebbi, what can we do to avert what might turn out to be a terrible tragedy?"

His unpretentious answer hit me like a punch in the chest in its power and simplicity.

"Go to shul five minutes earlier than you normally do and say *Korbanos*."

"That's it?"

"That's it?!" he shot back at me. "You know what it is to say *Korbanos*? Let's see you do it for a week!"

He always stressed the importance of getting to shul on time, so that a person will be able to daven with the proper *kavannah* and *derech eretz*. He also believed that one shouldn't go straight into davening without studying a little *mussar* first to prepare oneself for talking to Hashem.

"Five minutes of *mussar* when you arrive in shul," he would say. "Then *Korbanos*, then davening."

◆ ◆ ◆

One of the things that struck a person about Rav Brevda was his directness. For many years we held a private Rosh Chodesh minyan in Mishkan Esther, a shul in the Ramat Eshkol neighborhood of Yerushalayim. It was a "slow" minyan, everyone davening with great concentration, and we'd sing the entire *Hallel* from start to finish. Rav Brevda, who didn't live nearby, didn't usually daven with our minyan, but I do recall one Rosh Chodesh when he joined us.

During the course of the *tefillah*, Rav Brevda noticed that one of the people davening with us didn't stop walking around the room.

Rav Brevda took the man to task in his direct manner, explaining that this was simply unacceptable behavior during davening.

I once asked him about his relationships with wealthy people.

"I don't have relationships with *gevirim*," Rav Brevda replied. "They all run away from me because I tell it like it is."

This might have been the case with some people, but his penchant for not sugarcoating the truth appealed to me on a very deep level. It was clear to me that he considered the character trait of *emes* of paramount significance both for himself and for the people around him.

◆ ◆ ◆

For years, Rav Brevda's *talmidim* davened with him in a special minyan on Chol HaMo'ed Succos. Rav Brevda's interaction with his *arba'ah minim* was a completely unique sight. During the recitation of *Hallel* he would literally dance with his *arba'ah minim*, and watching him shake his *lulav* and *esrog* was like seeing a warrior in battle. He wielded the *arba'ah minim* fiercely, warding off the enemy with sharp maneuvers, as if he were destroying the Satan on the battlefield with his spiritual sword.

On the one hand, he was incredibly joyous.

On the other, he was intently engaged in battle.

It was a fascinating expression of dual emotions.

Watching him daven in general was akin to being in the presence of a master artist. He'd sculpt his *tefillos*, developing them and working on them, and I would find myself thinking, *This was probably what it was like watching Betzalel design the keilim in the Mishkan.*

The attention to detail. The incredible precision and talent.

He was a master.

An artist of prayer.

◆ ◆ ◆

Rav Brevda taught me that not all prayers are created equal.

The *sefer Sha'arei Orah* discusses a type of prayer, referring to it as "*bokei'a Shamayim*," breaking open the heavens. These are prayers that come from the absolute depths of a person's heart, and they have the power to shatter the thickest walls.

One of those times when I experienced this type of *tefillah* happened after I finished writing *Praying With Joy* and submitted it to a publisher for review. The editor who reviewed it rejected it, saying, "I don't think you are going to sell too many copies of this book."

"Why not?" I asked her, my heart sinking rapidly.

"Not enough stories, too much information. Plus we just published another book on prayer."

I was absolutely devastated. I had worked extremely hard and for a very long time on the *sefer*, the theme of the *sefer* was something very dear to my heart (having personally seen major *yeshuos* through *tefillah*), and here she was telling me that printing *Praying With Joy* was going to be a complete waste of time.

"How many copies do you think it will sell?" I asked her.

"I would be very surprised if it sold more than five hundred copies."

I was terribly shaken to hear her prediction.

How could this be true? I loved this *sefer*. I had put my heart and soul into this *sefer*. Could this really be its fate?

I closeted myself in a room and spoke to Hashem from the depths of my soul. "Hashem," I cried out, "I worked so hard on this *sefer*! Please make this *sefer* successful!"

It was an *emesdige tefillah*, true and pure, and somehow I "knew" that it had been accepted by Hashem.

After that prayer, I changed the format of my book — the idea for the changes suddenly flew into my mind — and published *Praying With Joy* with a different publisher.

The *sefer* sold out and was reprinted again and again. All in all, *Praying With Joy* ended up being one of my most successful books ever, having sold upward of twenty-five thousand copies — and it's still selling.

I believe that the book's success came through a *tefillah* that emanated from the depths of my heart. I have tried to copy the success of that *tefillah* on numerous occasions throughout my life, but I've been successful on only two occasions — both times literally feeling that my *tefillah* was accepted by *Shamayim* and that I had been granted a favorable response.

There were many times in my life when I davened and Hashem answered my *tefillos*, most notably after Rav Brevda wrote my very own unique *tefillah*. But these two prayers were unique for the fact that I knew while I was davening that my *tefillos* were being accepted in *Shamayim* as I said them.

◆ ◆ ◆

When I discovered that Rav Yechezkel Levenstein writes in the *sefer Ohr Yechezkel* on *Yamim Noraim* that even a newborn child is judged on Yom Kippur, I asked Rav Brevda, who had been a close *talmid* of Rav Chatzkel's in the Mir Yeshivah in New York, for his take on the matter. His response was startling.

"Why are you busy with such things?" he questioned me in his trademark direct way. "That's not what you should be focused on! Be nice to your wife, work on *shalom bayis*, just be a mensch... That's your *avodah*!"

Rav Brevda never hesitated to be firm with his *talmidim* and to correct them if he felt they could be making better and more productive decisions. It was all about the *emes*, the truth. At any cost. He demanded a lot from his *talmidim* and expected us to be constantly striving to improve ourselves. There wasn't even one iota of anything connected to falsehood. With Rav Brevda, it was truly a case of "*tocho k'baro*," of his inner and outer selves living in complete congruence and harmony with one another.

The *middah* of *emes* was not something new in his life. It had always been with him, even back when he was a young man.

"I recall giving a speech in a shul many years ago, when I was just a *bachur*," he told me once. "I was against Jewish youth attending university due to the almost impossible challenges they were exposed to — and I told the people in the congregation my thoughts on the topic, without stinting words. This was back in the days when attending university was a bedrock value of the American Jewish community, and the people sitting in the shul were decidedly not amused by my thoughts. They started shouting and throwing things at me, and I was forced to end my speech. But I had to tell them the truth about the situation."

That was Rav Brevda. A man who stood unflinching in the face of adversity. A man who didn't blink or back down from what he considered the *ratzon* of Hashem. His essence was that of unvarnished truth, melted through the crucible of his unique sense of mission.

But though *emes* was his defining character trait, there were other sides to him equally significant. Rav Brevda possessed an unbelievable sensitivity to people's *tzaros* and needs. I have seen this character trait in almost every *gadol* whom I have known, but in the case of Rav Brevda I found the sensitivity to be of almost superhuman capacity, as was his attunement to every nuance. While there were many people who tried to help us during our difficult days, it was Rav Shlomo Brevda who "descended into the seven levels of Gehinnom" to pull us out. He actually experienced our pain, and the extent of his empathy went very far to comfort us when we needed it most.

◆ ◆ ◆

Rav Brevda considered himself a *talmid* of the Vilna Gaon, and while listening to one of his *shmuessen*, I heard him say, "Anyone who doesn't study *Mishlei* with the *peirush* of the Gra has no chance of fighting the *yetzer hara*."

By that time in my life I had already known Rav Brevda for many years. We had shared dozens of private conversations, I had heard him speak numerous times in public, and I had listened to many, many of his speeches on tape. Yet this was the first time I had heard him make such a comment. The moment I heard this line, I glanced at my watch. It was eleven-thirty in the evening, but not too late for what I had in mind.

I left my apartment and knocked on the door of my neighbor, Reb Gershon Unger.

"Gershon," I greeted him, "I just heard Rav Brevda say that the only way to fight the *yetzer hara* is by studying *Mishlei* with the commentary of the Gra. Let's start right now!"

On the spot we began a learning *seder* that has lasted for over twenty years, accompanying us through various neighborhoods and life events. Every Friday, the two of us meet to learn *Mishlei* with the commentary of the Gra, and we've gone through it cover to cover more than twice. But the battle isn't over and the more time we spend on this *limud*, the more we understand the accuracy of Rav Brevda's statement. This *seder* of ours also developed into a Sunday morning *shiur* and a Shabbos *shiur* for women and numerous *shiurim* on *Mishlei* that are available on Torah Anytime.

In retrospect, I can see that Rav Brevda truly encapsulated the ideas presented by the Gra. The Vilna Gaon stresses the idea of dissecting the *yetzer hara's* methods and of being in control of one's actions, and Rav Brevda exhibited iron control in the way he lived his life, to the point that he would measure how much water he drank every day. Not ice cream or soda — even water! And he never took seconds of anything. He felt that taking additional food after you've already had a portion to eat was just the *yetzer hara* talking to you, and besides, a person only feels full when he stops eating. For all these reasons and more, Rav Brevda was adamantly against the entire concept of a smorgasbord at weddings. He urged me to limit my intake of cake and cookies as well, saying that it was easier to fast than to eat *"l'shem Shamayim."*

◆ ◆ ◆

Rav Brevda once told me, "The Gra saved Torah in *Klal Yisrael*."

When I asked him what was the basis of this statement, he replied, "Torah was turning into *pilpul* and *sevara*, and the Gra saved the Torah because he returned it to its *shoresh*, to its source."

It is known that at the end of his life, the Vilna Gaon concentrated on learning *Chumash* to the exclusion of everything else, tracing every particle of Torah he had learned back to the original sources. As much as Rav Brevda had many *rebbeim*, he was really a *talmid* of the Gra. He was a descendant of the Gra, and he was willing to work for months on end to achieve clarity in the Gra's Torah.

I remember when Rav Brevda was writing a commentary on *Shir HaShirim* according to the Gra, and he worked for an incredible length of time to understand what the Gra intended regarding one *pasuk*! He was willing to devote months to clarifying the smallest detail. Not days or weeks — months!

At one point he had been working for six months straight trying to comprehend the *pshat* of an explanation of the Gra, and when the curtain persisted in blocking out the light, he boarded a plane and flew to Vilna, where he davened for *siyatta d'Shmaya* at the Vilna Gaon's *kever*. He received the clarity he had sought immediately afterward. Where many people would have been satisfied with mediocrity, only pushing themselves so far, that didn't work for him. He needed to find the real *pshat* — the *emes* inherent in the words of Torah. If this meant he had to work for six months on one line, then he was willing to work for six months. If it meant that he would have to fly to Vilna to daven at the Gra's *kever*, then he would fly to Vilna.

Whatever he had to do.

He had an incredible collection of the Gra's handwritten manuscripts. One time he read in one of the *kisvei yad* that if you stand in front of the Kohanim during *Birkas Kohanim* you receive more of a *berachah* — almost as if there is a beam of *kedushah* emanating from the Kohanim, and standing in front of them means that the beam hits you head-on. There were other *talmidei chachamim* who didn't accept the validity of the idea, but Rav Brevda showed them the words — black on white — and to him the matter was closed. To Rav Brevda, if the Gra said something, then it became the reality, which was why he stood in front of the Kohanim during *Birkas Kohanim* from then on.

For me, seeing Rav Brevda and the way he lived his life was like seeing the return of the Gra. The Vilna Gaon's daily intake of food was two slices of bread soaked in water. When he went to sleep, he'd leave a piece of bread to soak in water and that was his breakfast. He would then leave another piece to soak in water and that was supper.

Rav Brevda's eating habits were not that extreme (at least not to the best of my knowledge), but his basic conduct and life philosophy was the same. Nothing extra, no candies, no anything. Just the basics that he needed to survive.

The same went for his sleeping habits. At times he would deliver five *shiurim* a day in different parts of Eretz Yisrael, each of them lasting between two and three hours. Needless to say, with a schedule like that a person doesn't get much sleep. And he kept his *shiurim* down-to-earth, though he was (on his own admission) a complete expert in kabbalistic matters (the Gra is constantly quoting *Zohar*). Rav Brevda deliberately kept things relatively simple, because he felt that including the loftier parts of the Torah would distance the very people he was trying to attract.

It was an amazing thing.

At Rav Brevda's *shiurim*, you could find both ten-year-old children and *roshei yeshivah*. He instinctively knew how to talk to everyone and utilized his unique talents to do so. And though his *shiurim* lasted for hours, the time flew by.

The way he built his *shiurim* was sheer genius. First of all, he possessed a phenomenal sense of humor. Listening to him, people found themselves rolling with laughter. Yet suddenly, right in the middle of the funniest story imaginable, he'd hit you with a point of *mussar* that was all the more powerful due to the fact that it was coming at you while you were doubled over with laughter.

"When you want to give a patient medicine," he'd say, "you have to tickle him. While he's laughing and his mouth is open, that's the best time to slip it in."

Mussar was his choice of medicine, and when he spoke, you found yourself at his mercy. He was just that good.

"You probably wonder why I speak with such sharpness at times in the *shiurim*," he'd say rhetorically.

"It's because," he'd say, answering his own question, "while some of the people listening to the *shiurim* are hearing me only once a week, they hear *shiur* from the 'Rebbi' (he was referring to the *New York Times*) every day."

He was able to make people laugh because he understood them so well. He knew how they acted and how they thought, and sometimes it felt like he knew more about you than you knew about yourself. He knew how you were feeling and how to talk to you. And he would deliver the same *shiur* to five people and to a thousand people with the same enthusiasm and *geshmak*.

I remember attending one *shiur* where there was a man sitting near the front who couldn't stop chewing gum. I was very upset with the man — not only was he chewing gum, he was blowing bubbles until they popped. Rav Brevda told me after the *shiur* that the man had a difficult job and needed to chew gum so he'd be able to concentrate.

"I told him to chew gum," he said to me.

"You told him to chew gum," I repeated incredulously.

"Yes. He asked me if he should, and I told him if that's what he needs to stay awake and focused, then that's what he should do."

◆ ◆ ◆

In 2012, I went to visit Rav Brevda in the hospital in New York, when he was first diagnosed with the *machalah*. He was weak but still had all his faculties. At some point, one of the nurses asked him how he was feeling.

"I feel like I can play for the New York Yankees," he replied, making a joke for the nurse's benefit.

"The Yankees aren't doing well right now," she said. "You would probably help them do a lot better."

I knew why he tossed that line at her. He was trying to make the nurse feel good. And it wasn't only with her. He acted the same way with every person he came in contact with at that hospital. Here was a person who was having difficulty moving, who was in pain. Yet he was constantly asking himself, *How can I help make the people around me feel good?*

There was one nurse in the hospital who was cruel to him. When the person with him wanted to confront her about it, Rav Brevda motioned him to keep silent and found something about her to compliment instead, mentioning in an offhand way that it would help him if she would change a certain thing she was doing — which she did. He knew how to overcome all the character traits that cause "normal" people to do the wrong thing, and his behavior won people over because they felt connected to him and were astounded by his selflessness. He knew how to uncover the *tzelem Elokim* in every individual — even someone who was cruel to him. The feeling I had watching him was that every single thing he did and every move he made was completely thought out and nothing was done off the cuff.

I remember how sad he was when the stock market crashed. Not for himself, but for the Jews who had lost significant sums in the crash.

"Put yourself in the shoes of the wealthy man who has to explain to his wife that he just lost the majority of his money," he said to me, trying to help me climb inside the mind of another Yid. He wanted me to be able to empathize with other people, to realize that feeling another person's pain is the greatest example of what being a spiritual person really means.

Rav Brevda liked quoting the Chazon Ish on this topic.

"My greatest accomplishment," the Chazon Ish used to say, "is when people leave my home feeling good, and my greatest failure is when someone leaves my home not feeling good about themselves."

Rav Brevda used to repeat those words over and over, as if trying to brand them into his very essence. He was constantly reminding himself of his priorities: learning, davening, and the way a person treats those around him.

Rav Brevda didn't allow outside society to influence him in the slightest. He lived in a small apartment with little more than the bare necessities. A person visiting might have thought that he'd just entered the Chafetz Chaim's house. All he needed and wanted was to be able to help the people around him feel good about themselves.

Chapter Four

Rav Brevda had many great *rebbeim* in his life, Rav Chatzkel Levenstein and the Chazon Ish among them. He was also one of the first *talmidim* of the Brisker Rav when he began saying *shiur* in Yerushalayim.

Rav Brevda used to say that the Chazon Ish's persona was akin to that of a *Tanna* from the Gemara.

"When you saw the Chazon Ish, you felt like you were seeing a person who wasn't at all affected by what was going on in the world around him. It was as if he were living within a protective bubble, and none of the negative influences of the world were able to infiltrate that protective layer."

When I would hear Rav Brevda saying these things about the Chazon Ish, I'd think, *And that's exactly how you are, Rebbi! You, too, are not affected by the world around you and by the norms of society and what they consider important.*

Politics didn't interest him in the slightest. He just didn't care. All he cared about was the *emes*.

"Truth and only truth" was the modus operandi of the Chazon Ish, and this was something that his *talmid* had imbibed until it became part of his blood. The Chazon Ish also didn't care what anyone said; all he cared about was fulfilling the *ratzon* of Hashem. The rest was just not important. The same was true of Rav Chatzkel Levenstein. With *rebbeim* like these, it was no wonder that Rav Brevda developed into a person who personified pure truth.

When you discussed something with Rav Brevda and he gave you his opinion, you felt intuitively that this was real Torah with no personal interests mixed in. It was very refreshing. Even when he "gave it to you," you knew he was doing it because this was what he felt he needed to do, and that after he tore the *shtusim* out of you, he would put you back together many times stronger than you had been before.

◆ ◆ ◆

I wrote a *hesped* on Rav Brevda in one of my *sefarim*, explaining that he was a person who lived with Hashem before his eyes at all times, in a constant state of "*Shivisi Hashem l'negdi samid.*"

As Rav Brevda used to repeat in the name of the Chazon Ish, "Whenever you need *anything*, you should make a *bakashah*, a request. After you finish making the *bakashah*, you should give *hodayah*, thanks to Hashem. Say you need a new hat. 'Hashem,' you pray, 'please help me find a good hat.' After you find the hat and leave the store, you thank Hashem for helping you find the perfect hat. And that's the way you live your life and go about your day."

The next time I went to buy a hat, I davened before I entered the store. It took me three minutes, and I found a hat that was perfect for me. Of course, I then thanked Hashem for helping me find the hat. The salesman in the store looked at me as if I had fallen off the moon.

"What's wrong?" I asked him.

"Nothing's wrong," he replied. "It's just that nobody in the history of this store has ever found a hat that quickly. What's your secret?"

"*Tefillah*. That's my secret."

I was in New York trying to hail a taxi for half an hour with no success. Suddenly it dawned on me.

Why don't you daven for the taxi to come?

I said a short *tefillah*, and a taxi pulled up a minute later.

This was one of the main lessons I learned from Rav Brevda and from the original *tefillah* he wrote for me. Many people think that after you daven, you're finished. You did what you had to do and it's done. Rav Brevda taught me that *tefillah* means devoting your entire life to Hashem on an ongoing basis. It's a recognition that Hashem controls everything that happens to us.

There is no question that the more we recognize His ultimate involvement and control, the more He reveals Himself in an obvious way. The *Nefesh HaChaim* agrees with this and explicitly states that the more you recognize that Hashem is running everything, the more it becomes clear how much He does for you.

I didn't truly grasp what *tefillah* was until I met Rav Brevda. *Tefillah* is not just a matter of reciting *Shemoneh Esrei*. *Tefillah* is your life — and an awareness that you are always in Hashem's hands.

◆ ◆ ◆

When my wife was expecting our son, I spoke to Rav Brevda quite often. Once he said to me, "You have no idea how much I'm davening for you or how much work I put in for you during the pregnancy."

From the way he said the words, I understood that he was putting his complete body and soul into the *tefillos* for the success of my family, and I had the distinct feeling that he was alluding to some sort of *gezeirah* that he had abolished for us with the power of his prayers.

Rav Brevda was extremely careful about whom he formed relationships with. When I first began coming to see him, he pushed me away. When I persisted in visiting him and seeking his advice, he made inquiries about me with Rabbi Fishman, the *mashgiach* in Toras Moshe, and with others who knew me. He wasn't willing to commit to a relationship with me until he felt that he knew who I was, because once he became close to someone, he formed an extremely strong bond with that person, almost as if he had adopted him.

He did this for many of his *talmidim*, though it became harder for him as he grew older. On one occasion, when he was already old and frail, I asked him if he could daven for something.

"When I was younger, I could have done it," he said. "It's too hard for me to do it now."

His words served as an interesting insight to me as to what *tefillah* was really about. I could have asked him, "What are you talking about? Younger, older, what's the difference? Just daven!" But there's davening and there's davening.

It's well known that the Chazon Ish put all his *kochos* into everything he did. Sometimes people would find him collapsed on the floor beside his bed. He thought that he'd left himself with sufficient energy to get from the table to his bed, but he collapsed on the way.

I found that Rav Brevda's approach to life came from a similar perspective — the perspective of someone who put one hundred percent of himself into every single thing he did and was never, ever satisfied with mediocrity. While it was true that a person might never reach a level of one hundred percent or even ninety-five percent in what he did, Rav Brevda strongly felt that one should recognize where he was and always keep in mind that he wanted to reach the sky.

I'll give you an example.

Rav Brevda was one of the original *talmidim* of the Brisker Yeshivah in Yerushalayim.

"One day," he related, "I walked into the apartment of the Brisker Rav and found him crumpling up some pieces of paper."

In response to his *talmid's* inquiry as to what he was throwing out, the Brisker Rav explained.

"This is a Torah thought that I have been working on for twenty years, and today I proved it wrong, so I'm putting it in the *genizah*."

More than anything else, Rav Brevda most remembered the Brisker Rav's joy at that moment — the moment when truth prevailed; the attitude that everything in life — and, of course, one's Torah more than anything else — had to be based on the purest truth possible.

As a rebbi, Rav Brevda could be critical. If you shared a Torah thought with him that he felt wasn't as developed as it should be, he didn't hesitate to share his misgivings with you. But when he criticized me, I didn't feel bad.

Sometimes I'd ask myself, *Why is it that you feel bad when this person makes a critical comment to you, but not when the criticism is coming from Rav Brevda?*

I thought about this a lot, and in the end I came to the following conclusion. When Rav Brevda criticized, he did it for one reason: because in an ideal Torah world matters were supposed to be a certain way, and you, the person talking to him, needed to know the ideal way to live. His intent wasn't to put you down, to make you feel bad, or to build himself up at your expense. He did it because you had to know the truth about life.

It was the difference between *tochachah lishmah* and *tochachah shelo lishmah* — rebuke for the right reasons and rebuke for one's own satisfaction.

Most important of all, he was treating you exactly the way he treated himself — stripping everything down to its essence and rebuilding it to the finest specifications.

That was his mission and goal: to never accept mediocrity, not in life, Torah, or *avodas Hashem*.

He used to point out how people like attending *daf yomi shiurim*, but davening is not as popular.

"Why is that?" he'd ask.

And he'd answer, "From learning the *daf*, you get *yedios* in Torah, you get the satisfaction of finishing a *masechta*. It's all about me."

The more he reiterated these points, the more I came to the realization that if a person isn't careful, he might just discover that his entire *avodas Hashem* is completely self-centered.

After 9/11 I remember feeling as if I'd been chopped into pieces, and I was trying to figure out why I was reacting so strongly. I thought about it a lot. In the end I realized what it was. As an American I had been raised with the idea of "*kochi v'otzem yadi*," that we have the power to control the world. Yet suddenly the United States of America, seemingly the strongest country in the universe, had been brought to its knees and struck in such a powerful way by nineteen men with paper cutters. And it hurt. Because *my* country was not as strong as I thought it was. And *my* pride was wounded.

He had a joke he often repeated.

"There are a lot of fish in America," he'd say. "There's white fish and there's salmon fish, but the most popular fish of all is selfish."

"America teaches you to be selfish," he'd bemoan, "and people don't even realize it. The entire culture is devoted to me. It's all about me, and what I have and more and more and more. It never stops."

◆ ◆ ◆

A short while after 9/11, there was a spate of deadly bombings throughout Eretz Yisrael, including Yerushalayim. A number of the bombings happened in restaurants and public areas. One morning I was in a taxi and heard an interview on the radio with an owner of one of the restaurants that had been destroyed in an attack and since rebuilt.

The talk show host asked the owner for his feelings on everything that had occurred.

"I think that we need to focus completely on the future," he said. "We can't look back at all! We need to rebuild without thinking of the past!"

His words shook me up.

Later that day I happened to be near the restaurant, and I decided to go in and have a conversation with the owner.

"I heard you on the radio this morning," I said, "and I was very impressed by your determination, but don't you think that it might be a good idea to learn something from the past? I mean, you experienced a miracle. Maybe, while focusing on the future, you should still give a little thought to what happened, what Hashem wants to teach you…"

"If it happens again," he said, "maybe I'll think about what happened."

I stood there dumbstruck, shocked by his words. The man's wife was also there listening to our conversation, and I could see by the look on her face that his words had hit her just as hard as they had hit me.

An hour later I went to hear Rav Brevda speak, and his words shook me to the core because they were so relevant to what had just happened with the restaurant owner.

"No one is going to change from 9/11," he told us. "People can see the biggest miracles and not allow themselves to be affected."

As always, his words were right on the mark.

◆ ◆ ◆

Rav Brevda was the classic example of what a real rebbi should be. One time I was sitting with him when someone approached to ask him for an *eitzah*.

Rav Brevda stared at the man, and I could see that he was looking straight into his *neshamah* as he tried to figure out the best guidance to give him. He then quoted a *Gra* on *Mishlei* and told the questioner, "It used to be that a person who wanted to know what to do in life would visit a *navi*, who would give him direction. We don't have *ruach hakodesh* or *nevuah* anymore, so today a rebbi has to rely on the *siyatta d'Shmaya* of his own feelings to guide him."

He studied the man for a few minutes more, then offered him an *eitzah* and *hadrachah* — directly from the inner workings of the visitor's *neshamah*.

It was something to see.

That sharp, penetrating stare, cutting through all the outer layers, to the core within.

My reaction: *This is what a real rebbi knows how to do.*

◆ ◆ ◆

"What do you think is the *gadlus* of *Mesillas Yesharim*?" Rav Brevda would ask his *talmidim*.

"When someone speaks to another person," he would go on, answering his own question, "it makes much more of an impact than when you read something. The *Mesillas Yesharim* knew how to write with the power and impact of someone giving a speech. When you write a *sefer*," he'd add, "write the words as if you're speaking them to your readers. They should feel like you're talking to them."

◆ ◆ ◆

A lot of people who get married (truthfully the vast majority of people) don't have the slightest clue what *shalom bayis* really is. But Rav Brevda drilled it into me. Once, a few days after Purim, I was talking to him and mentioned that I had gotten drunk.

"Mitzvah, not mitzvah," he said, "but you should know, if it bothers your wife, well, that's *kodesh kodashim*. *Shalom bayis* has to come before everything else!"

With that comment he was trying to help me understand the way to measure *shalom bayis* versus everything else in life.

"Sometimes I give five *shiurim* a day," he said to me. "I can give my first *shiur* in Netivot and my last in Acco, but my wife is always up when I return home at night."

He was traversing the entire country in one day. And the *shiurim* were each three hours long and he had no *ko'ach*.

"By the end of the day, I have no strength left. Zero. After the last *shiur*, people approach me to ask me questions, and I tell them, 'I'm sorry, I can't talk to you now. My wife is waiting up for me.'"

It's easy for a person to get caught up in "spiritual things," where you can justify what you do as being "holy," even if it bothers someone else. But Rav Brevda wanted me to understand that *shalom bayis* trumps everything, and if my "holy" *avodah* was bothering my wife, then maybe it wasn't an appropriate form of *avodah* for me at this current time.

He was also a major proponent of the idea that couples needed to feel chemistry for one another, because, he said, "a couple that marries without that chemistry will in many cases run into major *shalom bayis* issues. The importance of this should not be dismissed or downplayed. To give up on this aspect of marriage can lead to *machlokes* and discord within one's home, and this is nothing more than the work of the *yetzer hara* and should be avoided at all cost."

Mundane as it might have seemed, Rav Brevda saw this as a genuine part of *avodas Hashem*, and he stressed its importance — because it was just as much *emes* as any other part of life.

I remember davening in a minyan with Rav Brevda one time where there were ten men exactly. Before we started davening, Rav Brevda made an announcement, saying that since there were only ten of us, no one should take an overly long time reciting *Shemoneh Esrei*, because that would mean that the rest of the minyan would have to wait for him to finish.

Avodas Hashem might be the keystone of what it means to be a Jew, but Rav Brevda made it crystal clear that it should never come at the expense of someone else.

◆ ◆ ◆

I used to take luggage for Rav Brevda from New York to Eretz Yisrael during the years that he traveled from the United States to Yerushalayim for Pesach. Every time I did something for him, his *hakaras hatov* was unbelievable, something akin to my having done the biggest favor he'd ever received in his entire life.

He told me that he once merited carrying a bag for Rav Aharon Kotler, and how every time Rav Aharon saw him for the rest of his life, he'd express his gratitude for that small act.

"The *mahus*, the essence, of a Jew," Rav Brevda used to say, "is *hakaras hatov*."

◆ ◆ ◆

He was the ultimate *mechanech*, never hesitating to show me the error of my ways if something needed correcting.

One of the *sefarim* I wrote is titled *Yoreh Binah*, and it is an encyclopedia of the halachos of *issur v'heter*, containing all the concepts with which a person needs to be familiar with if he wants to study these halachos in depth. I worked very hard on the *sefer*; I rewrote several of the pages one hundred times. Many of the points are subtle, and I had to make sure that I was being as clear as possible. Every week for close to three years I stayed up the entire Thursday night working on the *sefer*. Needless to say, I was overjoyed when it was finally published and available to be used by people studying for *semichah*.

Right around that time, Rav Brevda's granddaughter was getting married, and I decided that I would present him with a copy of the *sefer* at the wedding.

Rav Brevda promptly handed the *sefer* back to me.

"Rav Daniel Yaakov," he said to me, "there's a time and place for everything, and this is not the time or the place to give me your *sefer*."

His words made a very big impression on me. While it was true that the publication of my *sefer* was a big *simchah* for me, his granddaughter's wedding was a big *simchah* for him, and Rav Brevda felt that my giving him the *sefer* at that precise moment was not correct behavior — and he told me as much without getting angry or upset at me. He made sure to say what needed to be said, and I understood his point and was able to accept it, learning that even if I was happy about something, thought had to be given for the people around me. The fact that I had come to his grandchild's wedding while still focused on my *sefer* showed that I wasn't thinking about the wedding, which was, after all, the real reason I had come.

It was a very important lesson for me, and, as usual, it took only a few words from him to bring it home.

◆ ◆ ◆

While I'm on the topic of *Yoreh Binah*, I want to share with you another story that happened to me at the same time, this one with Rav Nachman Bulman, *zt"l*. I came to know him when he served as *rav* in the last years of his life in the Nachliel shul in Neve Yaakov, where I lived at the time.

The day the brand-new *sefer* was delivered to my home, a few relatives were visiting me. I was filled with happiness at having had the *zechus* to publish such a *sefer* and excited that I was finally holding a copy of the *sefer* in my hands.

The relatives who had come to visit us were not *frum*, yet I showed them the *sefer* anyway, hoping they would be able to appreciate the amount of work that had gone into it. Perhaps they just didn't grasp the significance of what *Yoreh Binah* was, but they completely ignored the brand-new *sefer*. Obviously I felt hurt by their attitude, but there was nothing to do about it, since we can only change ourselves and not other people.

A short while later I left my house and headed over to Rav Bulman's shul where I set up a pile of my brand-new *sefer* for the other shul members to see and hopefully purchase.

There was a man standing there, someone who had the reputation of being a *talmid chacham*. Seeing the pile of brand-new *sefarim*, he picked one up and began flipping through it.

"Rabbi Travis," he said almost nonchalantly, "I thought that you were capable of publishing a Torah work of true quality."

A pause.

"But after seeing this, I have to say that I'm really disappointed!"

I had spent years on *Yoreh Binah*, writing every single line over and over until I was sure that I had explained the term I was discussing in the most simple and easy-to-grasp way — some terms I had rewritten twenty times, others forty times. It was finally in my hands, and now here was a *talmid chacham* who should have been able to appreciate how I had brought clarity to the most complex issues of *issur v'heter*, yet instead he had chosen to disparage the entire work after flipping through it for a mere twenty seconds!

Needless to say, it was a terrible moment, maybe even slightly akin to taking a gun and shooting me in the heart.

I was devastated, but instead of allowing this to ruin me completely, I picked up a copy of the *sefer* and headed over to the home of Rav Nachman Bulman.

He studied it for a while, his expression inscrutable.

"Wait here a minute," he said to me finally as he rose and went into his bedroom.

Handing me a thick envelope (I could feel the cash inside), he said, "Rav Daniel Yaakov, this *sefer* is worth a million dollars. I hope that one day I will be able to get you that kind of money, but meanwhile please accept this envelope as a token of my appreciation to you for putting out such a phenomenal work! Call it a down payment!"

He then walked me to his living room window and pointed down into the valley beneath us, which was filled with Arab homes.

"If they only knew what was going on here in Neve Yaakov," he said, "they would understand that there is no chance of them achieving their goals. If they truly grasped the quality of the Torah being learned, they would pick up their feet and run away!"

His words were one hundred percent *hatzalas nefashos*. With those few lines — words that left his heart and entered straight into mine — Rav Nachman Bulman saved my life.

When I left his house, I opened the envelope and counted the bills inside. There was a thousand shekels in the envelope!

Quite honestly, that thousand shekels was probably the sweetest money I have ever held in my hands.

From that day on, whenever a person approaches me with a new *sefer* that he wrote, I buy it, no questions asked. I buy it even if I don't need it, and I buy it even if I have no interest in the subject matter. A *talmid chacham* invested significant time in a Torah project, and I want to show him that I appreciate what he did and will pay money to own it. In my mind, I chalk it up to the everlasting impact that Rav Bulman had on me.

◆ ◆ ◆

For about ten years, Rav Brevda gave a biannual *shiur* in the *ezras nashim* of the Mishkan Esther shul in Ramat Eshkol a few days before the new *zeman* began. He told me that these were his favorite *shiurim*. He used to go out of his way to praise those in attendance for coming to a *shiur* during vacation. The room would be packed — there was usually over 150 people there — and he would go on for a few hours at a time. He'd speak about what Torah was really about and what a person had to do if he wanted to be considered a *ben Torah*. People loved that *shiur*, and every single seat was always taken. For the people sitting in that room, the *shiur* was calculated to get us through the *zeman*, like an injection in the arm that would last us until the next time he came to speak. "In many of the *shiurim* I give," he'd say to us, "I don't feel like I can say the whole truth. Here I say the whole truth!"

He would talk with honesty about the difficulties of being American born and bred and how the American culture and way of life had a pervasive influence on every person living there — many times in an extremely subtle way.

He told us that when the Mir Yeshivah left Shanghai for Eretz Yisrael, it ended up in the United States for two years before making its way to Yerushalayim.

"While the yeshivah was in New York," Rav Brevda said, "five *bachurim* were accepted to learn there. I was one of them. During that period I was *zocheh* to hear *mussar shmuessen* and *va'adim* from Rav Yechezkel Levenstein.

"Rav Chatzkel told us American boys that we didn't understand what Torah and *avodas Hashem* was all about, and at the time I didn't comprehend what he meant. It took me years to grasp what he was saying. Eventually I understood. When a person is raised in America, there are certain influences that take hold of a person that are very difficult to get rid of."

He would pause and say reflectively, "It can be very difficult to get America out of a person."

This is not to say that Rav Brevda didn't recognize the virtues of life in the United States because he did, as did Rav Elchanan Wasserman, who once commented that Americans have a lot of drive, which can be used to serve Hashem. At the same time, Rav Chaim of Volozhin stated that the Torah's final *galus* would be in the United States — with all its inherent challenges.

Rav Brevda had no problem recognizing the good parts of life as an American Jew. He lived in the States and was part of the fabric of Jewish life. But his main issue was with certain subtle norms of the American lifestyle that have become part of us and shape the way we think — and that are almost impossible to eradicate even if we wanted.

◆ ◆ ◆

Recently someone criticized me, saying, "Rabbi Travis, you spend too much time with *rabbanim*."

"I can understand why you might think that way," I replied, "but the truth is that a *rav* (or anyone really) cannot understand the Torah without seeing the way great *rabbanim* put halachah into practice. Seeing it come alive is a million times more powerful than reading about it in a book or learning dry halachos from a *sefer*. This is called *shimush chachamim*."

Chazal tell us, "How beautiful it is to see a person whose heart is one with the Torah and halachah." The only way to observe such a sight is by spending time with *gedolim* where you have the opportunity to see the way they live their lives and interact with people.

Someone asked me how a person is able to acquire the "fifth" section of *Shulchan Aruch* — the nonverbal part of the *Shulchan Aruch* that requires clear *da'as Torah*. The understanding and sense to properly apply the laws coded in the four sections of the *Shulchan Aruch*.

"You get that," I explained, "by watching *talmidei chachamim*. By studying the way they act in their everyday lives. As Rav Brevda once said to me, 'Studying the Chazon Ish gave me a glimpse into the concept of what being a Yid is all about.'"

People today are very concerned about halachah. Their tefillin have to be square to the tenth of a centimeter. But they don't really understand what the mitzvah of tefillin is, or what it means to be a Yid in the first place. This level of insight can be learned only from a *gadol*. Because to really be a Yid is so much more than what it says in the books! The written words give you a direction, but there is more to it than that. To penetrate the surface, a Yid needs to find someone who is able to show him what the words mean — or what to do when there are no words.

I was once with Rav Brevda in the grocery store when he purchased a few items that he needed. After he paid, the man behind the counter placed the items that he bought in a clear plastic bag.

"Can I please have a bag that isn't see-through," Rav Brevda asked.

"What's wrong with a see-through bag?" I wanted to know.

"It's not *derech eretz* for people to be able to see the food items in your bag."

Once again, Rav Brevda was teaching me through his behavior the subtle nuances of "*tzuras ha'adam*." When a Yid cultivates the self inside him, even non-Jews will recognize that beauty and respond to it favorably. This is something I could have learned only by seeing Rav Brevda in action.

◆ ◆ ◆

When Rav Brevda was diagnosed with the *machalah*, the non-Jewish staff in the hospital where Rav Brevda was being treated knew that Rav Brevda was a great person and respected him for who he was (that one unpleasant nurse I wrote about before was the rare exception). They were able to sense that he was a cut above the rest.

Rav Brevda told me a story about the Brisker Rav that illustrates this precise point.

The Brisker Rav was once visiting a spa when he was approached by a non-Jew.

"Rabbi," the man said to the *rav*, "after watching you for a few minutes, I realize that I don't know what's going on around me. Obviously there's something much deeper happening in life that I don't understand."

When a non-Jew sees a Jew who has worked on himself to a certain degree, it's the ultimate *kiddush Hashem*, because suddenly the non-Jew recognizes that Jewish people are special and living on an entirely different and lofty plane.

One of Rav Brevda's non-Jewish doctors told me, "I might have graduated from medical school where I was taught about the big intestine, the little intestine, the heart, and the liver, but I never learned what a human being is until I met this rabbi!"

But Rav Brevda was never satisfied with what he accomplished or how advanced he was in *avodas Hashem*. He always demanded more of himself.

"If you're sitting next to someone in shul," he said to me once, "and you don't say hello to him, that's *sinas chinam*. You are not allowed to be caught up with yourself to the point where you don't pay attention to the Yid next door. And you have to *fargin* people. You don't get extra credit for that. These are the basics of being a Jew!"

When a young boy named Leiby Kletzky was murdered in Boro Park, I had not yet heard the tragic news when I happened to call Rav Brevda that day. After informing me of the tragedy that had just hit our community, he proceeded to deliver an impromptu hour-and-a-half *shiur* over the phone.

"Hashem brings us together *b'tza'ar*, in pain," he said to me, clearly devastated by the news, "if we don't come together *b'simchah*. If there's no *achdus* in *Klal Yisrael*, then Hashem makes these things happen. This is the *pshat* in all the *tzaros* that we have!"

Later on I would come to find his words echoed in the *Abarbanel* on *Parashas Ki Savo*, who also writes, with total clarity, that when we don't come together in happiness, we will come together in pain.

Rav Brevda was an incredibly sensitive person, yet at the same time, he gave his close *talmidim* direct *mussar*, stripping them down and rebuilding them from the ground floor up. Watching him was watching a master at work.

Chapter Five

R av Brevda was the epitome of empathy. During that time when we were experiencing our unbelievable bout of *tzaros*, I visited many people and many *gedolim*. All were sympathetic to my problems; every one of them cared. But it was Rav Brevda who "climbed down into Gehinnom with me and bore the fire at my side." It was Rav Brevda who held my hand and helped me climb out of the darkest canyons, out of the places where there was no light. And even though there were times when I didn't speak with him for a month, I knew and felt that he was with me completely.

When my daughter was in *shidduchim*, the process lasted a year, but it took everything out of us. Many suggestions didn't work out, and it was a very draining experience. Of course I called Rav Brevda to unburden myself after each disappointment. He gave me *chizuk* and reassured me that he knew what I was going through.

As he had done during our most difficult moments years before, he penned another special *tefillah* for us. Rav Brevda's *tefillos* were always unique, and you were never quite sure if he was going to write you one. Sometimes he did, but many times he did not. All together he wrote us just a few, special *tefillos*, every one of them at a critical juncture of our lives.

It was toward the end of the year when he said to me, "You're finished doing *hishtadlus* for this year. The *yeshuah* will arrive at the beginning of next year."

During that critical period of my daughter's *shidduchim*, I also spoke with Rav Moshe a number of times.

Rav Moshe Shapiro used to give *shiurim* in the middle of the night, sometimes even at two in the morning. He explained that it was very difficult for him to sleep, which was how he came to rise for a *neitz* minyan at the Kosel every morning for decades. One of the conversations about my daughter's *shidduchim* took place at the Kosel after Rav Moshe's *neitz* minyan.

He thought for a second and said, "There's only one solution: daven. *V'zeh vadai ya'azor*. And that will definitely help!"

Needless to say, I took his advice very seriously, as I did anything involving *tefillah*. I felt like he was telling me not to get discouraged and the fact that there was nothing more I could do.

It was true. *Al pi derech hateva*, in the natural order of the world, there was nothing more I could possibly do that I hadn't done already.

But so what? Since when was Hashem bound by *teva*? He could do whatever He wanted to do, and nothing was beyond His reach. I followed his advice and redoubled my efforts when it came to davening for my daughter's *shidduch*.

Soon after these events, on Hoshana Rabbah morning, I was sitting in my succah with two friends. I had been close with one of them for many years. I had attended the Bronx High School of Science, a prestigious school in the States (many of my friends went on to Ivy League schools like Harvard and Yale), but I left it all when I was sixteen and went to learn in Eretz Yisrael. I had a friend who had been in my class at Bronx High and then went to Cooper Union College. Cooper Union is ranked number one among regional colleges in the north and is very selective in who they accept to their student body. Since we had been good friends, I began badgering this boy to come to Eretz Yisrael and give learning a chance. He was, understandably, resistant, but finally I wore him down. He flew to Eretz Yisrael and learned for a while. Eventually he'd had enough and wanted to go home.

"Don't think that you're leaving," I told him.

"I have to go home and finish college," he told me.

"You're not leaving."

We had a big fight, with me insisting that he couldn't leave everything that he now knew to be true and he insisting that he was in the middle of obtaining his education and had to finish before deciding the course of the rest of his life. In the middle of the argument, I davened to Hashem to put the right words into my mouth.

I pointed to all the *sefarim* on the shelves and *shtender*s (we were sitting in the *beis midrash* of Toras Moshe at the time) and said, "You see these *sefarim*? If you don't know them, you will never be able to get a really good *shidduch*!"

For some reason, that particular line made an impression on him, and he decided he would return to Eretz Yisrael, which he did after finishing college. Eventually he got married and moved to Bnei Brak. This friend in turn was *mekarev* another student at Cooper Union who ended up moving to Har Nof and becoming my neighbor. The three of us get together on Succos every year to discuss Torah and to catch up on the things that are going on in our lives.

That year, all that was on my mind was my daughter's travails in the world of *shidduchim*. There, in the succah with my friends, I said to them, "The whole *shidduchim* business is so difficult! But you know what? It's all a *nisayon* in *emunah*. The moment we're ready, Hashem will bring the *yeshuah*!"

I banged on the table to emphasize that I meant every word.

At that moment the phone rang.

It was a *shadchan*, and my daughter was a *kallah* eleven days later.

The *nisayon* was over. But my statement regarding *emunah* and the place it held in my life clearly came from Rav Brevda, who had unequivocally reassured me that salvation lay right around the corner at the start of the new year, and who was ultimately proven to be one hundred percent on the mark, just as he always was.

◆ ◆ ◆

I knew Rav Brevda for eighteen years. For seventeen of those years I tried to get a *haskamah* from him.

Although he never ended up giving me a *haskamah*, he also never refused me point-blank. He would say, "I have to think about it," but he would never say no, because he understood that his refusal would hurt my feelings. And although Rav Brevda always found a way to masterfully turn me down without turning me down, I kept on writing *sefarim* — and hoping that one day I would merit having his *haskamah* in one of my *sefarim*.

Years passed and I had already written many *sefarim*. In the last year of his life, I asked him again and this time he said yes.

It was for the *sefer* I wrote titled *Praying With Joy*, and Rav Brevda wrote something very nice — not a word of exaggeration, he would never do that, but it was a special *haskamah* and it meant the world to me.

He made a point of mentioning that my books were very well written, and he also wrote that "it's a very great source of *nachas* that I listened to him and followed his advice to turn to *tefillah* in a time of *tzarah*."

That he was finally willing to give me a *haskamah* was very significant to me, because I felt that I had been working to reach the point that he had in mind for me for the past seventeen years — and that I had made progress and he recognized that and was proud of me.

Rav Brevda (and Rav Shlomo Zalman Auerbach, too, for that matter) wouldn't give a *haskamah* for a *sefer* on *avodas Hashem* unless he felt that the person writing the *sefer* was on a level where it made sense for him to be writing such a *sefer*. These *gedolim* rarely wrote *haskamos*, and perhaps this is why it took seventeen years until Rav Brevda finally agreed to provide one for my *sefer*.

A point of interest: Rav Brevda never had any *haskamos* on his own *sefarim*, except for the first *sefer* he wrote, which was called *Ameilus HaTorah* and which he published anonymously. The story of how that first *sefer* came to be written is fascinating on its own.

The great Bnei Brak *gedolim* of the day — Rav Shach and the Steipler *zt"l* among them —decided that someone had to write a *sefer* about the importance of Torah learning. A meeting was held at the home of one of the *gedolim*, and Rav Brevda was tasked with the project, just as he had been tasked by Rav Shach to travel around Eretz Yisrael giving *shiurim*. This, of course, aligned with his own *hashkafah* and that of his primary rebbi, Rav Chatzkel, who said, "Never stop teaching! Your job in this world is to teach other people!"

About this Rav Brevda used to say, "My life is very easy because I have been given a mission and know what I have to do. Many people are constantly in doubt as to whether they are fulfilling their mission. I, however, have no doubts, because I was clearly told that I was supposed to spend my life teaching Torah to *Klal Yisrael*."

The *gedolim* of Bnei Brak clearly understood that the young Rav Brevda had what it took to spur people to change by dint of the words that came out of his mouth (and pen) and the masterful *shiurim* he was able to deliver with what appeared to be effortless ease.

◆ ◆ ◆

Toward the end of his life, Rav Brevda began speaking constantly about the coming of Mashiach. There was one line that he repeated all the time:

"I give you a *berachah* that you should be in the *beis midrash* when Mashiach comes. You should be in the *beis midrash* — that will be a safe place."

Rav Brevda was ill at the same time as Rav Elyashiv, which meant that the *olam haTorah* was devoting a lot of time to davening for them to have a *refuah sheleimah*. One Thursday, Rav Don Segal came to Mishkan Esther to give a talk. I approached him after the *shiur* and asked if we could arrange a special *tefillah* for Rav Elyashiv and Rav Brevda. I knew that Rav Don and Rav Brevda were close friends and therefore was not surprised when Rav Don thought my suggestion was a good idea. We held the gathering not long afterward, with the assembled pouring out their hearts in prayer to the Ribbono shel Olam.

When I called Rav Brevda later that day, he said to me, "Thank you for the *tefillah* you organized for me today. It helped very, very much."

Before I could get over my shock at the fact that he even knew about it, seeing as I hadn't told him what I'd planned on doing on his behalf, he said something else, almost as an afterthought — but to me it was earth-shattering: "And please don't tell anyone about our conversation." He was implying that no one had told him about the gathering and that he had come to know about it through unique ways of his own.

I kept my word until after he passed away.

◆ ◆ ◆

I always knew my rebbi was a *tzaddik*, but even I, who followed him around and went to hear him speak any time I had the opportunity, didn't imagine the extent of it. You'd think that hearing so many *derashos* from a person would give you more insight. You'd think that it wouldn't have come as a surprise. But it was a surprise. Even for me.

In the months leading up to his passing in 2013, Rav Brevda's body failed him, and his systems began shutting down. He was very sick, and everyone was sure that the end was near. Two months before he passed away, we were looking at a complete shutdown. Then something miraculous occurred, and Rav Brevda returned to himself.

It wasn't normal. We had all been sure that the end was at hand. When Rav Brevda was able to talk, he explained that his recovery had come about for two reasons.

"My first merit," he told his family, "is the fact that I have a close *talmid* in Kiryat Sefer who rises every evening at three and recites the entire *Sefer Tehillim* in my *zechus*."

When contacted, the *talmid* admitted that this was accurate information and told the family that he had been about to stop doing it because he was too exhausted to continue.

"But now that I know how much my saying *Sefer Tehillim* has been helping my rebbi, I will definitely continue."

Rav Brevda told his family that the second reason he'd been allowed to recover came about through another *talmid* who had recently organized a gathering to discuss ways and means to combat illicit usage of the Internet, and had generously handed over his merit for success in that worthy endeavor toward the recovery of his rebbi.

So Rav Brevda recovered, and life continued as usual, but the story was just beginning.

◆ ◆ ◆

In the days following his incredible recovery, Rav Brevda was visited by one Reb Menachem Lesser, the son of his close friend Reb Nosson from Bnei Brak. While they were conversing, Rav Brevda told his visitor about a series of fascinating visits that he'd received a short while before. If Rabbi Lesser first imagined that Rav Brevda was talking about visions he'd seen while asleep, he soon learned that this was not the case and that the visitors had appeared in the middle of a room filled with people, but they had been seen by Rav Brevda alone.

"Reb Menachem," his host said, "I need to give you regards from someone close to you."

"Regards from someone close to me?"

Reb Menachem was taken aback. Who could the *mashgiach* be referring to?

With a twinkle in his eye, Rav Brevda cleared up the mystery.

"Recently I was visited by four very distinguished guests on the same day. One of them was your father, Reb Nosson Lesser, who, as I'm sure you know, was a very dear friend of mine."

Reb Menachem was even more taken aback, since his father had passed away some time ago.

"But who were the other three?"

"One was my father," the *mashgiach* replied.

"And the other two?"

"One was Rav Chatzkel Levenstein, the *mashgiach* of Ponevezh, and the last guest was the Vilna Gaon."

Rav Brevda wasn't joking, and Reb Menachem accepted his words and the regards at face value. Yes, it did sound strange — most people don't merit visitors like these — but the *mashgiach* insisted emphatically that he had been visited by those four personages and that he hadn't been sleeping at the time of their appearance.

"Reb Menachem," he said as they concluded their visit, "please keep this information between us. At least for the time being."

Implicit in Rav Brevda's request was that the story of his four visitors should be kept quiet, at least until he passed away. Reb Menachem took his leave a short while later and returned to Bnei Brak. There the story might have ended if not for one thing. Reb Menachem had been shaken up by the regards he'd been given and found it extremely difficult to keep silent about the whole story. It sounded very far-fetched, and although he'd never known Rav Brevda to make anything up or embellish a situation in any way, in this particular case, he was having trouble keeping the story to himself.

After much soul-searching, he finally decided to share the story with one person: Rav Brevda's son, who also lived in Bnei Brak. In this way, Reb Menachem hoped to shed some light on the fascinating, yet somewhat bizarre incident.

◆ ◆ ◆

When the two of them next met, Reb Menachem shared the information he'd been told with Rav Brevda's son. He hadn't been sure what reaction he'd been expecting, but it certainly wasn't the reaction he got. Rav Brevda's son turned pale.

Was he surprised? Shocked? Taken aback? He knew his father very well. Why was he so shaken by what he had heard?

"I want to tell you something."

Reb Menachem waited to hear.

"Over the last few months, my father's health deteriorated drastically. I don't have to tell you how serious it has been. Just recently we thought we were losing him."

Reb Menachem nodded.

"Since my father is currently residing in the States, while I live here in Bnei Brak, I am unable to visit him. Of course, as soon as his condition began changing for the worse, everyone in America started calling me and telling me to get on the next flight so I could see him before the end."

A pause.

"There was one problem with getting on the next plane. You know what kind of schedule I adhere to. You know how much I try never to disrupt my learning. More than that, you know that my father himself wouldn't want me to leave Eretz Yisrael in the middle of the *zeman*. With all these considerations, I found myself wavering. On the one hand, everyone in the family was telling me to leave for the States as soon as possible. On the other, I personally felt that it might very well be the incorrect course of action for me in this case. To make a long story short, I didn't know what to do.

"Around the time I was struggling with making a decision, I received an invitation to attend a special *tefillah* that was being arranged for the sake of my father and his failing health. The *tefillah* was to take place at the graveside of Rav Chatzkel Levenstein, the legendary *mashgiach* of Ponevezh and my father's rebbi. I knew how close they'd been. My father speaks of the *mashgiach* often, and, I figured, can there be a better place to visit right now than the *kever* of Rav Chatzkel?

"So I went.

"We davened for my father to have a complete *refuah sheleimah*, and during the course of the davening, as I stood beside Rav Chatzkel's grave, I opened my mouth and made a personal request of the Ponevezh *mashgiach*.

"'Rav Chatzkel,' I began, 'you know that the family has been pressuring me to travel to the United States. You know that I almost never go anywhere and that all I do is learn. And you also know more than anyone that my father would much prefer that I remain right here in Bnei Brak, following my normal routine. We both know all this. But the rest of the family feels differently. I therefore respectfully make the following request.

"'Would you, Rav Chatzkel, please go visit my father instead of me? It would be much easier for you to get there than it would be for me. If you can do this, and you agree with me that it is more important for me to remain here in Bnei Brak, please do so along with at least one other person and let me know about it. Then I will have received confirmation that I made the correct decision.'"

Rav Brevda's son looked Reb Menachem in the eye.

"Now do you understand why I was so shocked? I asked Rav Chatzkel to visit my father and he did. I asked him to visit with at least one additional person, and he visited with three more people, all close to my father — and one of them among the greatest *tzaddikim* of *Klal Yisrael*! Can you blame me for turning pale?"

◆ ◆ ◆

I visited Rav Brevda in the Brooklyn hospital for the last time close to Chanukah. He wasn't himself anymore, and there were tubes and wires everywhere. The moment I entered his room, Rav Brevda shouted, "Do you know what *nissim* are? Do you know what *nissim* are?!"

At the time I hadn't yet heard the story about Reb Menachem Lesser's father and the Vilna Gaon and didn't know what *nissim* Rav Brevda was referring to.

Knowing instinctively that this was probably the last time I was going to have the opportunity to converse with him in this world, I waited until the room was empty and it was just the two of us. There was something I had been waiting to say to him for a long time, and the moment had arrived.

"Rav Brevda," I said, "I owe you everything in my life. Everything!"

He started crying.

That was the last time we spoke.

◆ ◆ ◆

I was up at three o'clock in the morning when someone called me from America to tell me the news.

I didn't think about what I was doing. I ripped my clothing as if my fingers were moving of their accord. There wasn't even a question here. This was Rav Brevda — my *rebbi muvhak*, my primary teacher in my *derech hachaim*.

He wasn't blind to my flaws. He knew my strong points and my weak points, but he cultivated the characteristics that made me, sculpting me like a work of art, like a lifelong project that needs constant direction. He knew my challenges, and he worked on me, smoothing out the edges and shaving off the rough spots. He recognized the inner potential and made it his mission to channel me in the right direction.

I'll give you an example of what I mean when I use the word *potential*.

When I was fourteen years old and still a student in the Bronx, I was just becoming *frum*, and one of my first stops on the journey was NCSY. As with everything I did in life, I became extremely involved in the program and decided that our chapter needed to win "Chapter of the Year." Having identified the goal, I set about attaining it.

How to do this?

The answer, it seemed to me, was by sitting down at my desk and writing a letter to Rabbi Nate Segal, who was then head of NCSY, every single day. I must have written him over a hundred letters explaining why I felt our chapter deserved to win the title.

In the end, we won second place.

Years later, I went to visit Rabbi Segal, who was now working for Torah Umesorah, establishing *kollelim* around the United States. After I introduced myself, he left the room and returned carrying a huge stack of my letters, which he had saved.

"You see these letters?" he said. "When you sent them all to me, I knew that you had real potential because it's a sign of greatness when a person can sit down and write a hundred letters!"

Sitting with him, I recalled what I was like at the age of fourteen and fifteen and how Rabbi Segal put me up at the home of Rav Dovid Feinstein and gave me *Chasan Bereishis* when I davened at his minyan on the Lower East Side on Simchas Torah.

Now it was fifteen years later, and he still had all those letters.

"This is a good *middah*," he said about my persistence, "if used in the right way."

Rav Brevda had seen my persistence — he knew what I was capable of achieving. He dedicated himself to teaching and honing me, to working with the raw material that comprised Daniel Yaakov Travis, whom he knew could go very far. What can I say? In my opinion, he acted exactly as a rebbi is supposed to act.

Rav Brevda used to say, in the name of his rebbi, Rav Chatzkel, "A rebbi is someone who can take the *talmid* and prepare him for the next generation."

What does that mean?

To me, it's obvious. There's no comparison between the world Rav Brevda inhabited and our world today. And that's okay. Because my rebbi brought me to the point where I was ready and prepared to face the world of today. Rav Brevda knew that nothing is static; nothing stays the same. He knew that the world was changing at a rapid-fire pace, and he was at peace with the situation — as long as his *talmidim* were equipped to handle whatever situations came their way.

◆ ◆ ◆

It was snowing heavily during Rav Brevda's *levayah*, snowflakes drifting downward from a darkened sky onto the crowd outside Yeshivas Torah Ore in the Mattersdorf neighborhood of Yerushalayim. The rain and snow intensified as we walked from the yeshivah to Har HaMenuchos, our feet trudging through slush and rain, pants soaking wet, tears streaming down our faces.

I carried the front of the casket (where Rav Brevda's head lay) for a great part of his final journey. Though my arms grew tired and began to burn from the fatigue of carrying the heavy box, I wouldn't exchange places with anyone else.

Rav Brevda carried me through life, I said to myself. *I have to carry him now.*

The snow didn't stop. It just kept drifting down to the ground, and I couldn't help but think it was very fitting: Rav Brevda had been someone (like the Kohen Gadol of old) who "whitened" the sins of *Klal Yisrael* and helped bring them to *teshuvah.*

◆ ◆ ◆

In the aftermath of Rav Brevda's passing, many people told me the same line: "I heard only one *shiur* from Rav Brevda, but it changed my life."

It made sense. Of course his *shiurim* changed lives. Every *shiur* he gave was calculated to help people change. He always stressed that people should not be content with how they are and that just because a person is a certain way one day doesn't mean that he couldn't become something completely different the next.

(Author's note: Rav Brevda spoke in my yeshivah on Shavuos night when I was eighteen years old. "You think you came into the world to eat cheesecake?" he said to the assembled in his typical humorous style. When davening was over that night and I went to eat my *seudah*, eating cheesecake gave me no peace. It is now over twenty years since he uttered that line, and it still comes to my mind every Shavuos when the cheesecake appears at the table.)

◆ ◆ ◆

Rav Shlomo Brevda is mourned by *talmidim* around the world who recall his incredible honesty, sincerity, erudition, and vast knowledge with poignancy and a sense of gratefulness that we were granted as much time as we had with our amazing rebbi — a rebbi who put on no airs and was accessible to anyone searching for the truth.

Rav Brevda was someone who never ceased to amaze me. And even though I was so close to him, I know that everything I witnessed barely scratched the surface because of the great pains he took to hide the extent of his *tzidkus* and connection to worlds that the average (and even above average) human eye does not see.

In the years following his passing, I tried to find another rebbi to take his place, but I wasn't able to do so. Every time I'd think that I found someone, something would happen and I'd realize that the person didn't have what enabled me to connect with Rav Brevda — and I wasn't able to call him my rebbi.

Because the person wasn't him.

I owe him my life and I am eternally grateful.

Encounters With

Rav
Shimshon Pincus
זצ"ל

The Unparalleled Oheiv

Yisrael of Our Time

"Because if you go to sleep like a Yid, you're going to wake up like a Yid!"

Chapter Six

I was a *bachur* learning at Yeshivas Toras Moshe when I heard that a yeshivah located in the southern town of Ofakim was looking for five serious American *bachurim* to join the student body.

"Who's the *rosh yeshivah*?" I asked the person who told me about the yeshivah.

"Rav Chaim Kamil."

Rav Chaim Kamil was a major *talmid chacham*, and everyone knew that he was a rising star in the yeshivah world.

"What do they mean when they say 'serious *bachurim*'?"

"*Bachurim* who don't listen to the radio."

That wasn't a problem for me. I hadn't listened to the radio in years.

I was invited to come down south to check the place out. Wanting to convince me that I was making the right choice, the organizers of the initiative put me up at the home of Rav Shimshon Pincus, *zt"l*, who was the *rav* of Ofakim at that time.

In the end, I accepted the invitation and traveled down south with another *bachur* for what turned out to be one of the most memorable Shabbosos of my life. The experience of spending Shabbos in the Pincus home was something a person could never forget.

Aside from the *divrei Torah* Rav Pincus spoke at the Shabbos table, there were many moments in his home that made a deep impression on my *neshamah*. For example, I remember Rav Pincus pointing at the clock on his wall, which was broken.

"Do you see the clock?"

I nodded.

"Do you know why it's broken?"

"Why?" I asked him.

"Because one of my children took a plate and threw it at the clock. Do you want to know what I said to that child?"

I shook my head. I had no idea.

"Absolutely nothing."

I stared at him, not understanding.

"The reason I didn't say anything to the child who broke the clock is because I do not punish children for infractions unless they have to do with matters of *ruchniyus*."

He then told me a story about a certain extremely *chashuve rav* who, when he was young, used to crawl under the dining-room table and bite people on their legs as a joke.

"Kids do all kinds of things, and we can't make a big deal about them. They'll grow up and stop doing those things, and we won't even remember when they used to act immaturely."

It was a *chinuch* lesson for life.

◆ ◆ ◆

I don't think I have ever met a man who loved his nation quite as much as Rav Pincus did. In many ways he was like a modern-day Rav Levi Yitzchak of Berditchev. He loved everyone — from the simplest Jew to the most intellectual. The Jews who could barely read a *pasuk* of *Chumash*, and the *lamdanim* who knew every "Rav Chaim."

One time Rav Pincus was walking down an Ofakim street when a nonreligious teenager passed by riding on a donkey. Back then,

Ofakim was a barely settled town, and the inhabitants were very much of the salt-of-the-earth variety. The teen on the donkey was clad in a pair of shorts and nothing more, prompting one of the people walking with the *rav* to comment, "A donkey on a donkey."

"Don't speak about my son like that," Rav Pincus shot back instantaneously and furiously.

He wasn't putting on a show. That was really the way he felt about every single Jewish child, no matter how removed or distant he might be. He took one look at them and was immediately able to recognize the spark within.

◆ ◆ ◆

When Rav Pincus arrived in town, Ofakim was literally a desert, both materially and spiritually. As the two of us discussed the yeshivah, Rav Pincus made the following emphatic comment.

"Reb Daniel Yaakov," he said, "a person should come learn in this yeshivah only if all he wants is Torah learning. There are no falafel stores here. You will be literally in the middle of the desert. All there is here is Torah. Nothing else."

When Rav Pincus assumed the position of *rav* there, Ofakim was almost completely nonreligious, yet his influence on the city was massive and undeniable. There was no trick or secret to his success; he loved every single person there — and they in turn loved him back.

Of course, there was much more to Rav Shimshon Pincus than that. He possessed an incredible ability to see things differently than everyone else. He more than anyone knew how to find a hook or a twist that allowed him to present complicated and intellectual ideas in a format that grabbed his listeners from the first minute.

Rav Shimshon (like Rav Shlomo Zalman Auerbach) was a master of the paradigm shift. If I came into a meeting with one of them looking at something one way, they were sure to change the way I saw things with a few well-chosen words.

During the course of that memorable Shabbos, one of the topics we discussed was how to converse with nonreligious people.

"How am I supposed to convince the average nonobservant Jew to attend the davening in a *frum* shul when his wife will be forced to sit behind a *mechitzah*?" I wanted to know.

"People make a big mistake," Rav Shimshon replied, "when they think that the *mechitzah* is the thing separating men and women. It's the exact opposite!"

"How can you say that? Everyone knows that women have to sit behind the *mechitzah*, which separates them from the men!"

"Let me give you an example," he said to me. "Say you want to heat water to make yourself a cup of tea. Obviously you can't take the water and throw it directly on the fire. That won't work. So what do you do?

"You pour the water into a pot or a kettle, turn on the fire, and place the pot on top of the fire. That's how you put fire and water together. The only way to bring two opposites together is with a separation between them.

"The concept of the *mechitzah* is the same thing. It is because there is a *mechitzah* in the shul that men and women may daven together when they wouldn't be able to do so if there were no separation."

It was such a different approach to a thorny issue, yet the moment he explained it in his unique way, it made complete sense. With Rav Pincus, everything he said was like that. Radical, fascinating, fresh, and mind-altering. He consistently explained the most difficult-to-grasp concepts with an approach that was 180 degrees different from that of everyone else.

◆ ◆ ◆

Later that same Shabbos, Rav Pincus and I discussed how a person can get rewarded for the mitzvos he does here in *Olam HaZeh*.

"I'll give you a *mashal* to explain how it works," he said to me. "Let's say a person is walking in the middle of a desert, and he is dying of thirst. And let's say that he finally reaches a house at the top of a sand dune, and when he knocks on the door and asks for a drink, the person living in the house offers him an ice-cold bottle of Coke.

"How much money would the hiker be willing to pay for that bottle of Coke? He'd pay a million dollars if that's what the owner demanded! And that's the way it works. Everything in this world works according to the degree of *chashivus* you attribute to it.

"It's all about how you relate to something right now from your *Olam HaZeh* perspective. A *rasha* may be rewarded with material things in this world — because that's what seems important to him right now. If a person thinks that Torah and mitzvos are the most important things in the world, then they become the things that he values most."

Then he took the concept a step further.

"How much is a *blatt Gemara* worth?" he asked me rhetorically.

He answered his own question: "It's worth whatever price you give it."

"Meaning?"

"Meaning that if you open your Gemara, and from the moment you begin learning you won't stop to talk to anyone or take a phone call or do anything but learn, then it's clear that a *blatt Gemara* is worth the world to you. But if you are willing to interrupt your learning to go make yourself a cup of coffee or buy yourself a slice of pizza, then your *blatt Gemara* is worth a cup of coffee or a slice of pizza. That's the concept of a person being rewarded in this world. One is rewarded with earthly rewards, because the person has chosen to treat the superficial as if it is really worth something."

◆ ◆ ◆

During the course of that memorable Friday night meal, Rav Pincus shared many ideas with us. At the time I didn't realize that this was a Shabbos I would never forget or that he was sharing kabbalistic concepts with us, ideas that originated in the world of *nistar*. It is only now — some thirty years later, when I am finally starting to delve a little more into that area of Torah — that I am beginning to appreciate and understand what he said then.

He spoke about the concept of Avraham, Yitzchak, and Yaakov — "*Avraham yagel... Yitzchak yeranein...*" — and about their influence in the worlds above and the worlds below. His words emanated from the highest spheres, yet he possessed the unique ability to explain the most esoteric and complicated concept and bring it down to my level of understanding, whose threshold at that time was very low. The words touched me deeply, knocking on the façade of my soul and begging entrance to take refuge in the depths of my spirit, only to emerge at the proper time.

◆ ◆ ◆

At the end of the *seudah* I couldn't help noticing that the Pincus children seemed to be in possession of quite an assortment of Shabbos treats.

"On Shabbos," he explained, "we are all guests at the King's table, and we need to buy the kind of foods one would find in a royal setting. Someone buying food for the palace would never think twice about whether or not to buy something. It should be the same with us.

"Besides, Chazal promise us that everything we buy for Shabbos is paid for! That's why I tell my children that they should buy whatever they want for Shabbos!"

In years to come I'd ask Rav Ezriel Auerbach about buying delicacies for Shabbos.

His response: "Whatever you would purchase for a *chashuve* guest you should buy for Shabbos!"

◆ ◆ ◆

Over the course of that Shabbos Rav Pincus fell into an introspective mood, and he shared some of his personal history with me, telling me how he had grown up in Washington Heights in Manhattan. I, too, had spent a year studying in Washington Heights. The neighborhood was changing then, and I remember being paid by one of the shuls to daven there so as to make sure they had a minyan daily. I told Rav Pincus about the experience and how there were barely ten men davening Shacharis in what was a gigantic space designed for four hundred.

"I know exactly what you're talking about," he said to me. "I used to go into those cavernous shuls with the empty balconies and the rows of barely used seats. I'd go up to the *aron kodesh* and give a *shmuess* to the four hundred people who used to be there. I'd scream, shout, and entreat the crowd — the crowd of people who were long gone from the streets of the city.

"The *shmuessen* that I delivered to the empty shuls of Washington Heights," said Rav Pincus, "is what helped turned me into the speaker I became."

There's no question that his technique worked, because Rav Shimshon Pincus was without a doubt one of the most powerful speakers I have ever heard. I remember hearing him give an hour-long *shiur* on the words "*l'susasi b'richvei Pharaoh* — like my mighty steeds who battled Pharaoh's warriors" (*Shir HaShirim* 1:9).

"The main thing in life is the battle," he said with great intensity. "It doesn't matter whether a person is successful or not, because ultimately that's not in a person's hands. The main thing is the battle and whether a person keeps on fighting — *no matter what!*"

In another conversation he made a shocking comment.

"One time I decided that I was going to learn *kol haTorah kulo* — the entire Torah. I began with *Maseches Berachos*, following the Gemara down to the halachah with the *Tur*. Right from the start someone heard about what I was doing and tried to discourage me from my plan.

"I didn't listen to him. I told myself that I have to keep on fighting, no matter what."

He smiled at me.

"Reb Daniel Yaakov, I want to tell you something. Even if you give up your great plan the next day, you have to keep on fighting the battle."

Another time he commented, "You know how many people have a *minhag* to say the *Tikkun* on the night of Shavuos?"

I nodded.

"There's something awesome about it."

"Why's that?"

"It's a chance to grab the entire Torah! A person has to think big in life. I'm not telling you to say the *Tikkun* or not to say the *Tikkun*. That's not my point. All I want you to remember is to think big and to grab the entire Torah when you have the chance.

"And I'll tell you something else. Not everyone is *makpid* to say *Krias Shema al HaMitah*. But it's a really big thing. You know why?"

I waited, sure that the line was going to be a classic.

"Because if you go to sleep like a Yid, you're going to wake up like a Yid!"

◆ ◆ ◆

In the end, I chose to remain in Toras Moshe for the time being. As much as I valued the ideas Rav Pincus had conveyed to me, and as rewarding as I knew it would be to live in a place where the sole thing to do was learn Torah, I didn't feel ready to leave my American yeshivah and immerse myself in a completely different culture.

Besides, the *hashkafos* of Rav Pincus and that of my *rosh yeshivah* at Toras Moshe, Rav Meiselman, were not that far apart, considering that it was Rav Meiselman who stressed time and again, "You learn Torah, you go to *Olam HaBa*, *v'zehu* — and that's it!"

Though I would eventually move on to other yeshivos, I would never forget the Shabbos I spent in that hot and dusty corner of the world, where there was absolutely nothing to do but learn Torah.

Chapter Seven

A
nother year went by. The fire Rav Pincus had ignited by dint of his larger-than-life personality was still burning. As the year came to an end, I decided that it was high time for me to return to the tiny town at the end of the world where there was nothing to do but learn. I wanted to board the Egged bus where the air conditioner barely worked and look out the window at the greens and browns of the landscape, watching the green hills give way to the stark desert. In short, I was ready to return.

This time, however, I decided that I wanted more than just one Shabbos. This time I decided to remain there for at least a week. The best time to do this was during the nine days prior to Tishah B'Av.

A friend of mine named Doron was learning in Ofakim at the time. A very serious *bachur*, he'd parked himself in the *beis midrash* when he arrived and learned twenty hours a day, pretty much dropping *Olam HaZeh* completely. Eventually he married the daughter of one of the *maggidei shiur* of Netivot. I was looking forward to spending time with him and to renewing my relationship with Rav Pincus. I wanted to sit at Rav Shimshon's dining-room table once again and to see the broken clock on the wall and hear about the currency conversion rate between this world and the next.

Since I was coming for a week, I went down there with my *chavrusa*, a *bachur* named Shimon. The yeshivah in Ofakim really wanted us to transfer from our yeshivah, but try as I might I just couldn't picture myself leaving the world of English speakers behind. I admired the Torah community of Ofakim no end, and I desperately wished that I could leave everything behind and throw myself into learning in the middle of the desert with no thought to the world around me, but it wasn't for me, and I was wise enough to know it.

At the end of the day, I was an American and even though Rav Pincus had been able to relinquish his childhood in America and trade it in for the privilege of raising a family who conversed in Ivrit among themselves, I didn't see such a future for me.

Besides all that, when Rav Pincus came to the yeshivah to deliver a *shiur* — naturally it was in Ivrit — I found that I had a difficult time following the *iyun shiur*.

Rav Pincus being Rav Pincus, he was, of course, attuned to my feelings and knew how I was down on myself for not being able to shrug off everything familiar for a life among the sand dunes (and for not being able to "get" the *shiur*) and made sure to approach me to give me *chizuk*.

"Reb Daniel Yaakov," he said, "the beauty of *iyun* is *bekius*. A lot of people give fancy *iyun shiurim* with the deepest *sevaros* and subtle nuances. But when a person knows a lot of Torah, that's a really beautiful thing because then he becomes a person who is able to converse in the language of Torah. A person has to really master a lot of Torah. That's the key. You should remember this in life: the beauty of *iyun* is *bekius*."

One of Rav Pincus's many talents lay in his ability to instinctively know the exact words to use with every person, and the words he told me that day would remain with me for the decades to come, giving me endless *chizuk* as I learned and reviewed and learned some more, trying to become a person who epitomized the beauty of *iyun*.

Of course, being Rav Pincus, he didn't stop with words of *chizuk*, but he gave me a personal example as well.

"Whenever my brother and I travel anywhere together," he said, "the conversation is *kulo divrei Torah* from start to finish. We drive from Ofakim to Akko talking Torah and words of *chizuk* throughout the entire drive."

In particular, the two of them enjoyed reviewing the entire fourth *sha'ar* of *Nefesh HaChaim*. They always strove to learn more and acquire more Torah for themselves, since, as Rav Pincus would say, "The beauty of *iyun* is *bekius*."

Words of wisdom to live by.

◆ ◆ ◆

Rav Pincus had a major impact on my life in many ways. Though he was taken away from us many years ago, it still feels like yesterday that I heard him speak in that powerful voice that shook the room. I remember many, many lessons that he taught me. But almost none of them were stronger than his personal example when it came to mourning over the *Churban*.

"When you go to a wedding," he'd say to a group of *bachurim*, "everyone's dancing and everyone's happy. You don't really know who the *chasan's* friends are. Maybe the people dancing 'round and 'round don't even know the *chasan* at all. Maybe they just walked in off the street and joined the circle because they like to dance!

"When you go to a funeral, on the other hand, and you see someone crying — there's no question in anyone's mind that the person crying loved the *niftar*!

"The person crying on Tishah B'Av is the person who really loves Hashem. That's when you really see what a Yid feels about Hashem and the Beis HaMikdash."

Until today, whenever Tishah B'Av comes around, I remember Rav Pincus saying, "The person crying on Tishah B'Av is the person who really loves Hashem."

As long as the Beis HaMikdash is still alive in our hearts, we're still connected to all the *doros* — to all the generations from back then until today. The moment the Beis HaMikdash stops meaning something to us, we become cut off from our past, from our heritage and our history.

◆　◆　◆

Rav Pincus also related the following Tishah B'Av–themed story about Napoleon Bonaparte.

Napoleon was once traveling through his empire when he came across a Jewish community. Extremely curious by nature, the French emperor decided to stop mid-journey and spend some time getting to know his Jewish subjects. To his great surprise, upon entering the local shul Napoleon saw all the Jewish people sitting on the floor weeping.

"Why is everyone so sad?" he asked the rabbi of the community.

"They are crying because the Temple in Jerusalem was destroyed."

Napoleon was confused.

"The Temple was destroyed?" he asked in surprise. "Why didn't anyone tell me about it?!"

The rabbi hastened to clarify.

"The reason that His Majesty didn't hear about the destruction was because it occurred a few thousand years ago."

Napoleon heard this and commented, with tremendous insight, "If the Jewish nation misses their Temple so much, it will yet be returned to them."

That line summed up Rav Pincus's philosophy and the way he related to life. If you really want something, he believed, then you'll get it.

Chapter Eight

Rav Pincus published his *sefer She'arim BiTefillah* not long after that Shabbos I spent at his home, and learning it changed my entire life. I had never read a *sefer* (with the possible exception of *Mesillas Yesharim*) that was so emotional — that cut through all the human deficiencies to speak to your heart. After reading that *sefer*, all I wanted to do was daven. Unlike the majority of the *sefarim* that were published by his children in the years following his death, *She'arim BiTefillah* was written by Rav Pincus himself, and his greatness of spirit shines forcefully through every line.

I recall one particular Yom Kippur when my davening was just not happening. Whatever I tried and whatever I did, I just wasn't into it. Right before *Ne'ilah*, I turned to Hashem and said, "Ribbono shel Olam, this is an emergency! I need help to turn this around!"

I happened to have had a copy of *She'arim BiTefillah* in shul with me (it was dog-eared and worn from use), and I opened up the *sefer* to the chapter on *"Tze'akah,"* on screaming. I read Rav Pincus's words with fascination.

"You don't have to scream to accomplish *tze'akah*," he wrote.

"A person can be sitting at his *shtender*, and he can scream without making a physical sound until the entire universe hears him! That's a real '*tze'akah*' from the depths of a person's heart."

Those words saved my Yom Kippur. Suddenly I understood that I didn't have to scream and that it wasn't about how loud I was. It was about connecting on the deepest internal level, and I could scream with massive force without making a single sound.

After reading those words, I experienced one of the greatest *Ne'ilah*s of my life!

◆ ◆ ◆

Rav Pincus was unique in numerous ways, but one of his greatest *kochos* was his ability to write and convey his heartfelt emotion in a way that the person reading his *sefer* felt like he was literally hearing him speak directly to them. Rav Pincus singlehandedly changed the way a generation related to davening.

One might have thought that Rav Pincus had a corner where he sat and wrote undisturbed. The opposite was true. Every month he traveled across Eretz Yisrael delivering *shiurim*, but that was only the beginning of his travels.

As a partner with Rav Ezriel Tauber, the two of them spoke to overflowing crowds in their Shalhevet Seminars, which were geared toward inspiring Jews of all ages and affiliations. The result of all this was that Rav Pincus found himself traveling to the States and to South America at least once a month in addition to all his speeches he delivered in Eretz Yisrael and his obligations to his Ofakim *kehillah*.

Which is how he came to write all his *sefarim* on the plane, surrounded by fellow travelers and the accompanying noise.

◆ ◆ ◆

As I mentioned earlier, my wife and I experienced an incredible degree of *tzaros* before Rav Brevda wrote our personal *tefillah*, after which there was a major change for the better. Once, while walking on a Neve Yaakov street with Rav Pincus, I unburdened myself.

"I hate to say this," I said to him, "but when my life was filled with hardship, I davened a lot better to Hashem."

He laughed and said, "What? You want the problems to return?"

Suddenly he stopped in midstep (I remember exactly where we were standing in Neve Yaakov) in the middle of a hill, and he said, "The Chafetz Chaim writes that the reason people have so many *tzaros* is because they aren't *makdim tefillah l'tzarah* — because they don't preempt the challenges with prayer."

He gave me a direct look and said, "You know something? If we'd daven when things were good, as if we already had a challenge, we wouldn't have any *tzaros*!"

A short while later, a *yungerman* passed us who was using crutches to get around. He was obviously a *ben Torah*. Also obvious was the fact that he was a victim of polio and that it was extremely difficult for him to walk.

Rav Pincus looked at me and then at the man on the crutches and said, "Do you see this man? He had polio, yet he's still living a life of Torah and makes no excuses for himself. He's a genuine *gibbor*!"

His words made a real impression on me.

As a teenager in New York City, I'd gone through serious training to run the four-hundred-meter hurdles for the Olympics. Even as a *bachur* in yeshivah I continued training, running to the Jerusalem Forest early every morning. In my mind, being in prime physical form was something to be proud of. Yet Rav Pincus, with just a few words, managed to show me that although physical fitness is important, the real heroes are people like the *avreich* who had been stricken with polio as a child, yet never gave up pushing himself to the limit every single day, on the street and in the *beis midrash*.

◆ ◆ ◆

Rav Shimshon Pincus told me personally that Hashem created the world in such a way that He doesn't get involved unless a person davens to Him.

"When you daven all the time, Hashem is always with you. That's just the way it is."

After he told me this, I began taking a minute at the end of my *Shemoneh Esrei* to think of all the things that I planned on doing until the next *Shemoneh Esrei* and to daven that I would succeed. In addition, I always try to daven for the things I am doing before I actually do them. For example, if I need to make a phone call, I will utter a short *tefillah* before I make the call. And that's in addition to having davened for my daily activities in the previous *Shemoneh Esrei*.

❖ ❖ ❖

When Rav Pincus was a young man, he learned how to check clothing for *shaatnez*. The reason he went out of his way to learn this somewhat rarely taught and unusual technique, was because he had heard that sometimes the fabrics used to upholster couches may contain *shaatnez*.

"Most people don't know about this," he said. "After I learned what to do, when I'd go to people's homes, I'd do a quick *shaatnez* test on the couch. That way, if I discovered that their couch did indeed contain *shaatnez*, I could let them know."

"Why did you feel like you had to do this?" I asked him.

"What do you mean? If Yidden are doing an *aveirah*, and I can help them avoid it, how could I possibly allow them to keep on living that way?"

It was obvious that if a Yid was doing an *aveirah*, and there was something to be done to stop them, Rav Pincus experienced a form of physical pain if he didn't do something to help them stop.

❖ ❖ ❖

Rav Pincus used to travel from Ofakim to Neve Yaakov twice a month to deliver *shiurim*, and I made sure to attend. Sometimes we'd run into each other at a *simchah* or an event, and I always approached him to exchange a few words. After all, even a minute with Rav Pincus could be sufficient to change a person's entire life.

One speech on *chinuch* took place a few days before summer vacation. A few days later, while on vacation, I had the opportunity to hear him again.

Though I seldom went away, the Jerusalem Municipality had organized a vacation for the families of *kollel yungeleit*, and I had decided to take my family. The vacation was affordable, took place at a hotel in Be'er Sheva, and the participants were given three months to pay. Many people grabbed the chance to spend a few days away for a good price, and Rav Pincus had been invited to address the guests.

After making a few vacation-themed jokes, he delivered his *shiur* — the same *shiur* I'd heard him deliver a few days earlier in Yerushalayim.

After he finished I went over to say "*shalom aleichem*." We shook hands, and I said, "Rebbi, didn't you just give the same *shiur* a few days ago?"

He nodded.

"Don't you lose out on getting to greater depth in Torah by just repeating the same *shiur* over and over again?"

He laughed. "I don't lose out at all! When you're giving to *Klal Yisrael*, you lose absolutely nothing! This *shiur* contains an important message — important for the people in Yerushalayim and important for the people here — and I lose nothing by repeating it again."

Many years have passed since that *shiur* in a Be'er Sheva hotel lobby, and today I find myself traveling often around the United States. At times I will repeat the same *shiur* fifteen times over the course of a few days. Now I'm the one repeating the same ideas over and over, and while this does allow the speaker to polish the *shiur* and hone it to a level of perfection, after saying the same thing over and over you don't get that much from it.

At the same time, as Rav Pincus told me, you don't lose anything from it either — because you lose nothing by giving to people.

His words were an example of his *bitul*, his self-negation. Rav Pincus honestly felt that he had been placed on this earth for the benefit of *Klal Yisrael*. If that meant repeating the same *shiur* fifty or a hundred times, then repeat it he would.

◆ ◆ ◆

I was standing outside Rav Tzvi Kushelevsky's yeshivah in Givat Shaul one evening when Rav Pincus drove by and offered me a ride to the Central Bus Station, where I'd be able to catch a bus to Neve Yaakov. Happy to have the opportunity to spend even a few minutes in his company, I accepted his offer and climbed in beside him. He told me that he was on his way to Jerusalem's International Convention Center for the annual citywide *shemiras halashon* gathering that evening. He was to be one of the speakers.

I volunteered that my wife would be attending, and I wondered if he could give me a taste of what he planned on saying.

Rav Pincus focused his gaze on me and replied, "You think I have any idea of what I'm going to say tonight?"

He dropped me off a few minutes later, and I wished him *hatzlachah* with his speech.

My wife returned home later that night, eager to recap what Rav Pincus had said. "Rav Pincus stood on the stage and started speaking in his trademark singsong manner," she began. He then commenced his speech with the following interesting line.

"I met a *yungerman* on my way here tonight, and he asked me what I was going to say…and I replied, 'Do you think I have any idea what I'm going to say?!'"

Rav Pincus then proceeded to deliver the most incredible speech, blowing everyone away with his words of *chizuk*.

It was a classic example of a dictum Rav Pincus used to repeat: *Lev darshanim b'yad Hashem.* The heart of a speaker is in the hands of Hashem, and it's up to Him to decide whether a speaker will find the words that will inspire his listeners.

That was Rav Pincus. When he spoke, he connected to Hashem, plain and simple. He was like a pipe with one end located down on earth and the other situated up above in the loftiest realms of Heaven.

Is it any wonder that his words were able to penetrate our hearts so deeply?

◆　◆　◆

"People don't understand what Hashem is," he told me once.

"They see Hashem as a G-d Who epitomizes mercy, and they don't understand how He allows 'bad' things to happen to them.

"What they're missing," Rav Pincus continued, "is that Hashem doesn't get involved unless you ask Him to! Hashem set up the world in such a way that a person has to daven. That's what he's waiting for, and that's what we need to do."

There was a man who had been married for a long time and hadn't been blessed with children. He used to come and see Rav Pincus from time to time and ask for a *berachah*. This went on for a long time with no results. One evening the man returned again.

"I want you to come somewhere with me," Rav Pincus told him.

"Where to?" the man wanted to know.

"You'll see."

They got into Rav Pincus's car, and without another word, he drove them out of Ofakim and into the utter darkness of the desert roads of Israel's south. They drove for a long time. The man had no idea where he was being taken, but he trusted the *rav* and knew if Rav Pincus was taking him somewhere there was a good reason for it.

After driving for about forty minutes, Rav Pincus pulled over at the side of the road.

"It's time to get out," he told his passenger.

The man looked around him. They were in the middle of the desert. There was nothing to be seen for miles around. Up above, the sky was filled with a million stars. Otherwise they were surrounded by an inky darkness.

"Why are we here?" he asked Rav Pincus.

"I am going to leave you here for an hour," Rav Pincus said. "This is the middle of nowhere. You can scream as loud as you want, and nobody will hear you. This is your chance to scream out your heart to Hashem! Scream out all the pain. Scream out all your hopes and dreams. Scream out the suffering of all your years of emptiness. Scream to *Shamayim*. This is your night and your chance to break the wall that has been erected around you. Make the silence of the night your own! I will return for you in an hour."

Rav Shimshon Pincus ♦ 93

Then Rav Pincus got back in his car, made a U-turn, and drove off, leaving the man in the middle of nowhere.

When Rav Pincus returned an hour later, he found a man with a face that was streaked with tears and a heart that had been emptied of pain. There was a glow of inner happiness in his eyes, and he looked at peace with himself. He had found himself and his voice in the silence of the night.

It wasn't long before the couple was celebrating the birth of their child.

It happened in the desert. It happened in the silence.

◆　◆　◆

Speaking of sound and silence, I have always been a person of words — as a *rosh kollel*, speaker, and author. Rav Pincus was also primarily a man of words, as was the legendary Rav Moshe Shapiro. But although Rav Moshe Shapiro had a major influence on *Klal Yisrael* with the dissemination of his Torah, he was at the same time — interestingly enough — a master of silence as well.

Rav Moshe was one of the people asked to address the crowd at the *sheloshim* of the children of the Sassoon family, seven of whom perished in a fire that broke out in their house on a Friday night. Reb Gabi Sassoon is a dear friend of mine; we went to yeshivah together, and he learned in my *kollel* years later. It was only fitting that I organize such an important event in the very *kollel* where Reb Gabi had spent so much time learning. (I would also come to write a book about the tragedy that happened to my friend and his family.)

When Rav Moshe stood up to address the gathering, tellingly he chose to speak about silence — a subject that was obviously very dear to his heart.

"Too many people are speaking," he said. "There's too much talk being spread around. When such a tragic event happens, there is nothing anyone can say! The only thing is silence."

Then, for over half the *shiur*, Rav Moshe stood in his spot and said not a word. He was quiet. Silent. His quiet was incredibly intense, because you could see that he was holding himself back from speaking. You could hear the power echoing through his silence. His silence fairly crackled with emotion and raw energy.

He stood there, staring at his hands, thinking, weighing, deciding what words to use and most of the time coming to the conclusion that it was better not to speak.

The person recording the speeches used a device that stops recording automatically when the person speaking is quiet — which meant that half the speech went unrecorded. When Rav Moshe learned that all the silence had been deleted, he said, "You missed the best part of the *shiur*."

Speaking of silence, Rav Moshe used to say that the Alter of Kelm would wait twenty years before finally sharing a particular *yesod* or *machshavah* that he'd long wanted to say.

"The reason he waited so long," Rav Moshe explained, "is because it takes a long time for a concept to truly become part of a person. You have to give ideas time to become imbued in a person's essence."

Rav Aviezer Peltz, *rosh yeshivah* of Yeshivas Toshiah in Tifrach, eulogized Rav Moshe Shapiro when he passed away, quoting the words from a *pasuk*, "*kol demamah dakah* — a still, small voice" (*Melachim I* 19:12), to describe the fallen lion. Rashi there explains that the words refer to a voice emanating from the silence, or like the echo of the silence.

"Noise," Rav Peltz continued, "is limited, it's finite. At some point, it fades away. Silence, on the other hand is infinite. Hashem's essence is clothed in silence because Hashem is infinite. Rav Moshe Shapiro," he concluded, "was the faint voice connecting us to that infinite silence."

◆ ◆ ◆

Rav Pincus was against newspapers of any kind, especially secular newspapers.

"It's not so much what they say," he'd explain. "It's how they say it. They're giving over their world outlook, and sometimes their agenda is so subtle that the reader doesn't even realize how much of an effect they're having on the way he thinks."

◆ ◆ ◆

He was always smiling and full of joy, with a playful twinkle in his eye that radiated outward, touching every person he met. He loved kids — he was always giving out candies to children. He loved everyone. In truth, he loved life! He was completely alive in every way.

During one period, there was a problem with robberies in Ofakim. After homes were broken into more than a few times, Rav Pincus accepted the role of security guard upon himself by studying Torah all night and providing complete spiritual protection, in addition to the remainder of his scores of responsibilities.

Being the self-appointed "head of security" for the religious community of Ofakim meant that Rav Pincus barely slept. Instead, he'd doze on a mattress just outside the *beis midrash* (this was after learning the entire day with barely any rest, or food for that matter) and took the responsibility of protecting his people with extreme seriousness.

It worked.

He continued in his role of security consultant for a year, after which he gave himself permission to return home at night.

◆ ◆ ◆

I remember him asking in a *shiur* why it is that women aren't required to daven more. Then he answered his own question.

"Women do daven. They daven all the time. They are *yotzei tefillah* (fulfill their *tefillah* obligations) when they say, 'Oy vei.'"

The *Magen Avraham* writes a similar idea, stating that women fulfill the obligation of prayer just by making a request of Hashem.

Keeping all this in mind, Rav Pincus was very much in favor of women taking the time to daven, even if it was too hard and the kids were running around and they weren't able to concentrate.

"It's very important that the children see their mother davening," he'd say. "This is the example that you're giving and the tone that you're setting."

Rav Pincus had certain stories that he really liked, and he'd repeat them over and over. One such story was about the Ba'al Hafla'ah, Rav Pinchas HaLevi Horowitz.

"I want to give you an example about the difference between this generation and previous generations," he'd say. "Take the Ba'al Hafla'ah and his brother, Reb Shmelke. The two brothers used to learn together. Unlike most *chavrusos*, who learn for two or three hours, the two brothers used to learn until they collapsed…"

One day they were learning together when Reb Shmelke rose from his place to go get a particular *sefer*. When he didn't return after a reasonable amount of time, his brother went searching for him, only to find that Reb Shmelke had collapsed on the floor from sheer exhaustion.

Most people would have looked at the sight of their brother stretched out on the floor after having learned to the point of zero energy and smiled with *nachas*. Most people, however, were not the Ba'al Hafla'ah.

The Ba'al Hafla'ah took a closer look at his brother. In particular, he studied the position of his right arm. Was it positioned beneath Reb Shmelke's head or just flung in any direction?

You may be wondering what difference it made, but to the Ba'al Hafla'ah the difference was huge.

If his brother's arm was flung any which way, it meant that he was one hundred percent exhausted. If it was positioned beneath his head, it would mean that Reb Shmelke still had some energy left — the energy he'd used to place the arm beneath the head — and that meant that he could still be learning.

The Ba'al Hafla'ah looked at his brother closely and found that, indeed, his arm was lying beneath his head.

Raising his voice to full volume, he called out, "Shmelke! What's going to be in the *kever*?!"

It was a really powerful story and Rav Pincus loved it, telling it and retelling it many times. While this level is light-years away from the majority of *Klal Yisrael*, it was good to see someone who constantly aspired to reach such heights and related to it as something eminently obtainable.

In truth, this epitomized Rav Shimshon Pincus.

At the end of his life, Rav Shimshon kept an apartment in Yerushalayim for the days when he was away from Ofakim. It was in the basement of a building, dark, dank, and dismal, with only a rickety table, a chair, and a bed for furniture. And, of course, he had his *sefarim* to keep him company. When one of his sons came to the apartment to learn with his father, Rav Pincus said to him, "You must be thinking, *Wow! My father is such a tzaddik to be living like this!*

"Don't think that. Because it's not difficult for me. I'm happy living like this!"

He just didn't care about *gashmiyus*. It wasn't important to him. The only thing that was important was getting out there and fighting to succeed in *avodas Hashem*. Perhaps that's why he related to the Ba'al Hafla'ah and Reb Shmelke with such intensity.

◆ ◆ ◆

Rav Pincus gave a speech in Neve Yaakov a few days before he passed away in the fatal car accident that claimed his life. During the *derashah* he repeated a variation of one particular line seven times.

"When I get to the next world… When I get to *Olam HaBa*…"

Was he prescient?

Did he have a premonition of what lay ahead of him in the near future?

At the time, it struck me as strange but I didn't think too deeply into it.

And then he lost his life in that fatal car accident, and it all made sense.

◆ ◆ ◆

Rav Pincus might have been the *rav* of Ofakim, but on a number of occasions I asked him halachic *she'eilos* and he refused to answer, telling me that he wasn't a *posek*. He knew exactly who he was. Rav Pincus was the *mashpia*.

His relationship with Ofakim was somewhat akin to that of Rav Chaim Soloveitchik and the town of Brisk. Happy to serve as the town's moral conscience, Rav Chaim brought in another *rav* to serve as its *posek*. So it went in Ofakim as well.

The people of the town loved Rav Pincus and respected him totally. Under his leadership, the commencement of a *sheva berachos* party could only happen after the third *seder* of the day had ended. Those were the kinds of *takanos* he instituted as a *rav*, turning his town into a place for serious *bnei Torah*. And yet, while Ofakim was a town where men spent their days immersed in Torah learning, it was a place that was filled with joy. It was a happy place, and it was Rav Pincus who set the tone.

Once, when we were having a conversation, Rav Pincus mentioned how Chazal write that it's better to give someone a smile than a glass of milk.

"What was Chazal telling us with their comment about smiles and milk?" he would ask.

"Milk," he said, answering his own question, "is the substance that keeps a baby alive. And while that is obviously so, smiles keep people alive even more than milk keeps the child healthy. Smiles are completely life-sustaining on the deepest, most emotional level."

Rav Pincus had made the art of smiling his own. When he smiled, the smile emerged from deep within his *neshamah*. His mouth curved upward, but that was just the beginning, because his eyes smiled too, as did his entire being in an authentic and captivating fashion. It was the smile of a truly happy man.

How sad it is that so very few people think the way he did.

How lucky I was to have been blessed with the time we spent together.

◆ ◆ ◆

Rav Shimshon Pincus's *levayah* took place on the night of *bedikas chametz*. The entire world was in shock. No one could believe that a *tzaddik* who was the personification of vibrancy could just be gone from one moment to the next.

When Rav Shlomo Zalman Auerbach passed away, I was in the hospital struggling with meningitis and was released on the day of his *levayah*. I could barely stand up at the time, but there was no way in the world that I was going to miss Rav Shlomo Zalman's funeral.

But when it came to Rav Shlomo Zalman, at least we knew that he was sick. At least we'd had the time to prepare for his departure — mentally and emotionally.

With Rav Shimshon Pincus, none of us could believe what had happened. It was like our worst nightmare had just come true. Slowly the crowd started to gather outside Yeshivas Torah Ore on Sorotzkin, the same dazed look on every anguished face.

Could it be that we would never see his smiling face again? Never feel that incredible energy? Never hear another heart-stirring *shmuess*? Or that powerful voice? Could this be actually happening?!

The truth? Very few people knew the real him — that was definitely the case outside Eretz Yisrael. Rav Shimshon Pincus was in the category of *tzaddikim* who become much more well known after they pass away. In the years since he was taken from us, I don't think I have been in an American house that doesn't have some of his *sefarim*. His words and ideas have made a phenomenal impact on the entire Jewish world.

Baruch Hashem, I merited knowing him before his fame spread throughout the world — when he was "just" an incredible lecturer for Shalhevet and the *rav* of a tiny town down south in the middle of nowhere.

How lucky I was.

A close relative told me that when Rav Shimshon was young, he used to ask his mother to cover his eyes with her hand so that he wouldn't see anything improper in the city streets. The sensitivity to *kedushah* that so epitomized him in his later years was already there when he was just a child. Is it any wonder that he grew up to become the *Mesillas Yesharim* of our time?

Like I said, how lucky I was.

Encounters With

Rav
Don Segal
שליט"א

Yedid Hashem

"Being shomer Shabbos means that you hold on to the holiness of Shabbos throughout the entire week and allow it to penetrate your neshamah. Being shomer Shabbos should also affect the way a Yid enters Shabbos and the way he ends Shabbos. It's a lifelong process."

Chapter Nine

Since Rav Don Segal is the head of a *kollel* in the Mishkan Esther shul in Ramat Eshkol, our *kollel* has had the privilege to join in and hear *shiurim* from him every Thursday for the past fifteen years. The *shiurim* are devoted to learning *sefarim* from beginning to end. He taught us *Orchos Tzaddikim* and *Mesillas Yesharim*, and when the *shiur* was over, I'd stay behind and take advantage of his presence to discuss a wide range of topics with him.

Like many of the *gedolim* whom I'd eventually come to know, our first point of contact was when I approached him regarding my *sefer* on *hoda'ah*: I asked him to contribute a Torah thought, and he in turn was very excited about the project.

At the time, Rav Don commented, "Genuine *hoda'ah* is a lot harder to achieve than anything else."

When I asked him why he felt that way, he explained.

"Everyone davens. People daven when they aren't feeling well, and they daven when they need a *shidduch* for themselves or their child. You see people standing at the Kosel crying. But as soon as they receive what they want, they forget all about what happened before. A lot of people ask me to daven for them, but forget to tell me about the *yeshuah* when it arrives."

Consequently he was very happy that such a *sefer* was being written.

◆ ◆ ◆

Rav Don used to repeat many stories about *gedolim*.

"We know about the four sections of *Shulchan Aruch*," he would say. "But there is also a fifth section, and how is a person supposed to learn that part of *Shulchan Aruch*? That," he'd explain, "is where *shimush talmidei chachamim* comes in. This is also why you would hear Rav Shach and the Brisker Rav relating stories about *gedolim*."

As an aside, Rav Brevda used to say that when it comes to *gedolim* books, whether they are a worthwhile use of time depends on how you relate to them. If you put your feet up and read them to relax, they will have a lot less impact on you than if you treat them as you would a Torah discourse in a *sefer* — what you are reading should have an impact on you.

During one period, a certain family member of mine was not well, and I sought counsel with Rav Don on a regular basis.

One time I returned from a visit to the doctor, who was feeling extremely pessimistic about the situation and didn't hesitate to make his opinion known. Rav Don was uncharacteristically upset by the doctor's behavior.

"It says in the Gemara that doctors were given permission to heal. Really we shouldn't have doctors at all, but we were given special dispensation to use them. But to act as if they are privy to Hashem's inner plan?!"

Rav Don himself rarely visited doctors. I do recall him going to a doctor when he came down with a severe bout of pneumonia and was in serious danger, but that was a rare occurrence for him.

"A doctor was given permission to heal," he'd say. "He was not given permission to predict the future!"

Rav Don insisted that I not rely on what the doctor had said, and in the end, everything turned out to be okay just as he'd said, but I would never forget his reaction and how strongly he felt about the proper role of a doctor in this world.

Before someone went into the hospital for treatment, Rav Don would give him *berachos* that rang with an explosion of love for the person. You could see that his *ahavas Yisrael* was constantly bubbling under the surface. While giving the actual *berachah*, it was almost as if his heart would emerge from inside his body to take part in the event.

During a *hesped* that he gave at the *levayah* of Rav Chaim Kreiswirth, a former chief rabbi of Antwerp, Rav Don said the following *vort*.

In *Parashas Shemos* the Torah tells us that Moshe Rabbeinu left Pharaoh's palace to take part in the burden of his people. "Moshe Rabbeinu went out and gave a *krechtz* for the Jewish people," he said. "A Yid has to know how to feel for his fellow Yid."

He went on to show how Rav Chaim Kreiswirth had demonstrated the same qualities.

Those words made a huge impression on me because of their inherent truth. A Yid really does have to know how to feel for his brothers when they're in pain and how to give a *krechtz* for *Klal Yisrael*.

On a similar note, Rav Don told me what happened when Rav Shach eulogized Rav Beinish Finkel, *zt"l*.

He began his *hesped* with the word *dodi*, "my beloved." Rav Shach couldn't move past the word. He just kept on repeating it. It was obvious that Rav Shach loved his friend with all his heart and soul and couldn't get over his loss. *Dodi*, my beloved. *Dodi*, my beloved. That was the love Rav Shach had for the *rosh yeshivah* of the Mir, that's the type of love Rav Don has for *Klal Yisrael*, and that's the love a Yid should ideally feel for the Ribbono shel Olam.

It's the love that Rabbi Akiva portrayed for Hashem when he would recite *Shir HaShirim*. The *poskim* discuss how he'd say the words, and tears of love for the Master of the world would stream from his eyes (*Taz, Orach Chaim* 288:2).

◆ ◆ ◆

There was a girl in the hospital who was very sick, and Rav Don was asked to daven for her. Rav Don contacted the girl's mother shortly afterward and asked her if she had ever considered naming her daughter Nava.

The mother was taken aback.

"Nava was one of the names we considered for our daughter," she admitted. "Why do you want to know?"

"Because," Rav Don explained, "I am saying *Tehillim*, and I just can't get the word Nava out of my mouth."

"I don't understand," the mother said.

"Whenever I reach the word *na'avah* in a *pasuk*," Rav Don said, "it won't come out. I can't say it."

"What does that mean?"

"I think it means that your daughter is supposed to be called Nava."

They changed her name to Nava and she recovered.

◆ ◆ ◆

A close family member of mine was having trouble maintaining his sense of balance. He would fall repeatedly and get hurt. Wanting to ease his pain, I declared that I would accept his suffering and *yissurim* on myself if I could.

Immediately following my grand statement of altruism, I suffered from leg injuries on six separate occasions! I broke my ankle, hurt my knee, and even suffered from a torn meniscus during my daughter's wedding! On top of all that, the ladder collapsed from under me while I was building my succah and I was injured again.

In desperation, I went to Rav Don and told him the whole story.

"There's no question in my mind that this is happening to you because of what you said. This is a classic example of *ko'ach hadibbur* — of the power of words. This shows that Hashem really takes what you say seriously."

Now I was really anxious. "What should I do now? Things are really getting out of hand!"

"Get up in public," he advised me, "and say that you are no

longer willing to take on that person's *yissurim* — and that you don't want them to return to the original recipient either."

I followed his advice, and the injuries stopped — for both of us.

One of the lessons I learned from that story was the power of speech and how a person has to be so careful of the words that come out of his mouth.

Rav Don himself imbues everything he says with a feeling of *romemus*. He is uplifted and he uplifts. Just hearing him utter the word *romemus* — just that word alone — is a lesson in what it means to be a person permeated with *kedushah*. You feel him elevating you just by hearing the word coming out of his mouth. His words are not mere words. They are vehicles of holiness, calculated to lift his *talmidim* out of the drudgery of the "real" world and into a place of exalted spiritual feeling.

◆ ◆ ◆

"I think I am doing too many things and spreading myself way too thin," I told Rav Don one day. "I'm afraid that I am burning myself out."

"On the contrary," Rav Don rejoined, "you should do more! You should know that the more you do, the more *ko'ach* Hashem gives you."

Once I heard those words, I was no longer afraid. I had Rav Don's reassurance on my side.

Along similar lines, Rav Don told me the following story.

The Brisker Rav once had to make an emergency visit to an Israeli government office on *erev Yom Kippur*. When he approached the civil servant at the desk, the man turned down the Brisker Rav's request with the words "*Kevod HaRav, eini yachol.*" Rabbi, it's *erev Yom Kippur*. I cannot help you.

The Brisker Rav's response: "Don't say, '*Eini yachol.*' Say, '*Eini rotzeh.*'" Don't say, "I can't do it." Say, "I don't want to do it."

They repeated this interchange three times, until the clerk gave in and took care of whatever it was that the Brisker Rav wanted him to do.

"There's no such thing as *eini yachol*, I can't do something," Rav

Don stressed. "*Eini yachol* doesn't exist. It all depends how much you want something! If you want it badly enough, you can get anything done!"

Quoting Rav Chatzkel Levenstein, Rav Don told me that one of the most important *sefarim* to study is *Nefesh HaChaim*. It happens to be that *Nefesh HaChaim* is not the easiest *sefer* to learn. There are a lot of kabbalistic ideas in it, and it's not always easy to grasp. But I followed his advice.

The author, Rav Chaim of Volozhin, describes the unlimited potential within every one of us and how we are connected to the upper worlds and the *sefiros* and how we are not limited in our potential.

"*Chevel nachalaso*," the *Nefesh HaChaim* teaches. Every Jew is tied completely to the Ribbono shel Olam, and you can go as far as you want. But you have to really want to get there! As Rav Don had told me, "If you decide to do more, Hashem will give you more strength."

At the time I found myself slightly shocked by the simplicity with which he portrayed this deep concept.

◆ ◆ ◆

As a sign of *aveilus*, I don't wear a tie during the Nine Days. This decision can lead to embarrassing situations at times, since there are citywide *shiurim* on *hilchos lashon hara* during the Nine Days, and I am often asked to address the crowd. Being tieless makes me feel awkward. Every other speaker wears a tie while I sit there in my white shirt and jacket like an Israeli politician from the seventies. If I were wearing a "frock coat" it would be something else. Then not wearing a tie wouldn't make me stand out as much. But since my normal attire is more or less like that of everyone else, a hat and jacket, the absence of a tie is quite obvious.

(When Rebbetzin Twersky, the wife of Rav Mosheh Twersky *Hy"d*, who was killed in the Har Nof massacre, showed me a picture of her husband without a tie because it was *erev Shabbos* and he wanted to appreciate his Shabbos clothing to a higher degree, I stopped wearing a tie on *erev Shabbos* as well.)

Regarding my tie dilemma, I decided to ask Rav Don what he thought about my decision.

Rav Don was very much in favor of my practice, and then told me about a *yungerman* who had the habit of shining his shoes on a daily basis — except for the Nine Days when he left them unshined. Rav Don felt that this was a huge thing.

"Little actions, like not shining your shoes or not wearing a tie, make an indelible mark on a person's *neshamah* because they are literally connecting him to the *aveilus*. Choosing to give something up that's important to you for the sake of the *Churban* makes a real impression on your *neshamah*. It doesn't have to be something that's important to other people, as long as it's important to you. Then it becomes a personal gift."

◆　◆　◆

Whenever I left Eretz Yisrael to fundraise for the *kollel*, I'd ask Rav Don for a *berachah*. He'd give me a *berachah*, remarking enthusiastically, "It's such a great thing that you're going to *chutz la'aretz* to collect for the *avreichim* of the *kollel*! You're helping them learn and supporting them in their mission. This is the best thing you could possibly be doing in the world!"

Inevitably, not only did he give me his typical (atypical) *berachah*, but he'd also insist on accompanying me as I went on my way, starting me off on my journey, as it were.

As everyone knows, fundraising is not a job for the faint of heart. It's difficult. It's filled with humiliating moments. But listening to Rav Don, I'd feel a sense of happiness and gratitude for the fact that the Ribbono shel Olam had chosen me to get on a plane and solicit funds so that many young men would be able to sit and learn in Yerushalayim.

This is Rav Don. He knows how to turn a situation around so one viewed it from the proper perspective.

There was a tragic story where the father of a *chasan* was killed in a car accident on the way home from his child's wedding. People, of course, reacted with horror at the timing.

Rav Don had an entirely different slant on the situation.

"Think of the *rachamim*," Rav Don said. "Imagine if the father had been killed before the wedding! The wedding would have been postponed..."

We have to learn how to find *rachamim* even within the *din*, the mercy within the judgment.

In the aftermath of a pogrom, Rav Baruch Ber Leibowitz instructed his yeshivah to hold a special *tefillah* to praise Hashem for giving them the Torah.

"It's not Shavuos," one of the *talmidim* pointed out. "We should thank Hashem for being saved."

"We have to thank Hashem for giving us the Torah," his rebbi replied, "because without the Torah we would be just like them."

◆ ◆ ◆

Rav Don's worldview is such that the entire universe boils down to Torah and *Klal Yisrael*. One day I heard him make the following fascinating observation:

"The whole women's lib movement," he posited, "was because of Torah and *Klal Yisrael*."

When I questioned him, he was happy to explain.

"Currently there are many *avreichim* who spend their days learning full-time in *kollel*. This is something both the husband and wife want. In many cases, the only way *kollel* families can support themselves is if the wife works. A hundred years ago it would have been pure heresy for a woman to go to work. So the women's lib movement was established, giving women the legitimacy to pursue a career, and now *kollel* wives can work (if they so choose) without any impediments.

"In a similar vein," he went on, "the Quakers don't use electricity. This has had a wonderful outcome for the Jewish people because we need a hand grinder for baking matzos, and the Quakers have designed the best and most effective hand grinder — one that is perfect for our needs.

"If you think about it, everything in the world is for Torah and *Klal Yisrael*."

Chapter Ten

I f someone were to ask me to describe Rav Don, I would use the words *"yedid Hashem,"* Hashem's friend. Talking to him, I always walked away with the feeling that he had a certain elusive *yedidus* with Hashem completely unique to him.

Rav Don told me that Rav Shach used to give him *mussar* for not accepting an official position, either as the *mashgiach* of Ponevezh or something similar.

"What can I do?" he said to me. "I have such *simchas hachaim* in my relationship with Hashem. How can I take on an official position?"

Today two of his sons run *kollelim*, but Rav Don is still unencumbered by an official position, more than content to be referred to as *"echad mehamashgichim"* — as one of the *mashgichim* of the generation.

In an interesting twist, Rav Brevda lived his life exactly the same way — as a roving ambassador, delivering *shiurim* around the world and helping draw Yidden closer to Hashem — but never in an official position of authority. Both Rav Brevda and Rav Don were *talmidim* of Rav Chatzkel, content with their roles of *eved Hashem* and *yedid Hashem*.

And, of course, when *tzaddikim* run away from *kavod*, everyone pursues them and is constantly running after them for *berachos* and *eitzos* and listening to their every word. There are numerous people like this. Individuals who never held a position. And yet they are sought after by the entire world. They are the *yedidei Hashem*.

They have a job to do.

Their job is to assist Yidden in making a connection with the Creator of the world.

Who better than a *tzaddik* like Rav Don who is capable of imposing a *ta'anis dibbur* on himself from the beginning of Elul until after Yom Kippur? Of course, delivering *shiurim* is considered *divrei kedushah*, and he still speaks to the *tzibbur* during this period, but if he has anything to say that is not Torah, he will write it on a piece of paper.

This is Rav Don. He asks for nothing. The world seeks him out, because they know the truth and desire to touch holiness when they see it.

◆ ◆ ◆

In one of his *shiurim,* Rav Don told us, "A person has to be so careful when it comes to business."

"What do you mean?"

"I mean that it is incredibly easy to be pulled into doing the wrong thing with regard to money. Not long ago someone came to ask me about getting involved in a financial deal that was somewhat on the shady side. After they described the deal to me, I asked them how they could even consider such a deal. But then after they left, I said to myself, *Wait a second. Maybe it's not so bad…*

"*Baruch Hashem*, I caught myself in time, but the fact that I entertained the idea even for a second only reinforced the power of this particular *yetzer hara*."

It's an interesting phenomenon that a person like Rav Don, who is almost wholly removed from this world, is a man whom many consult when it comes to matters of business. Many people attribute their success in business to his guidance. Someone told me how his father kept on asking Rav Don whether he should sell a certain stock. The stock's value was on the rise, and the man asked Rav Don time and again whether he should sell.

Finally Rav Don told him to sell the stock.

The market crashed the next day.

The fact is, it's obvious to those who know him that Rav Don Segal is a *ba'al ruach hakodesh*. Once, in a *shiur*, Rav Don said that if a person follows a certain course of spiritual action, then he could "personally testify that the person could achieve *ruach hako —*"

The words were coming out of his mouth when he caught himself and moved on to a different topic.

Yet, though he may have saved himself from a direct statement on the subject, his *talmidim* know that he possesses a certain sense of *kedushah*, that he "knows" things that a common person really has no way of knowing...

◆ ◆ ◆

Having to raise funds for my *kollel* means that I am a person who spends more time than I would like on the road. As a result, I have enjoyed many a conversation with a host of unlikely people over the years.

Rav Don, too, saintly though he may be, attracts all sorts of people and doesn't discourage people's inevitable questions.

"Not long ago," he said to me, "I was on a plane and the non-religious steward approached me with a question:

"'Are you Rav Don Segal?'

"I nodded in the affirmative.

"'My brother goes to your *shiurim*.'

"His brother had become religious and was now a *talmid*.

"One thing led to another, and the steward invited me on a tour of the cockpit. I wouldn't have accepted the invitation, but I was hoping that maybe our conversation would have a positive effect on his life as well."

I asked Rav Don what he said to the man.

"While we were in the cockpit, I asked him one question: What makes this plane fly?"

"Why that question?"

"For a person who spends the majority of his time in the sky, I could think of no better question, especially since there is only one real answer. As a *posek*, there is no question in my mind that a Jew has to recite the *berachah* of *hagomel* when he steps off a plane. After all, he has just spent hours flying thirty thousand feet above the ground!"

"What was his answer?"

"He cut my visit short and sent me back to my seat."

◆ ◆ ◆

Rav Don often uses stories of *gedolim* as a tool to teach invaluable lessons to his listeners.

"Watching Rav Baruch Ber learning a piece of Gemara," he liked to say, "was like seeing a person enjoying a meal of the finest cuisine. Imagine a person cutting a piece of perfectly broiled steak in the finest restaurant. Rav Baruch Ber enjoyed a *sugya* more than that. Way more."

He'd quote the Chazon Ish, who wrote, "If we were free of sin, we would go out of our minds with pleasure whenever we learned Torah. The intensity of merely uttering '*amar Abaye*' would afford us such a level of pleasure that a person wouldn't know what to do with himself."

◆ ◆ ◆

Rav Don stressed the fact that a person can be successful in his learning only if he does his best to keep himself pure.

There was a *maskil* who asked to be able to deliver a *derashah* in Rav Chaim Brisker's shul. Of course, his request was denied.

"But I will quote only pure Torah sources," he protested.

"Kosher food in a *tereifah* pot is still *tereifah*," he was told.

It's not enough to learn Torah. A person has to turn himself into a utensil worthy of being filled with Torah learning.

◆ ◆ ◆

When Rav Chaim Brisker was very young, many *gedolim* from all over Europe gathered to hear his first *shiur*. After he finished delivering the *shiur*, the *rabbanim* were so overcome by the brilliance of his words and his method of delivery that they broke out in a spontaneous dance to celebrate the *gadlus* of Torah that the next generation had to look forward to.

"That absolute joy of Torah is missing today," Rav Don lamented. "When Rav Aharon Kotler uttered the word *Torah*, you could see the incredible joy just saying the word gave him. Hearing him say *Torah* was so uplifting that his *talmidim* would try to get their rebbi to say the word."

A *kollel yungerman* shouldn't just get used to the fact that he is sitting and learning. He needs to stay cognizant of his good fortune at being part of such a world. Not just focus on the idea that learning is a mitzvah, but feel the immense joy that learning can give a person who allows it to become part of him, and recognize its sweetness and the complete pleasure it gives him.

I remember hearing Rav Don comment, "We don't feel happy about learning Torah today. When a person reaches his seat in the *beis midrash*, he should start dancing!"

◆ ◆ ◆

Another *gadol* story that I heard Rav Don relate involved the Chafetz Chaim.

"The Chafetz Chaim was very afraid of receiving *kavod*. When questioned as to why he detested this pursuit more than all the rest, the Chafetz Chaim explained that unlike food or money, which are pursuits limited to this world, *kavod* takes away from a person's *Olam HaBa*, because it is a spiritual pleasure. The Chafetz Chaim therefore begged people not to give him any honor."

"A *rosh kollel* gets a certain amount of honor from his *talmidim*," I pointed out. "Not much, but some. This means that now he has an obligation to 'repay' what he has received in the *kavod* department. How does he do that? By going to *chutz la'aretz* to raise money — facing embarrassing situations and thereby repaying whatever honor he received."

◆ ◆ ◆

Rav Don told me that when the Chazon Ish passed away, the Brisker Rav said that a world with the Chazon Ish and a world without the Chazon Ish are two completely different worlds. Rav Don made the same remark when Rav Elyashiv passed away. "A world without Rav Elyashiv is a different reality," he said.

Rav Elyashiv passed away during a time of loss. Fifteen *gedolim* were *niftar* within a few months. Rav Don took every additional passing to heart, explaining to me that the world we had known for so long would never be the same again.

◆ ◆ ◆

Rav Don was very against people learning by themselves without a *chavrusa*.

"Chazal say people who learn by themselves are *'mitapshin'* — their learning becomes much weaker. On the other hand," he continued, "it's not good to lose your individuality either. A person should be part of a program, but must make sure to maintain his individuality."

Rav Don was not in favor of a person forgoing his talents and capabilities in order to become part of the *klal*.

It says, "*Kabeid es Hashem b'honecha.*" The simple meaning of the word *b'honecha* means "with your money," but Rav Don translated it as "anything that Hashem bestowed you with," including personal talents of any kind.

Rav Shlomo Zalman Auerbach was once invited to a *sheva berachos*. From the moment of his arrival, the *gadol* made the assembled laugh. A *talmid* who was there couldn't understand what was going on. After all, Rav Shlomo Zalman was a fairly serious person, and this behavior was out of character.

When he asked his rebbi for an explanation, Rav Shlomo Zalman explained.

"It happens to be that Hashem blessed me with a good sense of humor. I don't often have the opportunity to use it to its fullest, but I felt that a *sheva berachos* was the perfect time to make the guests laugh and use a gift that I was granted by the Ribbono shel Olam. Everyone has strengths and unique talents. The issue is finding the right way to showcase those talents in our lives, but we have an obligation to use the gifts we were granted by Hashem."

◆ ◆ ◆

Rav Don has a special love for Shabbos. He told me how he was once visiting a *gadol* and heard him instructing a family member to "bring something in to him from the Shabbos room."

A little questioning and all became clear. The family ate their meals during the week in the kitchen. On Shabbos, however, they ate in the living/dining room, which was consequently called the "Shabbos room."

"These people were living Shabbos the entire week," Rav Don said, "and since their entire lives revolved around Shabbos, it made sense to call the room after the most important day of the week. We have to do whatever we can to remain connected to Shabbos all the time."

Rav Don related how Rav Chatzkel just couldn't understand it at all when someone came late to shul on Shabbos. He would exclaim in wonder, "A *Shabbosdige* davening! A *Shabbosdige* davening! How can a person be willing to miss such an incredible thing?"

"People say that they are *shomer Shabbos*," Rav Don says. "'We are *shomer Shabbos*. We don't do *melachah*.' That's not what *shomer Shabbos* means. Being *shomer Shabbos* means that you hold on to the holiness of Shabbos throughout the entire week and allow it to penetrate your *neshamah*. Being *shomer Shabbos* should also affect the way a Yid enters Shabbos and the way he ends Shabbos. It's a lifelong process."

◆ ◆ ◆

While spending Shabbos once in Teveria, Rav Don davened in a Sephardic shul. When I saw him next, he commented on how impressed he had been with the people and their *hanhagah* within the walls of the shul.

"They treated their shul the way a shul is supposed to be treated," he said. "Do you know how careful a person has to be inside a shul?" he asked me. "Even to give *mussar* in a shul is not a simple thing."

"Why is that?"

"Because you start off with a *mussar vort* and that leads to a story. One thing leads to another, and it is very easy to forget where you are and the sanctity that surrounds you.

"Your *dibbur* in the shul has to reflect the *kedushah* of the place."

On a similar note, the halachah demands that a parent not kiss a child in shul because while in shul a person is supposed to show love only for Hashem. The Ponevezher Rav, however, would kiss *talmidei chachamim* in the *beis midrash*. When asked why he was overlooking what was ostensibly a simple halachah, the *rav* explained that by kissing *talmidei chachamim* he was visibly demonstrating his love for Hashem.

Eilu v'eilu divrei Elokim chaim.

Encounters With

Rav
Shlomo Wolbe
זצ"ל

Mussar Giant

"If something is going too easily, then it's not really going at all! If there are no growing pains, then you're probably not growing. Avodas Hashem is about overcoming challenges and reaching the next level. The Torah way of life is the best and the sweetest, but that doesn't mean you won't find it difficult. Especially if you want to move up to the next madreigah."

Chapter Eleven

I was a student at Yeshivas Heichal HaTorah, the yeshivah of Rav Tzvi Kushelevsky, on Givat Shaul Street, for the first five years of my married life. That was where I spent my days and that was where I almost lost my life, on that memorable Friday afternoon. But Givat Shaul Street is memorable to me for another reason as well: one of *Klal Yisrael's mussar* giants lived right across the street from the yeshivah, affording me access to his home on a regular basis.

Rav Shlomo Wolbe would daven at a nearby shul known as Perushim, and I made a decision to speak to him at least once a week. The first time we met I asked him if we could converse in English.

"If you speak the Queen's English," he replied with a twinkle in his eye, "we will definitely be able to converse. But if you speak like a New Yorker, I won't be able to understand you at all, and then speaking in English might prove to be slightly challenging."

◆ ◆ ◆

Rav Wolbe named his most renowned *sefer Alei Shur*, explaining that he chose to name it thus based on a midrash that details how the women in Egypt would climb up on the walls (*"alei shur"*) to catch a glimpse of Yosef HaTzaddik due to his outstanding (spiritual) beauty.

"A true *ben aliyah* is someone who is constantly working on himself," Rav Wolbe writes, "and that is something that even the nations will recognize and will climb walls to look at."

The more I got to know him, the more I felt that he himself epitomized what it meant to be a *ben aliyah* in his own life, and I also came to understand that one of our goals is spreading *kavod Shamayim* throughout the world.

Egypt was a country steeped in licentiousness, but even they, the most immoral people in the universe at that time, were able to recognize the greatness of Yosef HaTzaddik and wanted to acquire some of what made him so special for themselves, because Yosef was the essence of a *ben Torah* and that's the level all of us should be striving to achieve.

Rav Wolbe himself was all about building every person and bringing out his *gadlus*, to the point where every Jew should be worthy of having people climb the walls to catch a glimpse of his shining spiritual countenance.

◆ ◆ ◆

Rav Wolbe was one of the *talmidei chachamim* I approached to ask for a Torah thought when writing my first *sefer*, *Mizmor L'Sodah*. He graciously acquiesced. In the piece he gave me, he explained the value of silence and wrote that it was just as important as giving thanks with words. He wrote that a person can use the power of speech in multiple ways: he can daven and thank Hashem; he can make a *chasan* and *kallah* feel good with a heartfelt *berachah*. "However," he continued, "staying silent is no less important, and a person must be constantly thinking about what to say and what not to say."

He himself was a true master of *shtikah*, of silence, a quiet person who used his speech sparingly — to the point where you almost had to pull words out of him.

Rav Wolbe's mode of behavior fit with the concept of *"mezukak shivasayim"* — purified to the nth degree (a concept he referred to fairly often), which is used regarding the oil that was burned in the Menorah. The same concept can be used with speech when a person sifts through his words before uttering them, considering the outcome and ramifications of what he says to the people hearing them. Rav Wolbe was completely in control of his speech, and you could sense that he was almost molding his sentences into the most effective tools possible.

It shouldn't be surprising that I found his davening very meaningful. He didn't move at all throughout, standing completely still. His stillness seemed connected to his *shtikah* — to the profound silence that he maintained so religiously.

◆ ◆ ◆

During our hard times, Rav Wolbe was very sympathetic to our situation and tried his best to help us in a number of ways. The majority of the *gedolim* we consulted gave us practical *eitzos* for how to deal with our challenges, and Rav Wolbe was no exception.

On one occasion he recommended a certain homeopathic doctor that he felt might be able to help me with certain recurring health issues.

"This doctor helped me a lot," he said. "I want you to go see him."

I followed his advice and visited the doctor, who prescribed treatment for me — treatment that actually was beneficial in many ways.

◆ ◆ ◆

In addition to *Alei Shur*, Rav Wolbe wrote a *Kuntres Chasanim*, where he provides a wide range of insightful comments, advice for a successful marriage. To my mind, his *kuntres* was like a *Shulchan Aruch* on the laws of marriage.

In the yeshivah world, the majority of *bachurim* hear one main *chasan shmuess* before being expected to embark on what is possibly the most important relationship of their lives. Here, however, was a *sefer* with vital principles for a happy and stable marriage, and I felt that it should be required reading for every *bachur* before leaving yeshivah to set up a home.

We have to remember something.

Our *bachurim* and girls do not spend time socializing together. And while it's true that brothers have sisters and vice versa, that in itself will not prepare a person for marriage because the average *bachur* does not relate to his sister in the way he will relate to his future wife. Rav Wolbe wrote *Kuntres Chasanim* so that young men would know how to act and what to expect in the days following the *sheva berachos*. He believed in preparing people for marriage, and I feel this is especially important in this day and age when all too many marriages do not last. Maybe if all our young men and women were getting the proper *hadrachah* as Rav Wolbe envisioned, we would see a change in that area.

◆ ◆ ◆

Rav Wolbe was a *ba'al mussar* whose approach to the way he lived his life was very much "by the book." One winter's day we were walking together, and he noticed that I wasn't wearing a coat. Although it was winter, it wasn't that cold and I hadn't taken much notice of the weather.

"Where is your coat?" he asked me sternly.

"It's not a cold day," I responded meekly.

Rav Wolbe was not impressed with my arguments and brushed them aside.

"In the winter, you wear a coat," he said with finality.

To Rav Wolbe it was obvious that you do what is necessary. This meant wearing a coat in the winter and not taking a chance with your health, no matter what.

The truth is, Rav Wolbe was hitting the nail on the head here. I had never been one for toeing the line. (Perhaps that is why I had never gotten along with *dikduk*.) Giving me such a command was *mussar* of the highest order.

The winter I came down with meningitis, which developed into pneumonia, was a tough winter, to put it mildly. In the winter's aftermath, when my health had begun to stabilize again, I told Rav Wolbe about the past few months.

"I must have pushed myself too hard," I told him.

Once again, Rav Wolbe took me to task.

"What does that even mean?" he asked me. "I don't understand! You have first *seder*, second *seder*, and night *seder* and then you go to sleep!"

Beneath his simple words was an underlying message that he made sure to reinforce time and again: There are rules in life, and it is our job to obey them if we want to flourish and be successful. If you push yourself beyond your limits, there are repercussions. Remain within the boundaries set for you by the Torah, and you will be just fine.

Rav Wolbe was so fine-tuned in his *avodas Hashem* that it was as if he couldn't even grasp how a person could possibly place himself at risk with his behavior. Slowly but surely his message began to sink in and eventually to resonate within me, until I began hearing his voice inside my mind gently directing me in the right direction.

◆ ◆ ◆

While walking together in Givat Shaul one afternoon, we noticed a crane towering over the Yerushalayim skyline, and Rav Wolbe stopped to gaze at it for a few seconds, fascinated and amazed that Hashem had granted human beings the ability to create something so fantastic. Rav Wolbe's somewhat intense reaction reminded me of the way a child is amazed and delighted by everything new that he sees. His childlike excitement and appreciation of the world is what so many of us are missing in our lives — lives where everything has become dry and nothing moves us.

I have an aunt in California who signs her emails with the words "Stay Amazed," and it reminds me that this is a sentiment many people are lacking.

Rav Wolbe's *mussar* approach gifted him with a certain freshness, and this was revealed to me in his appreciation of the workings of a crane, something to which most adults have already long stopped paying attention, perhaps to our detriment.

◆ ◆ ◆

When I started to learn halachah, Rav Wolbe warned me against being a *posek* who leans toward *chumros* in halachah.

"*Chumros* are not halachah," he said to me, conveying his point of view in as clear a fashion as he could. "If a *posek* gets caught up with *chumros*, he's missing the real point, which is to do *ratzon Hashem*."

He also mentioned to me that he was very impressed with *Shemiras Shabbos K'Hilchasah*, a work that he considered a genuine halachah *sefer*, as opposed to so many others, which he referred to as "*likutei chumros*," a compilation of *chumros*.

My approach to making a *psak halachah* was honed by Rav Shlomo Zalman Auerbach, who told me clearly that "it's *assur* for a person to keep *chumros* unless he learned the *sugya* himself and arrived at the conclusion that a particular *chumrah* is the right way for him to go. However, if *Klal Yisrael* follows a certain approach or halachah, then for a person to decide to be more stringent is against *minhag Yisrael*. If a person didn't learn the *sugya* himself and is just taking on *chumros* because other people are doing them, it's completely fake behavior."

"When the Brisker Rav took on a *chumrah*," Rav Wolbe said to me, "that was a great thing, because he knew what he was talking about, he had worked out the reasons for doing it, and he had come to the halachic conclusion that this was the proper course of action. That is a special thing. What's not special is when people take on *chumros* just because it makes them look *frum*."

Once, the Brisker Rav was seen drinking water outside the succah. When asked how he was able to do such a thing, considering the fact that it says, "*Ba'al nefesh yachmir al atzmo*" — that it is praiseworthy to be stringent about not eating or drinking anything outside the succah's four walls (*Shulchan Aruch, Orach Chaim* 639:2) — the Brisker Rav replied, "It's a *chumrah*. Everything I do is *me'ikar hadin*. It is the basic halachah to follow."

"What about the fact that you are often so *machmir*?" he was asked.

"That's because I learned the *sugya* and understand that the *Rishonim* rule a certain way."

If a person goes through a *sugya* from start to finish and reaches a conclusion that he should act in a way that seems in line with the more stringent course of action, then he should do so by all means because he got there on his own and can back his opinion with halachic proofs. But he should keep in mind that once that occurs, it will no longer be considered a *chumrah* for him but rather the halachah.

◆ ◆ ◆

Rav Wolbe stressed that whatever a person does in life (helping your wife is a good example) should be viewed as an act of *chesed*, and thought and concentration should be put into it. You may be doing a simple action, but you should keep in mind that you are doing *chesed*.

"*Olam chesed yibaneh*," he'd say. "You should be constantly thinking about the different types of *chesed* available to you. When you get on the bus or into a taxi or walk into a grocery store — in all these scenarios there is possible *chesed* involved. Just the fact that you have chosen this taxi driver is a *chesed*..."

This type of behavior is the antithesis to the way most people live their lives, yet it will make your life so much more enjoyable! We give and give and give all the time; we may as well have the *kavannah* that we're doing *chesed* at the same time and turn what we're doing into the mitzvah that it is!

Two people can do the exact same action, and one will receive reward for it and the other won't — because one had the *kavannah* that he was doing a mitzvah and the other didn't.

◆ ◆ ◆

When I spent time in conversation with Rav Wolbe, it reminded me of stories I'd read about the great *ba'alei mussar* of the past — men like the Alter of Kelm and the Alter of Novardok. I'd see them in him; the behavior he exhibited was such that I knew they would have acted the same way. I'm an American, and I have long felt that although the United States has many *ma'alos*, there are major deficiencies as well. One of those flaws is the lack of dignity.

Ba'alei mussar are saintly men who strive mightily to develop the inner dignity that is the essence of a prince. When you see a Jew who has spent much of his life working on his *middos*, there is such dignity and such attention given to every detail of the person's life in the way he speaks, eats, and carries himself. That was Rav Shlomo Wolbe — a prince of Torah, with incredible inner dignity that bore witness to years of working on his *middos*.

◆ ◆ ◆

On one occasion I asked Rav Wolbe about learning *Mesillas Yesharim*.

"*Mesillas Yesharim* is a very difficult *sefer*," he said. "If you want to study *Mesillas Yesharim*, then you have to focus on the first chapter, where he discusses '*chovas ha'adam b'olamo*' — a man's obligations in this world. Once a person understands what he is doing here, the rest is easy."

Rav Wolbe was telling me that a person has to really crystallize what he wants out of life. Say a person wants to travel from New York to Passaic. He types his destination into his MapQuest, and a second later he has a clear route in his hand. If a person knows where he's going, then it's easy.

This idea of a person knowing what he wants and who he should be is encapsulated in the opening words of the first chapter of *Mesillas Yesharim*: "*Yesod hachassidus v'shoresh ha'avodah hatemimah hu sheyisbarer v'yisameis eitzel ha'adam mah chovaso b'olamo* — The foundation of piety and the route of pure service is that a person should clarify and verify what his obligation is in Hashem's world."

"Sometimes," Rav Wolbe said, "I feel like you can put a hat and jacket on a stick and that's a *yeshivah bachur*. Everyone's copying everyone else. This is why the *Mesillas Yesharim* says that a person's obligation is to understand '*mah chovaso b'olamo,*' *his* obligation in His world. Every person has to know who *he* is."

Knowing who you are and what you want from life is step one to making a success of your time in Hashem's world.

"Once you know what your mission is," Rav Wolbe liked to say, "life becomes so much easier."

Rav Wolbe encouraged me to write — both *sefarim* and poetry — and to use my unique set of talents because those were my own personal gifts from Hashem.

◆ ◆ ◆

Rav Wolbe once asked the following question in a *va'ad*:

"How many people find themselves in the middle of reciting *Shema* and feel that they cannot continue until the end, basically saying to themselves, 'You know something? I don't want to do this anymore!'"

Obviously no one sitting in the audience responded.

"The fact that nobody feels that way," he continued, "is a sign that people are not really accepting the yoke of Heaven upon themselves, because if they were, then they'd know what they were saying and they'd be afraid to say the words. They'd be afraid of the contract they're agreeing to with every additional word.

"Let's be honest," he went on. "If a person doesn't have the inner opposition to the promises that he's making when he recites *Shema*, then he's fooling himself."

And indeed, as Rav Wolbe made clear, it's very easy to fool yourself.

When I say *Shema*, what am I doing? I'm accepting the yoke of Heaven upon myself. That means agreeing to keep 613 mitzvos *d'Oraisa* and all the *mitzvos d'rabbanan* and *divrei sofrim* and *minhagim*, and all the multiple details that come with each mitzvah and *minhag* — by saying *Shema* I'm agreeing to abide by all of these obligations on a daily basis! There's also *emunah* in Hashem and *ahavah* for Hashem. It's a tremendously complicated and binding contract for a person to agree to sign. If you just blithely say the words and your acceptance doesn't make you nervous at all, then what are you agreeing to and what are you accepting on yourself?

To really accept the yoke of Heaven, you need to be honest about what it's going to demand from you!

Which is why, when a person is saying *Shema*, he should be apprehensive and unsure of himself. Because this is a major challenge that we accept upon ourselves every single day of the year!

Rav Wolbe stressed how honest we need to be with ourselves regarding our life challenges and our *avodas Hashem*. How *Yiddishkeit* is not a game — it's a serious commitment for life, and it's supposed to be challenging. When Chazal use the words "*kabbalas ol malchus Shamayim,*" the implications are that this is supposed to be a struggle. It means thinking about what you as a Jew are accepting upon yourself, and that you are accepting those obligations with happiness and the knowledge that you are going to have to really work to get it right.

Many times he'd say, "If something is going too easily, then it's not really going at all! If there are no growing pains, then you're probably not growing. *Avodas Hashem* is about overcoming challenges and reaching the next level. The Torah way of life is the best and the sweetest, but that doesn't mean you won't find it difficult. Especially if you want to move up to the next *madreigah*.

"When a person begins a workout regimen of pushups or weight lifting, he begins slowly and is challenged at every step (until he reaches his goal and finds that his muscles have developed and are much more powerful than before). The same is true when it comes to weight lifting in the Torah arena."

◆ ◆ ◆

There's another very important point: the struggle in this case is referring to a *positive* struggle. When a person lifts weights, he begins with lighter weights before progressing to heavier weights and it hurts him to do it — his muscles ache and it's difficult — yet he still enjoys it and wants to do it because at the end, he will have achieved a goal. It's the same thing when it comes to the challenges of being a true *ben aliyah*. The challenge may be great, but it's one of positive development with true goals and incredible rewards.

For many years I learned one day a week with boxing middleweight champion Yuri Foreman. At the time Yuri was one of the top boxers in the world. Yuri was from Russia, he was a *ba'al teshuvah*, and had competed in twenty-eight prize fights undefeated, culminating with a dramatic win in Yankee Stadium. We learned *issur v'heter* together, and Yuri eventually received *semichah*, a fascinating and unprecedented development in the life of a professional boxer.

Many of the religious people in Yuri's life were against him boxing, but I felt that it was completely permissible for him to continue in his chosen field. I even wrote a *teshuvah* about it in one of my *sefarim*. Not only did I hold it was permissible for him to box, I was convinced that Yuri Foreman was making a tremendous *kiddush Hashem* when he stepped into the ring, in a way that nobody else does. The fact is, the world respects professional sports more than almost anything else, and here was a man at the top of his game who was openly keeping Shabbos in a way that reminded me of the pride that so many Jews felt when Sandy Koufax refused to play in the World Series on Yom Kippur.

But here I want to focus on the intensity of Yuri's training. When you ask an athlete who trains for hours every day if he enjoys the training, he will tell you that he doesn't necessarily relish the challenge and the struggle of the six-hour workouts, but he does take pleasure in emerging the winner at the end of the game — or the boxing match at Yankee Stadium.

At the end of the day, we're here to work. Obviously it would be much more pleasant and relaxing if we could just lie in bed all day reading books and drinking iced tea. But if you know what you want and you're focused on achieving the goal, there is no other option but to go for the gold.

When I was fifteen years old I ran my first race. I came in 497 out of 500 runners. After that loss, I said to myself, *This is not going to happen again. From now on I'm going to win!*

I continued running and pushing myself until I became one of the top runners in New York (to the point where the black guys I used to train with said about me, "Travis, if you wasn't white, we'd say you were black!" "You are white on the outside but black on the inside!"). Those guys were incredibly talented athletes, and they treated me with respect because they saw how hard I worked and the level I reached. In my mind, I was not prepared to lose.

When I was 15, at the height of my running days, I was running a hundred miles a week and sometimes I felt like I was tearing my body apart. I used to literally collapse on the floor after my races. And then I'd get up and go on because I had a goal and a mission, and I was driven to the point where I was willing to do anything to get where I wanted to go.

This is the same drive one needs if he wants to find true greatness in the realm of Torah.

This was what Rav Wolbe was telling me. Ignoring the things we need to work on is much easier than changing ourselves. But we're here to grow, and it's imperative that we don't take the easy way out.

The *Mesillas Yesharim* points out that people who love one another are always searching for ways to show it. The authentic *ben Torah* is anxiously waiting for the moment when he can show Hashem what He means to him. The *Mesillas Yesharim* says the same thing about the general of an army. He, too, is waiting for the chance to prove himself, despite the challenges of battle and the possible and probable dangers involved.

When the pilot of U.S. Airways Captain Chesley "Sully" Sullenberger made his famous emergency landing on the Hudson River after his engines failed shortly after takeoff, he saved the lives of his passengers and earned the admiration of every American citizen. When questioned how he felt about his actions during those fateful moments, Sully replied, "I've been waiting all my life for this moment."

His entire life Sully had been developing the skills necessary for precisely such a situation, and he had been ready for just this type of challenging opportunity where he would be forced to use them. The skills were there, but without the challenge no one would ever have known about them.

◆ ◆ ◆

I carry a check for one hundred thousand dollars in my wallet. It's a check I wrote to myself. As I mentioned previously, I've been learning the *Gra* on *Mishlei* with my *chavrusa* for twenty-five years, ever since Rav Brevda told me how important it is for a person's development. One of the things Shlomo HaMelech writes in *Mishlei* (2:4) is that if you pursue the Torah like you would silver and gold, then you'll eventually know what *yiras Hashem* is.

That *pasuk* got me thinking, and I said to myself, *You know, Daniel Yaakov, you'd be prepared to do a lot of things for a hundred thousand dollars.*

I fundraise a lot. Some people give me checks for a few hundred dollars, some for five thousand dollars; sometimes a person will give me a check for ten thousand. But I would be willing to put in a lot of work for one hundred thousand dollars.

I put on tefillin in the morning like every religious man. If someone offered me a check for one hundred thousand dollars on the condition that I put on tefillin the way a person is supposed to put on tefillin — say the relevant *tefillah* before putting them on, think about what I'm doing as I do it, have all the proper *kavannos* — how would I react?

One morning I said to myself, *If I manage to put on my tefillin today the way I would put them on if someone offered me such a check, then I will write myself a check for one hundred thousand dollars.*

That morning I put on my tefillin the way a Jew is supposed to put on his tefillin, and then I took out my checkbook and wrote myself a check for one hundred thousand dollars, which I examine every morning before I take my tefillin out from my tallis bag.

And the truth is, the mitzvah of tefillin is worth way more than one hundred thousand dollars.

It's all about the clarity, as Rav Wolbe stressed over and over, adding that when it comes to clarity the *ba'al teshuvah* has the advantage over the "FFB": he has already fought the battle of deciding what's important to him and achieved a high level of clarity about the importance of being a Jew.

Of course, even if you have clarity, without the discipline needed to do the work, the clarity will not help you achieve your goals.

Clarity. Acceptance. Discipline. Desire.

You must want to reach those goals. Really want it. And you have to remember that real growth involves struggle and be prepared for that.

In other words: challenge + struggle = growth.

Encounters With

Rav
Moshe Meiselman
שליט"א

The Epitome of Integrity

"You learn Torah, you go to Olam HaBa, v'zehu — and that's it!"

Chapter Twelve

I n retrospect, Hashem prepared me at an early age to take the leap of coming from almost no religious background to learning Torah in Yerushalayim. From the time I was very young I had been into learning and personal growth. I attended the Bronx High School of Science, which was ranked third-best high school in the United States and seemed to provide every prospect for a successful life in whichever field I chose. I was involved in the very prestigious Westinghouse Project, which offers high school students full scholarships for innovative projects in the areas of science and social sciences, The teachers at the school regularly impressed upon us that we were the future leaders of America and that every single one of us would go on to the best of Ivy League universities.

All this talk about our glowing futures gave us students the feeling that we could accomplish anything we set out to do. Our teachers were trying to instill in us a feeling of "*romemus*," of being one of the chosen, of the exalted few.

"There are no limitations" was something we were told on a

regular basis. Being fed this type of diet can be dangerous because it encourages a sense of superiority and arrogance. On the other hand, being told that you are part of the best group of students in the country makes you realize that you are destined for greatness and can push you to strive for the heights.

I took my teachers seriously, was chosen editor of the school paper, and spent a lot of time considering my professional future. Everything was moving along just fine when a rabbi was invited to my high school to address the student body. No doubt I would never have dreamed of going to hear him, but someone put up signs (with a picture of him carrying a machine gun) warning students not to attend. In retrospect, I think he was the one who put up the signs, but seeing those signs piqued my curiosity and I decided to go and listen to what this rabbi had to say.

The auditorium was packed when I arrived. There must have been hundreds of students there. The rabbi didn't speak for very long, but his speech made an incredible impact on my *neshamah*. The theme of the talk was the importance of Torah learning, and the truth of his words scorched my soul with their intensity.

Directing his words to the Jewish kids sitting in the auditorium, the rabbi said, "All of you are in the wrong school! You should get on a plane immediately, come to Israel, and study Torah full-time!"

I sat there stunned. Never in my entire life had I heard someone speaking in a way that was completely sincere.

He then turned around, picked up a piece of chalk, and wrote his phone number on the blackboard at the front of the room.

"When you arrive," he concluded, "be in touch with me and come for Shabbos."

Bear in mind that this was the first time I had ever seen an Orthodox rabbi in my life, and I instinctively understood that this man's message was crucial to the way I wanted to spend the rest of my life.

By that time, I had already achieved a healthy dose of what the world considered success. Despite this, I felt completely empty inside. The more I searched, the more desperate I grew, because it seemed to me that there was truly nothing out there. And it wasn't as if the people around me were content and satisfied with their lot. Nobody seemed happy, nobody seemed fulfilled — and these were kids who were being groomed for American leadership positions.

When I met *gedolim* years later, I was struck by the glaring contrast between those uplifted people who were filled with Torah and *yiras Shamayim* and those I had associated with in the past, be it my fellow students or even the professors. It was like seeing two opposite extremes.

Rav Yisrael Salanter writes that if Darwin had met R' Yisrael's rebbi, he would have never been capable of originating his theory of evolution. On a similar note, there are quite a few reasons why a person should find the time to attend *talmidei chachamim*. We learn Torah every single day; many of us spend many hours learning Torah every day. But you don't really understand what a life of Torah is until you spend time with *gedolim*. Attending a *gadol* — what we call "*shimush*" — allows a person to really witness what Chazal meant by the things they wrote. It's one thing to read a line in a *sefer*; it's something else entirely to see the words come alive in an actual person!

But there's another reason relationships with *gedolim* are so imperative. Simply speaking, being involved with *gedolim* elevates a person and gives a person *she'ifos*, ideals toward which to strive. Small people tend to have small aspirations, while being around big people gives us big aspirations and at the same time allows us to internalize the idea that we, too, can become like them if we are willing to work hard enough. This can actually be you! How's that for something to think about? But in order for that to occur you need to develop relationships with *tzaddikim*. It's a prerequisite.

The day the rabbi walked into my high school was the first time I had ever met a *talmid chacham*, and I was simply blown away by him. All he talked about was learning Torah, and his message went straight to my heart, especially in light of the fact that this was my very first exposure to the concept of learning Torah.

Experiencing anything for the first time makes an extremely powerful impression on a person, and so it was with me.

◆ ◆ ◆

The road to becoming *frum* was strewn with obstacles. It's not easy to just pick yourself up and change your entire life. But I have always been a very determined and stubborn individual, and at that point in my life, my stubbornness was a character trait that served me well, helping me forge ahead, despite the opposition coming my way. I began developing connections with the world of religious Jewish people and soon found myself discovering Judaism through NCSY.

One *erev Shabbos*, I left my home with plenty of time to spare for a Shabbaton that was being held in Brooklyn. Having grown up in Queens, I was no stranger to the New York subway system, and that Friday I opted for what I imagined would be a smooth and relatively rapid way of reaching my destination. When I boarded the train that Friday afternoon, Shabbos was about four hours away, leaving me plenty of time.

At first, the journey went fine, with the train making good time. Suddenly, however, everything changed as the train came to an unexpected halt. Looking around at my fellow commuters, I saw that nobody was concerned. This was normal for people used to taking the subway and no reason at all to be nervous.

For the first twenty minutes, I didn't even think twice about the cause of the delay or pay any attention to the infrequent announcements coming across the loudspeaker in conductorese. But as twenty minutes turned into forty-five and then an hour, and as the sun outside the subway car window began descending, I started getting slightly concerned. On a regular day, this would have been mildly inconvenient, but nothing I hadn't been through or couldn't live with. But this was *erev Shabbos*, and for a boy like me, who was in the process of becoming *frum*, the last thing I wanted was to be forced into a situation where I'd end up being *mechallel Shabbos*, even by default, and even if there was nothing to be done about it.

Hours passed. The people around me were upset, everyone was grumbling, the conductor apologized, the air was stifling…and finally, finally, finally, the train began moving once again. But it was really close to Shabbos. Really close.

As the train pulled into a Brooklyn station, I said to myself, *Either you get off the train right now, or you'll be riding a train on Shabbos!*

Needless to say, I got off the train.

◆ ◆ ◆

The station was one where I had never alighted before. Come to think of it, I had never even been in this part of Brooklyn before that Friday afternoon. With New Yorkers rushing past me on every side, I left the underground station, walking down a passageway tiled a dirty white and plastered by advertisements. I ascended to a busy street via a steep staircase, and found myself in the middle of a New York traffic jam. Shabbos was coming any second, and there was no time to lose.

The problem was this:

I was holding a couple of bags in my hand. In a few minutes I wouldn't be able to carry any longer, and then I'd be forced to abandon all my belongings on the street. I didn't want to contemplate such a scenario. I needed an alternative, and at that point, any alternative would do.

It was then that I spied the bowling alley.

Located a block away, it was lit up by a neon sign that flashed orange and white in the shape of a bowling ball and pins. Being flat out of options, I hoisted my bags over my shoulder and headed straight toward the bowling establishment, not sure what I was going to say to the man in charge and uncertain of my reception. It wasn't long before I stood in front of the long, low building, which I now saw was called "Tony's Bowling Alley." Pushing open the door leading into the alley, I found myself hoping that Tony was a nice guy.

As I entered, I could hear the sounds of bowling balls hitting the wooden floor and speeding down the lane to hit the pins with a clatter and a bang. I smelled the aroma unique to bowling alleys everywhere, a mixture of floor polish, fast food and Coke, popcorn, and leather shoes, and relaxed just a tiny bit. I saw the kids playing with their parents and the teenagers standing at the arcades. It was Friday afternoon, and everyone was getting ready for the weekend. Music was blaring on the loudspeakers, and somewhere off to the side a group of people was singing "Happy Birthday" to some kid who'd just turned six.

Ignoring everything bombarding my senses, I went in search of Tony. "I need to speak to Tony," I blurted to the kid manning the front counter.

"Tony!" he called out. "Someone here to see you!"

Tony came out to the counter, and I found myself face to face with a middle-aged Italian man with a slight paunch and a Brooklyn accent.

"Can I help you?"

"Sir," I began, "my Sabbath is about to begin any minute. On the Sabbath I will not be allowed to carry my belongings outside in the street. I need a place to leave my things, and I was wondering if you would allow me to leave my bags here at the bowling alley until tomorrow night, at which time I will come to pick up my stuff."

The truth is, it wasn't just my bags. I also had three hundred dollars in my wallet, given to me by my aunt that day.

Tony gave me permission to leave my things in one of the offices, and watched as I unzipped the top of the bag and carefully placed the three hundred-dollar bills inside. Then, after promising to return the following evening, I left the alley and headed out into Brooklyn.

Unfamiliar with the neighborhood, I had no idea where I was, but I found a little *shtiebel* and davened Minchah, *Kabbalas Shabbos*, and Maariv. I wasn't at all sure what to do next, but I finally remembered a friend of mine who lived in Brooklyn and who I knew would be happy to help out. It took me about an hour and a half to find his home. I finally knocked on his front door at nine-thirty that Friday night. I told him the entire story — how the train had broken down and I'd been forced to leave my belongings at Tony's Bowling Alley. He welcomed me in, and I joined the family who were still at their *seudah*.

In the morning, my friend accompanied me to the Shabbaton, which was a good hour away. All in all, I received a very large dose of exercise that Shabbos. The Shabbos itself was very pleasant, and I enjoyed the singing and dancing as I always did. On the other hand, I couldn't help wondering whether my bags and belongings were still going to be there when I showed up at the alley that night. Tony didn't owe me anything, and if any of my belongings were missing I'd have no way of proving it, since it would be my word against his. But it was Shabbos, and I did my best to put the whole thing out of my mind and celebrated with my usual vigor.

◆ ◆ ◆

The moment *Havdalah* came to an end I borrowed a few bucks, called a taxi and asked the driver to take me to Tony's Bowling Alley. I don't know what exactly I was expecting when I walked through the doors and into the alley, but it was definitely not the sight that hit my eyes. Instead of the sound of bowling balls crashing into pins, there was silence. The place was deserted, completely deserted.

That, however, was nothing compared to the mess. The alley was in a complete shambles. Chairs had been broken into tiny pieces. The machines that returned the balls to the top of the lane had been jammed by pieces of the chairs and were clearly in need of a major emergency operation. Bowling balls had been scattered everywhere; they had obviously been used by whoever had done this to destroy the glass-fronted cabinets where the bowling trophies from past championships had been displayed.

The bowling alley was destroyed. I stood there, in the midst of the carnage, trying to hold myself together in the face of the terrible scene and figure out what to do. Should I run? Maybe the people who had wrecked the place were still around! Was there any chance of retrieving my belongings?

Suddenly a man stepped out of the back office.

It was Tony.

"You're back."

"Yes, sir."

He was pale and looked as sick as a person could look.

"They took everything," he told me. "The cash box, everything of value."

"I'm sorry, Tony."

Other than that there was nothing for me to do but stand beside him in silent commiseration for his pain and losses.

"There's only one thing they didn't touch."

"What's that?"

He led me into the office where I'd left my bags and cash.

"This," he said, pointing down at the floor where my bags sat undisturbed, notwithstanding the wreckage and destruction throughout the alley. Reaching down to one of my bags, he unzipped the zipper and opened the bag. My three hundred dollars lay there, innocent and untouched, as if everything that had transpired in every other part of the bowling establishment had absolutely nothing to do with them at all.

Tony looked at me with a world-weary gaze.

"They didn't touch your bags," he said at last. "It's because you kept your Sabbath. The Jews are a holy people. G-d bless you!"

Then he handed me the bags, and I left the bowling alley and headed out into the muggy *motza'ei Shabbos* summer night.

◆　◆　◆

As time passed, I became more and more involved in NCSY and other *kiruv* initiatives, and I even spent a summer with kids my own age picking peaches on a religious kibbutz. Eventually I came to the conclusion that it was time for me to move on in life.

In my senior year, I left the Bronx High School of Science and transferred to a yeshivah college program. Academically it was fine, but I didn't connect to any of the *rebbeim* there. There were many classes taught by many teachers, but nobody whom I could call "Rebbi."

I was still a kid for all practical purposes and had no direction or real *hashkafah*. One thing that saved me was that I had a *chavrusa* with whom I learned *Mishnah Berurah* at mealtimes. I liked the fact that the two of us were accomplishing something on a daily basis.

Another thing that helped me was that I wrote my end of term paper on a topic from a biography I had read about Rav Chaim Soloveitchik. The book stressed the concept of seeing life through the prism of halachah and how this was the way Rav Chaim related to the world. The idea of using halachah as a person's yardstick to go through life resonated with me, and I knew that I wanted to learn as much halachah as possible. As he put it: "The Halachic Jew stands by a river and sees not water but forty *se'ah* (the amount of water a *mikveh* needs to be kosher)." This concept moved me, and I wanted to reach a level where I was honestly familiar with what halachah expects of a Jew.

It was this recognition of what halachah is that gave me the push I needed to make it to Eretz Yisrael.

◆ ◆ ◆

It wasn't long before I found myself in Yerushalayim for the summer. I hadn't yet done any major learning yet, but I knew enough that I was asked to tutor a few kids who had come to learn in Ohr Somayach during their vacation.

One day I was sitting in the *beis midrash* when a rabbi entered the room to give a *shmuess* to the students. It was one of the first real *shmuessen* I had ever heard in my life.

"What is *mussar*?" he asked the assembled.

He waited a few long seconds to allow the question to penetrate our minds before providing an answer.

"Yaakov Avinu was forced to hide his daughter Dinah in a box when faced with the knowledge that Esav was on his way to confront him. Chazal tell us that Hashem was unhappy with Yaakov for taking such an action. The question is obvious: Yaakov knew his brother and what he was capable of. Since that was the case, what did Hashem want from him? What should he have done differently?

"The complaint against Yaakov Avinu," the speaker explained, "was not that he hid Dinah in a box. He had no choice but to hide her, and he did what he had to do. That wasn't the *ta'anah*.

"But when he closed the lid of the box, he shouldn't have done it so emphatically. He should have shut the box with a *krechtz* and a sigh.

"He should have shown how heartbroken he was that his brother was on such a low *madreigah*: This is my brother. I wish my daughter would be able to marry him! Maybe she'd be able to bring him back to Hashem...

"That's what Yaakov Avinu should have been thinking when he closed the box on his daughter, and that's what *mussar* is — getting to know the fine points of your personality. Not just doing the mitzvos but doing them with heart and meaning while caring about the little details that make them so special."

Hearing that *shmuess* sold me on *mussar*. This was most probably due to the fact that the rabbi who gave the *shiur* that evening was the famous *mashgiach* Rav Naftali Kaplan.

◆ ◆ ◆

I knew that I wanted to continue learning in Eretz Yisrael, but I had no idea where. I did have a number of *chavrusos*, but not any one person who gave me consistent guidance. Every time I'd ask someone where he thought I should go learn, I'd get a different answer. I didn't know the differences between any of the yeshivos and could have gone anywhere. In the end, someone convinced me that I would become a real *talmid chacham* if I went to learn at Yeshivas Toras Moshe in Yerushalayim.

I called the yeshivah and made an appointment to meet with the *rosh yeshivah*, Rav Moshe Meiselman.

Rav Meiselman opened a Gemara and told me to read it for him.

I could barely read Gemara at that point. I had been in a yeshivah for all of one year, and in that yeshivah Gemara learning had been a very small part of the day. In sum, I didn't know how to learn.

It took Rav Meiselman exactly twenty seconds to understand

that for me learning Gemara was like trying to read a foreign language.

"I heard good things about you," he said to me. "You're accepted. But you have to dress yeshivish and remember you're not in the Bronx High School of Science anymore."

Rav Meiselman was a great-grandson of Rav Chaim Brisker, a grandson of Rav Moshe Soloveitchik, and a nephew of Rav Yoshe Ber Soloveitchik, and it didn't take me long to recognize that he was a person who, like his ancestors before him, related to the world through the eyes of halachah. He was a person who exemplified the concept of the "Halachic Jew," and I knew that I'd found a role model whom I could look up to and emulate.

◆ ◆ ◆

I had left high school a year early to begin college and learn in yeshivah, and four of us came from the same yeshivah that year, and we were all welcomed into Toras Moshe, which had a very small student body. There was a major emphasis on longtime learning in the yeshivah, and I found that the concept struck a chord deep within my soul.

A few weeks after I joined Toras Moshe, I spent Shabbos by some friends at a yeshivah that was ideologically way more to the left. There the stress was on secular studies and college and how the Rambam states that he wouldn't have been able to write his *sefer* on *Kiddush HaChodesh* without secular knowledge.

I returned to the yeshivah all confused and unsure of myself. What was the right path to take? The path of Torah learning combined with higher education or a genuine devotion to undiluted Torah learning?

I told Rav Meiselman everything I had heard over Shabbos. His response remained with me forever.

It was focused, honest, and direct.

"You learn Torah, you go to Olam HaBa, *v'zehu* — and that's it!"

At that moment I recognized the clarity with which he viewed the world.

Later, during a *shiur*, he remarked that some people claim that they want to go to college because having secular knowledge would help them learn better.

Rav Meiselman didn't agree. "The amount of secular knowledge that a person needs for his Torah learning can be acquired in two weeks."

He wasn't against going to college if someone feels he needs it for his *parnassah*, but he did not agree that a person needs it to aid his Torah learning. In his mind, it would always be that "you learn Torah, you go to Olam HaBa, *v'zehu* — and that's it!"

In my particular case, Rav Meiselman would later advise me to finish college. Years afterward, when my son was in elementary school, he didn't want to spend time learning secular studies, preferring to learn *limudei kodesh* instead. I conferred with a *gadol*, who told me that he should stay where he was: "*Limudei chol* is not a bad thing. It's good for a *ben Torah* to have a handle on general knowledge in addition to his Torah learning."

My son stayed right where he was.

◆ ◆ ◆

I remember thinking shortly after my arrival in Toras Moshe how much I admired Rav Meiselman and how I wanted to be like him and the other *rebbeim*, because to me they epitomized what life was all about. Though I had attended one of the most prestigious high schools in the United States, I had constantly felt a sense of emptiness. Learning Torah at the yeshivah was like emerging from a vacuum into a sea of meaning.

During my first year at the yeshivah, I didn't eat or sleep enough. Having spent the majority of my formative years involved in the regimented study of secular education, I felt an extraordinary need to catch up with the others my age. This meant that sometimes I felt tired and weak, but I was in the process of discovering who I was, and along with that came the desire to learn until I had mastered it all.

After a year at the yeshivah, however, I came to the realization that it was preferable to eat three meals a day and get a good night's sleep — that by following the rules that govern us, I would have a much better chance of becoming the *ben Torah* I so wanted to be.

This realization was brought home to me when I came across a *tefillah* written by Rav Shmuel Hominer, *zt"l*, in his *sefer Olas Tamid*. He writes that before eating or sleeping, a person should pray that he should be *"bari v'chazak la'avod es Hashem"* — that he should be healthy and strong in order to serve Hashem.

Rav Meiselman, quoting the Netziv, put it best.

"Daniel Yaakov," he said to me, "what's a *masmid*?"

He answered his own question.

"A *masmid* is someone who eats when he's supposed to eat, sleeps when he's supposed to sleep, and learns when it's time to learn. That's a *masmid*."

Even after I moderated my behavior, I still spent almost all my time in the *beis midrash*. I seldom left the yeshivah for Shabbos, and I used my *dirah* just for sleeping. I had come to yeshivah to learn, and I wanted to maximize my time.

◆ ◆ ◆

This is not to say that there were no challenges along the way. One summer my brother came to visit. He was a student at Columbia University at the time. I also had several cousins living in Eretz Yisrael. And all of them were planning on flying to Switzerland to spend time with relatives.

My choices were simply this:

I could join them for what promised to be a very enjoyable family vacation in picturesque Switzerland, or I could remain in my *dirah* in Yerushalayim and make a *siyum* on the *masechta* I was currently learning.

I could not do both.

(That's the thing about life. You always have to make choices. It's just the way it is.)

It was very difficult for me to make the decision. I could picture the vacation: waking up in the morning to the crisp air of the Swiss Alps, enjoying the sight of the lush green mountains and timber chalets, hiking along the narrow trails of the mountain peaks and valleys.

I sought counsel with Rav Meiselman.

"Daniel Yaakov," he said, "you can do whatever you want. There's nothing wrong with spending a few weeks in Switzerland. I just want you to remember one thing."

Then he repeated his favorite line.

"You learn Torah, you go to Olam HaBa, *v'zehu* — and that's it!"

Rav Meiselman was teaching me a very important lesson here. Of course I could go to Switzerland. I could go on vacation. There was nothing wrong with any of it. On the other hand, he knew my dreams of becoming a genuine *talmid chacham*, and he understood my personality. For me, a trip to Switzerland could mean a great setback in my progress.

There is no question that he knew what to say to every *talmid*, and he recognized what I needed to hear. In the end I decided to remain in Yerushalayim over summer vacation. That move turned out to be a major game changer for me. It was when I said, "*V'zehu* — and that's it," for myself. That decision was a real commitment on my part and helped cement for me exactly where I wanted to be for the rest of my life.

There would have been nothing wrong with my going on vacation that summer. It was *bein hazemanim*, and many people go away during that period. But at that point in my life, choosing to remain in Yerushalayim to learn helped lock everything I had been doing up until that time into place — for life.

One of the most powerful ideas I ever heard Rav Meiselman say was about how the Satan appeared to Avraham Avinu at the *Akeidah* to persuade him to fail the test. The Midrash (*Bereishis Rabbah* 56:4) tells us that the Satan sent fire, wind, and water to stop him, yet nothing stopped Avraham and he carried on, not allowing himself to be distracted by anything in his path.

The Satan sent the same set of obstacles to Yitzchak Avinu — fire, wind, and water — and nothing. Yitzchak didn't waver for a moment.

Finally the Satan reached the end of his rope. He had given the mission everything he had, but nothing worked.

Mustering his final argument, he said to Yitzchak, "If you allow your father to kill you, Yishmael will inherit all of your playthings!"

After all those obstacles, why should Yitzchak care about the toys he played with as a child?

Said Rav Meiselman the following:

"People come to Eretz Yisrael. They are willing to give up everything — college, secular studies, the chance to make the big bucks, the huge house with the pool, the fancy car. They are willing to forgo it all, to give it all up and sit and learn. Sometimes, however, they lose the battle and end up returning home.

"What gets them?

"The toys, the playthings, the comforts they grew up with and from which they are unwilling to part."

I remember that he gave two examples.

"There was a boy who came to learn in Eretz Yisrael. He was an incredible *masmid*. Brilliant, insightful, kind, thoughtful. He had everything it took to go all the way. But he gave it all up and returned home. The reason? Yerushalayim's streets are much more dusty than in America and he couldn't keep the dust off his shoes.

"Another boy went back because the cottage cheese wasn't good enough.

"They were willing to give up everything," Rav Meiselman concluded, "but they just couldn't give up the toys. And that's where the real test hits a person."

His words resonated with me on a deep level. They were so true. *Mesirus nefesh* may be difficult and demand much from a person, but you feel so good afterward.

Suffice it to say, I didn't go to Switzerland and made a *siyum* on *Maseches Gittin* that year.

❖ ❖ ❖

Rav Meiselman was not in favor of learning without depth just to finish *sefarim*. The style of learning at Toras Moshe was very much *b'iyun*, concentrating on getting to the core of every *sugya*.

"You want to finish *Shas*?" he'd say. "No problem. Just turn all the pages..."

❖ ❖ ❖

Rav Meiselman once shared with us that he had a *mesorah* about a certain *Shabbos niggun* called "*Odeh LaKel*," which he taught us. A beautiful *piyut*, "*Odeh LaKel*" describes, in poetic language, the journey of the *neshamah* coming into this world.

"If you sing this *niggun*," he said, "your children will grow up to be *talmidei chachamim*. I have a *mesorah* for this from the Ibn Ezra, through Rav Chaim of Volozhin and the Beis HaLevi, all the way down to me."

I once heard about a Yerushalmi Yid named Rav Frank whose five daughters all married extremely *chashuve bachurim* who later became *rabbanim* and *roshei yeshivah*. When asked how he had merited raising such a family, he attributed some of his *siyatta d'Shmaya* in marrying off his daughters to his weekly singing of the relatively obscure *piyut* "*Odeh LaKel*." Some of the expanded *siddurim* have it, but the average *zemiros* booklet does not.

Later I discovered that the *niggun* had been recorded on an album produced by Modzhitz. I purchased the album, made sure to learn the song, and have been singing it every Shabbos for the past twenty-five years. My feelings on the matter is that it is less a person's singing a particular song and more a person's willingness to commit to doing something every single Shabbos of his life because he really, really wants to see his children become *talmidei chachamim*. In my opinion, this is akin to a self-fulfilling prophecy. If you want something enough and are willing to be *moser nefesh* for it, then it usually does come.

On the other hand, perhaps it really is the song…

◆ ◆ ◆

The Gulf War broke out while I was at Toras Moshe. The government brought gas masks to the yeshivah and had someone demonstrate how to use them, but the overall feeling was one of complacency. Though Iraq was threatening to shoot their Scud missiles throughout Eretz Yisrael, no one really believed that a missile would strike us.

I went to sleep that night at about two in the morning.

At three the siren went off.

There was complete panic in the dorm as we ran around trying to remember the instructions we'd been given about taping the doors, using the masks, and soaking the towels (to be placed at the bottom of the doors) with cleaning fluids. I remember shaving my friend's beard off with one hand — the gas masks didn't fit over beards — while undoing a roll of duct tape with the other and screaming at the top of my lungs.

In short, complete and utter pandemonium reigned.

We found a radio and turned it on, but we must have been tuned in to a local Arab station. Maybe it was Radio Jordan, because we could hear people speaking English with Arabic accents, and they were saying things like "Tel Aviv is burning" and "Jerusalem is in flames."

Needless to say, hearing that didn't improve our mood much, and we raced around the rooms like mice on steroids screaming words of *Tehillim* at the top of our lungs, trying to do a million things at once and accomplishing close to zero.

In the middle of everything, Rav Meiselman knocked on the door.

"Who's there?"

"Rabbi Meiselman. Don't open the door. It's dangerous out here. I just wanted to make sure you're all okay."

In the end, only one Scud fell in the middle of nowhere that night, but I will never forget that first hour when the siren rose and fell and our hearts nearly jumped out of our chests imagining dozens of gigantic Scud missiles streaking across the skies straight for our apartment.

And then the knock on the door and the sound of his voice, reassuring and calming. *"Is everyone okay? Good. Don't come out now. It's dangerous out here."*

Maybe it was dangerous. But as our *rosh yeshivah*, he was prepared to take the risk.

Chapter Thirteen

As I wrote earlier, I have experienced a wide range of *tzaros* in my life, *tzaros* that resulted in my developing relationships with many *tzaddikim* from all walks of life as I searched for the answers and for clarity.

The chain of *tzaros* truly began on the tenth of Av, just as I was about to go daven Maariv at the end of the fast (Tishah B'Av was a *nidchah* that year, having been postponed to Sunday instead of Shabbos). I was a *chasan* at the time; the date of our wedding a mere three days after the *ta'anis*. As I walked into the *beis midrash*, someone told me that I had a phone call. It was my *kallah's* aunt on the line.

"Your *kallah's* father just passed away," she informed me.

This didn't come as a complete shock, since he had been sick for a while. I had even gone to Rav Chaim Pinchas Scheinberg *zt"l* for advice, explaining about my future father-in-law's illness, and asked him whether to change the date of the wedding.

"No," he said. "Leave the date as is."

When I heard the news of my father-in-law's passing, my face turned white, and I went into panic mode. My mind began to whirl as I considered all the possibilities. If my father-in-law had passed away, then my *kallah* was in *aveilus*. This would mean postponing the wedding, and once a wedding is postponed anything could happen. Just the thought of having to change the date of the wedding and get in touch with all the people who had received invitations and were planning to attend, as well as the band and the caterer... The idea was overwhelming. Pushing off the wedding would mean endless complications of every kind, not the least of which was the fact that it would be extremely difficult for a *kallah* to dance with happiness so soon after her father had passed away. The implications of pushing off the wedding made me shudder.

In desperation, I called Rav Meiselman and told him what had happened. Rav Meiselman dropped whatever he was doing and met with me as soon as humanly possible. He kept the absolute latest *zemanim* — at times he'd finish Shabbos a few hours after everyone else — and arrived still wearing his slippers.

Upon his arrival, the two of us went to see Rav Shlomo Zalman Auerbach at his home in Shaarei Chesed. Rav Meiselman told Rav Shlomo Zalman the story, and to my surprise, the eminent *posek* was not even slightly fazed by the complex *she'eilah*.

His response: "There's a way around the situation. Just don't tell the *kallah* what happened."

It wasn't even a *safek* for him. He just wanted to make sure that she hadn't yet heard the news.

I reassured him that my *kallah* still didn't know what had happened. We then got in touch with my future mother-in-law, who agreed not to inform my *kallah* of the fact that her father had passed away.

In the end, we were married on the designated day.

Keeping this secret from my *kallah* was not as difficult as it may seem since her father had been very sick and she hadn't been expecting him to fly in from Brazil for the wedding. On the other hand, she had been expecting her mother to come, and it was difficult for her to grasp why she had chosen not to attend. What's more, even if her parents couldn't come because of her father's illness, she'd expected them to call, but to her great surprise the wedding day arrived with no phone call from home. My *kallah* was completely baffled at the incredibly loud silence of the phone that never rang.

Several of the guests cried throughout the wedding. My wife has many family members living in Eretz Yisrael, and they were all at the wedding and crying over the fact that her father whom they loved hadn't lived to see this important day. To the *kallah*, the fact that people were crying made sense since this was a wedding and people cry at weddings. But after the wedding was over, my wife really wanted to call her mother in Brazil, and I had to come up with all kinds of ways to stall her from making the call until the *sheva berachos* were over.

◆ ◆ ◆

During the *sheva berachos*, I spent my free time studying *hilchos aveilus* and trying to work out who would be willing to break the news to the *kallah*, who still had no idea that her father had passed away. I must have asked fifty people, who all turned me down. Nobody had the heart to tell a *kallah* that she had to start sitting *shivah* on the last day of her *sheva berachos*. In the end, Rebbetzin Fried from Kiryat Sanz accepted the mission and broke the news with sensitivity and caring, explaining that we had been following Rav Shlomo Zalman's unequivocal *psak* that the *kallah* not be told until the end of the festivities.

Seven days of celebration segued into seven days of mourning. This turn of events heralded the return of the same people who had come to celebrate with us at the wedding, now visiting to be *menachem avel*; the same people who had known the secret and hadn't given it away and had danced with her and smiled and laughed, all the while knowing that soon enough they would have to return to cry together. It was like a replay of the wedding, only from the opposite perspective.

In retrospect, what amazed me most about the whole story of our wedding was the absolute composure exhibited by Rav Shlomo Zalman when Rav Meiselman brought me there for a *psak halachah*. It was a true example of pure *da'as Torah*, and I remember deciding at that time that he was going to be our *posek*.

Thus ended my first encounter with Rav Shlomo Zalman Auerbach.

◆ ◆ ◆

My wife and I purchased airline tickets and left for Brazil on the final day of her sitting *shivah* so that we would be able to spend some time with her family at this crucial juncture.

We remained in South America for about three weeks, during which time I experienced one of the scariest moments of my life.

I had always heard that the Brazilian beaches are some of the most beautiful beaches in the world, with feathery sands of the softest white and water so blue it could melt your heart. For obvious reasons I wasn't able to visit the beach during the regular hours most people frequented it, which left me two options — very late at night or very early in the morning. Late at night meant I wouldn't be able to see the water, which left an early-morning visit as the only viable option.

I left my in-laws' home early in the morning while most of Brazil slept and headed to the beach, drinking in the absolute beauty of my surroundings. I planned on immersing myself in the ocean (which can serve as a *mikveh*), followed by davening. It was Elul, I had just gotten married, our entire life lay ahead of us, and this was the perfect place to daven. The beach was completely empty, and I found a spot and prepared myself to enter the tranquil early-morning waters.

One moment everything was fine, relaxed, nonthreatening. The next moment, two extremely tough-looking Brazilians approached me, seemingly from nowhere. One grabbed me, placed me in a headlock, and stuck my head into the sand and held it there, while the other man began going through my belongings, searching for money.

"Where's your money, amigo?!" he bellowed at me.

I hadn't brought any money with me, but the absence of financial incentive wasn't stopping them from killing me. I literally couldn't breathe. At first I still had a little bit of air in my lungs, but after about a minute, there was nothing left and I felt my body beginning to slow down as all systems went into shutdown mode. Brilliant shapes and colors swam before my eyes as the last remaining oxygen left my brain. Everything receded and a black light began filling my head — a black light that spread farther and farther, taking over everything in its path.

I had left the house that morning just wanting to immerse in the ocean and purify myself in honor of Elul, and here I was literally moments away from death.

Suddenly my brain recalled a story I had heard a few weeks before about the Brisker Rav's escape from the Nazis during World War II. I don't know how I was able to focus sufficiently to remember anything, but the details filtered through my consciousness.

Every time the rav and his family had been in danger of discovery by the Nazis, the rav concentrated on the words "ein od milvado," that there is nothing in the entire universe besides Hashem, and every single time he did this, it was as if the entire family had become invisible. Thus the family survived the war.

At that moment, as the very last vestiges of oxygen disappeared from my brain, I concentrated for a millisecond on the words "*ein od milvado.*" Even as I saw the words in my mind's eye, I felt the absence of the pressure that had been weighing me down, as my would-be murderer released me from the chokehold and allowed me to turn over and open my mouth. Fresh air had never tasted so delicious as I took deep breaths of salty, tangy, ocean-scented breeze. With every breath, I felt my brain regaining its functions.

Meanwhile, the two Brazilians, having finished riffling through my belongings with nothing to show for their efforts, shouted, "Mafioso Brazil!" and raced away, leaving me still gasping for breath on the soft, sandy carpet. They were gone and I was still alive.

It was difficult to comprehend how very close I had come to losing my life on that forsaken stretch of beach. It took me time to recover, but eventually I was able to stand without shaking, the recipient of a miracle and still as determined as before to immerse myself in Hashem's ocean in honor of Elul. Which I did.

When I made it back to my in-laws' apartment not long afterward, it was difficult to find the words to relate to my wife how close she had been to losing her brand-new husband. Though I appreciated being granted a new lease on life, I couldn't help but wonder why such terrible *tzaros* were being visited on us.

◆　◆　◆

Our flight home from Brazil ran into trouble before we had even left the ground. Instead of taking off at the appointed time, the plane just sat on the tarmac for six hours until we were informed that there was something the matter with it. Next thing we knew, everyone on board was being taken to one of the fanciest hotels in Rio, where we would stay until the next day. In the morning I woke up and, wanting to daven with a minyan, I left the hotel with my tallis and tefillin.

I hailed a passing cab and asked the driver to take me to the nearest shul. Unfortunately, the driver didn't understand the address I had given him and dropped me off in the middle of nowhere, after assuring me that this was where I wanted to be. But it wasn't. I found myself in an utterly strange neighborhood, where nobody spoke a word of English and the people exuded a vaguely menacing air. And all the time I couldn't help remembering that our flight was leaving in a couple of hours. It took me about ten anxious minutes until I found someone who spoke my language and helped me get back to the hotel.

I learned a lesson that day: be extremely careful when visiting a foreign country where the people don't speak your language.

Chapter Fourteen

When I think of Rav Meiselman, the word *integrity* comes to mind. If ever I have a question about an issue of integrity, he is the address I turn to.

When I first arrived in Eretz Yisrael, changing dollars into shekels was a real experience due to the fact that in 1985 one American dollar equaled more than one thousand shekels. Imagine how much money you'd get when you changed a hundred dollars.

The first time I flew with El Al the airline lost my luggage, and they reimbursed me for it to the tune of three hundred dollars, which is how I came to be walking the streets with more than three hundred thousand shekels in hand. I still have the picture where I'm holding an incredibly thick wad of bills, smiling from ear to ear, even though I knew very well that it wouldn't get me very far. Of course, everything changed when the Israeli Treasury issued the New Israeli Shekel, but that was still in the future.

One day Rav Meiselman had to go to the doctor for something. The visit cost sixty dollars — sixty thousand shekels. Someone at his non-Jewish insurance company in the States made a mistake and sent him a check for sixty thousand dollars, not shekels. Of course, he didn't dream of cashing the check and returned it to the insurance company, who were shocked out of their minds that someone would return sixty thousand dollars of their own volition.

That was just one example. But I have seen the same straightness in Rav Meiselman time after time.

◆ ◆ ◆

I had a donor who was on the verge of selling a property he owned in New York. The price of the property was one million dollars, and the donor pledged to donate the full amount to *tzedakah* on the successful conclusion of the sale. He had asked me to distribute the money once he made the sale and I could use ten percent for my *kollel*. However at some point he called me up and said, "Listen, I want you to give my son the majority of the money (he told me how much) and a small amount to my sister as well."

The rest would go to the designated *tzedakah*, but this meant that he was basically using my *tzedakah* exemption to transfer untaxable money to his family members. It was like a small breakdown in morality — going from one million dollars of *tzedakah* to money laundering.

When I realized what he was up to, I conferred with Rav Meiselman, who heard me out and told me, "I understand that a *tzedakah* organization stands to benefit from part of the money, but do not touch these funds with a ten-foot pole!"

It wasn't even a discussion. With Rav Meiselman, the question was open and shut. If money is tainted, you stay away from it. The end.

There was another person (for the sake of the story I'll call him Jason K.) who began giving the *kollel* five thousand dollars a month. One day my phone rang with an international number.

I answered. It was the FBI.

"Is this Rabbi Daniel Travis?"

"Speaking."

"This is Agent McNeal. I'm with the Federal Bureau of Investigation, and I want to know if you are a friend of Jason K."

"I wouldn't say that we're friends exactly, but I do know who he is. Why do you ask?"

"Well, Rabbi Travis, it turns out that your friend Jason is involved in all sorts of shady business. Did you know that he is wanted for millions of dollars of stock fraud?"

"I had no idea."

"We raided his apartment and found a brochure that explains all about your study program. That's why we're calling."

At the time of the call from the FBI, my daughter had been in the hospital and I had been sleeping on the floor for a week. Friday morning I returned home after being away the entire week, only to receive a phone call from McNeal.

Our conversation continued for a few minutes. Before we got off the phone, I asked the FBI agent, "Can I continue accepting donations from this person, or do I have to stop immediately?"

"You can continue accepting contributions from him, until he's proven guilty."

I asked Rav Meiselman whether I should continue taking money from Jason, explaining that there wasn't a problem from a legal standpoint.

"Definitely not," he said. "You can't receive any benefit from such money."

"Do I have to return all the money I received so far?"

"You don't have to give it back, but you should not accept any more."

"But do I have to start suspecting everyone who gives me big money?"

"No. But be circumspect. Be aware of what's going on around you."

It wasn't easy for me to turn around and tell Jason, "Thank you for all your help, but I don't need it anymore." His contribution had been covering virtually all my monthly expenses! Besides, the FBI agent had given me permission to continue taking his donations.

But Rav Meiselman had given me a clear directive and I obeyed.

A few weeks later I was in the States on a fundraising trip, and someone told me to go meet a certain individual. I wasn't sure if the meeting would be worth my time, but in the end I decided to meet him. Five minutes into the meeting, the man wrote me a check for five thousand dollars. Not only that, he would go on to become a regular donor.

Coincidence?

I didn't see it that way. At the end of the day, you never lose from being honest.

I remember asking Rav Meiselman about using credit card miles. "You're allowed to utilize whatever loopholes the airline built into its system," he replied, "if you have the kind of brain that knows how to maneuver the system. That's not dishonest. You can't lie or steal, but you can definitely work within the system the airline set up."

◆ ◆ ◆

Another very interesting thing about Rav Meiselman is how he straddles both worlds. The brilliant grandson of Rav Moshe Soloveitchik, Rav Meiselman earned a doctorate in abstract mathematics at MIT. He learned with his uncle in Boston twelve hours a day while earning a doctorate at the same time. Rav Meiselman went on to establish YULA — Yeshiva University of Los Angeles.

At a meeting about the construction of an *eiruv* in a certain American city, Rav Meiselman stated with confidence that "it would be mathematically impossible to build."

A woman at the meeting responded by saying, "Rabbi, why don't you leave the mathematics to us?"

"Not a problem," he replied. "I would just like to point out that I do have a doctorate in mathematics from MIT."

For some reason that piece of information quieted her down.

◆ ◆ ◆

When my *kollel* was studying the *melachah* of *kotzer*, the prohibition against reaping on Shabbos, I learned Chazal's statement that says that removing moss (a living entity) off the side of a bucket on Shabbos would fall under the category of *kotzer* (*Shabbos* 108a as cited by *Shulchan Aruch Orach Chaim* 336:5). Using the Gemara's logic, I wondered if removing a layer of mold (also a living entity) from the side of a piece of bread would be considered *kotzer* as well.

I discussed the question with Rav Ezriel Auerbach and Rav Shlomo Zafrani, who both gave me the same answer: mold may very well be a living entity, but since human beings do not perceive it as a plant, removing it would not fall under the category of *kotzer*.

Rav Meiselman disagreed completely.

"It is imperative that one understand the science here," he said emphatically. "If mold is a living entity, then mold is a living entity, and it doesn't matter how people perceive it."

He then mentioned a Rambam that discusses the prohibition of *kotzer* with regard to water lilies, even though they are seemingly just sitting on the water and not a "real plant."

As we talked, I could see that glint in his eye — the glint that he gets when he discusses something that presents a fusion between matters of science and matters of Torah, a partnership he truly comprehends on the deepest level.

Seeing that glint in his eye reminded me what had first attracted me to his approach to learning all those years ago when I joined Toras Moshe, just a short while after having been a student at the Bronx High School of Science. I, too, had been coming from a background in science, and the fact that Rav Meiselman had such a strong scientific understanding demonstrated that it's possible to be a genuine *talmid chacham* and appreciate the wisdom of math and science at the same time. From Rav Meiselman I realized that it is possible to mesh the two (seemingly unrelated) worlds into one cohesive unit. This knowledge was a big *chizuk* for me.

◆ ◆ ◆

In the fashion of grandchildren of great *tzaddikim*, Rav Meiselman used to tell me stories about his *zeide* Rav Chaim.

"My *zeide* didn't understand how a person could have money

and keep it for himself. One of the challenges the Soloveitchik family faced was that a few days after Rav Chaim had received his monthly salary, there would be almost nothing left, because Rav Chaim had already given everything away to *tzedakah*. The community went so far as to appoint '*shomrim*' to stand in front of his house whose job was to make sure that Rav Chaim wasn't left penniless due to his penchant for giving everything away."

Of course, Rav Chaim didn't accept this move on the part of those who paid him, and he ordered those trying to prevent him from giving *tzedakah* to leave in no uncertain terms.

"His house was always filled with people," Rav Meiselman would say. "Everyone knew that you could come and go as you pleased in my *zeide's* home. People even put up advertisements on the walls! With my *zeide*, there was no concept of self at all."

When I heard this, it came to me that Rav Meiselman was the same way, giving his entire self to the yeshivah.

◆ ◆ ◆

Rav Meiselman used to deliver a *shmuess* to the yeshivah every other week. The *shmuessen* basically consisted of a number of *Rambams* that he repeated in one form or another over and over again. After I had been at the yeshivah for a while, I knew exactly what he was going to say and which *Rambam* he was going to quote when.

One time I approached him and said, "Rebbi, you're saying the same *Rambams* over and over."

"You think I don't know that?" he replied. "In thirty years you'll come back to me and thank me for this. These *Rambams* are going to change your life!"

He was one hundred percent right. Those *Rambams* were drilled into us, and we never forgot them.

One of his most oft-quoted *Rambams* was "*Lo shevet Levi bilvad...*" — where the *Rambam* explains that anyone can become a genuine *talmid chacham*. Another *Rambam* discussed the laws of *mikva'os*, where the Rambam explains that if a person wants to become pure, the only way to do so is by immersing himself in the water entirely; not even a hair can be left on the surface.

The messages that Rav Meiselman reinforced again and again remained with me throughout the years. If I close my eyes today, I can still picture him standing at the front of the *beis midrash* giving those *shmuessen* to the boys, repeating the same *Rambam* that I had already heard twenty times before and that he had resolved I should hear another twenty times before I left the yeshivah.

Another thing Rav Meiselman used to say was that one of the wonder kids of Wall Street (he will remain unnamed) and Rav Moshe Feinstein had one thing in common: they both used to get up at four in the morning. This one for learning and that one for money.

He also used to say that many people want to have a lot of money. The basic desire, he explained, is in truth a spiritual thing — similar to a person wanting to have a big portion in *Olam HaBa*.

There was another memorable *shmuess* that stayed with me until today, this one delivered by Rav Elchanan Fishman, the *mashgiach* of Toras Moshe.

I had the key to a small room in the yeshivah's attic where I used to learn for many hours straight. One evening another *bachur* asked me if he could use the bed there to lie down for half an hour.

I gave him the key and he went upstairs.

That night happened to be at the beginning of Elul *zeman*, and the *mashgiach* gave a *shmuess* to the *bachurim*. The *mashgiach* related how the venerable Rav Chatzkel Levenstein once arrived at a wedding in the middle of Elul where he'd been asked to speak.

Rav Chatzkel did give a speech — consisting of one word. He let loose a scream: "ELUL!!!" His scream was impossible to miss, and the entire hall heard Rav Chatzkel's emotional outburst.

When our *mashgiach* came to the part in the story where Rav Chatzkel cried out "ELUL!!!" he, too, raised his voice to its full capacity and yelled, "ELUL!!!" loudly enough that the walls themselves seemed to shake.

The *bachur* who had borrowed the key to the attic was already sleeping when the *mashgiach* roared like a lion, and he later told me that he literally hit the roof (it was a very low ceiling) when he woke up from the shout that shook the room.

◆ ◆ ◆

When Rav Meiselman spoke at my *vort*, he related an idea from Rav Chaim of Volozhin about the many *nissim* that occurred in the Beis HaMikdash. One of them was that the smoke on the *Mizbei'ach* always ascended in a straight column and never shifted from the wind or any other factor.

"What was the point of that miracle?" Rav Meiselman asked, quoting Rav Chaim. "How did the fact that the fire was always straight help anyone?"

Rav Meiselman explained.

"The reason for the fire's straightness in the Beis HaMikdash was to give an important message: that this is the way a Jew is supposed to be. Straight. One hundred percent straight, not able to be moved by the wind." (Or, in other words, "Learn Torah, go to Olam HaBa, *v'zehu* — and that's it!")

◆ ◆ ◆

I found myself spending Shabbos at Hadassah Hospital one week. During the communal *shalosh seudos* offered there by dedicated volunteers, I ended up at a table next to another man, and the two of us started talking. Inevitably, he asked me where I had gone to yeshivah.

"Toras Moshe," I said.

"You went to Toras Moshe! I want to ask you a question!"

Now I became a little nervous. Such an introduction usually precedes criticism of some sort, and I was not in the mood of being put into a position where I had to defend my yeshivah.

I was pleasantly surprised when he followed this by asking me, "Why is it that everyone who learns in Toras Moshe is a mensch?"

The truth is he was right. *Derech eretz* was stressed at the yeshivah until it became ingrained in every *talmid*.

◆ ◆ ◆

The Rambam writes in the second *perek* of *Moreh Nevuchim* that before Adam ate of the *eitz hada'as*, there was a concept of *emes* and *sheker*. In the aftermath of the *eitz hada'as* debacle, the world was introduced to the idea of *sefeikos* — of doubt. Black and white disappeared, and gray took its place.

I had grown up with a lot of gray in my life.

With Rav Meiselman, however, there is no room for moral ambiguity. He possesses an integral sense of clarity that precludes doubt. He is able to cut straight through any confusion a *talmid* may have had and lead him down a clear path with a sure hand and strong guidance.

His honesty and integrity are a cut above, and I see him as a prime example of the "Halachic Jew" — a person who sees the world through the prism of halachah.

Encounters With

Rav
Asher Arieli
שליט"א

Legendary Maggid Shiur

"What's the secret of being successful in your Torah learning?"

[Rav Asher Arieli] thought for a while, then said, "I really don't know."

Suddenly his face lit up with an inner glow, and he called out enthusiastically, "Tefillah — that's the secret! The Gemara says a person has to daven if he wants to succeed in his learning!"

"As a rosh kollel," I continued, "how can I help my yungeleit find that inner power and drive?"

"You have to build an inner excitement inside them." He then lifted his face up to Shamayim, and that glow returned as he quoted the standard words Tosafos uses to ask and answer a question — "v'im tomar... v'yeish lomar..." (if you say... one must say...) — repeating the phrases over and over as if he were on fire and the words he was saying were the most exciting things in the world, which to him they clearly were.

Chapter Fifteen

There are two types of people in the world: those who have met Rav Asher Arieli and those who haven't met Rav Asher Arieli.

When I was in the process of writing *Mizmor L'Sodah*, and I began making the rounds of *gedolim* to ask them for Torah thoughts on the topic of giving thanks to Hashem, a good friend of mine named Reb Ariel Greenberg was learning in Rav Asher's *shiur* at the Mir. Rav Asher gave a *shiur* on Chanukah at the time, and my friend transcribed it and then asked Rav Asher if we could include it in the *sefer*. Rav Asher gave his permission and even rewrote it so that it would fit better with the *sefer's* theme.

Up until then, Rav Asher had never published anything, which was why there was an immediate run for the *sefer* when it was finally printed and people in the Mir realized that Rav Asher had contributed. Interest surged since in the piece he disagreed with an opinion of the Brisker Rav. Of course, being Rav Asher he didn't actually write that he was disagreeing with the Brisker Rav, managing to phrase his own opinion in a way where he disagreed without sounding like he was disagreeing. It was pure humility cloaked in genius.

Two or three days after the *sefer* was published, the phone rang in my house. I answered the phone and heard the voice of Rav Asher Arieli.

"Thank you so much," he said to me, his voice thick with emotion.

"For what?"

"For including me in your *sefer*."

I was completely taken aback by how grateful he was. However, he wasn't finished yet.

"It's such a *kavod*," he continued. "You have an entire *Shulchan Aruch* on the *inyan* of *nissim*..." He went on and on and he was really sincere.

The fact is, Rav Asher is an incredibly humble human being, and he is the *maggid shiur* for what is arguably the largest *shiur* in the world, which should serve as proof that Hashem is in charge.

What do I mean by this?

Take the way Rav Asher's *shiur* even started. He didn't put up signs or gather a *chaburah* together. The sequence of events leading up to his historic *shiur* occurred in a way that can only be described as organic.

It began when Rav Asher was learning with his *chavrusa*, and someone overheard what Rav Asher was saying and asked if he could join them and listen in. Then a few more people asked if they could join in, and Rav Asher agreed. Why not? If they wanted to sit there and listen as he learned out loud, where was the harm? There was no reason not to agree.

The group grew, and it wasn't long before someone offered Rav Asher the use of his dorm room, which the *shiur* outgrew in a very short time. One thing led to another, and today there are upward of a thousand people attending his *shiurim* on a daily basis.

Yet he remains completely oblivious to the fantastic happenings that are occurring around him. In his mind, everything is still the same. He walks the hallways of the Mir in his sweater — no frock, no *rosh yeshivah* garb, just another *yungerman* hurrying up the stairs to his place in the *beis midrash*. It's obvious that he doesn't consider himself a cut above anyone else, despite the fact that thousands of people are following him from morning till night.

When I asked him what title to use when writing his name in the *sefer*, he adamantly refused to allow me to identify him as a *maggid shiur*.

"Just write 'Yeshivas Mir,'" he insisted.

I remember thinking, *Well, that makes sense. After all, Rav Asher is Yeshivas Mir!*

Yet I couldn't help asking myself, *Is he really not aware of who he is?*

I gave the matter a lot of thought, and eventually I came to a conclusion that I felt was the truth. It's not that Rav Asher doesn't know who he is and what he does. He sees how many people flock to listen to him, and he knows how his method of learning has impacted an entire generation. The reason that he is able to remain so genuinely humble is because he's on such a high level that he knows how far he still has to go before he'll maximize his incredible potential. He knows what he is capable of and what his obligations are. And that kind of understanding allows a person to remain truly humble.

◆ ◆ ◆

Twenty years later Rav Asher came to wish me *mazel tov* at my daughter's wedding. During our brief exchange, I mentioned my *sefer Mizmor L'Sodah*, which was when we had really connected for the first time, and Rav Asher's face lit up.

"*Mizmor L'Sodah*," he said, reacting with enthusiasm. "What a wonderful *sefer*! I have it on my bookshelf! A *Shulchan Aruch* for *hilchos nissim*!"

It was as if no time had passed at all, as if the *sefer* had been published the day before.

At a bris we both attended, I watched him talking to his mother for five minutes. I have never seen a person talk to his mother like that. It was pure *avodas Hashem*. It's impossible to accurately describe the respect that emanated from his entire being during that short conversation.

Which is why I say there are two types of people in the world — those who know Rav Asher and those who haven't had the good fortune to meet him. When you meet him, you understand that he is a person who lives his life at all times as if he's standing before Hashem.

◆ ◆ ◆

On a recent Purim visit to Rav Asher's home, I found a good 150 people already crammed into the apartment. Obviously everyone there wanted to speak with Rav Asher. However, when I was finally able to talk to him for a few minutes, I felt like it was just the two of us in the room despite the fact that there were so many other people there. Somehow he possesses the incredible ability to make every person feel like he is the only one in the world, and Rav Asher can do this even when surrounded by other people and even on Purim, when everyone around is being loud and boisterous. It's as if everything stops — as if time recedes — and you and Rav Asher have been transported to a distant island where nobody can get to you or disturb you.

And then your turn is over and someone else gets a chance, and when you leave his apartment it's with a feeling of utter incredulousness because you just cannot understand how on earth he manages to pull it off.

The only explanation is his utter humility.

◆ ◆ ◆

Another year I decided that I would beat the five o'clock crush and visit him soon after davening and the Megillah reading. It was early in the morning when I arrived, and the atmosphere was relaxed and peaceful. Sitting with Rav Asher at the dining-room table, I took advantage of this special opportunity to ask him a question that had been on my mind for a while.

"What's the secret of being successful in your Torah learning?"

He thought for a while, then said, "I really don't know."

Suddenly his face lit up with an inner glow, and he called out enthusiastically, "*Tefillah* — that's the secret! The Gemara says a person has to daven if he wants to succeed in his learning!"

"As a *rosh kollel*," I continued, "how can I help my *yungeleit* find that inner power and drive?"

"I can tell you that the result you want will *not* come from offering them more money and incentives."

"Then how?"

"You have to build an inner excitement inside them."

He then lifted his face up to *Shamayim*, and that glow returned as he quoted the standard words *Tosafos* uses to ask and answer a question — "*v'im tomar... v'yeish lomar...*" (if you say... one must say...) — repeating the phrases over and over as if he were on fire and the words he was saying were the most exciting things in the world, which to him they clearly were.

At that moment I understood that when you have a rebbi like Rav Asher, you have *talmidim* who are excited, and if I wanted my *talmidim* to be excited I had to work on building that excitement within me.

Or, as the famous saying goes, "Charity begins at home."

◆ ◆ ◆

After the terrorist attack on Rav Rubin's shul in Har Nof, I wrote a book about my friends who were murdered. Wanting this *sefer* to be read by as many people as possible, I approached many *gedolim* and asked them to sign on in support of the project. Rav Yitzchak Berkovits signed, as did Rav Dovid Cohen, Rav Reuven Elbaz, Rav Zalman Nechemia Goldberg, Rav Yaakov Hillel, Rav Shmuel Kamenetsky, Rav Ze'ev Leff...

All in all, it was a very *chashuve* group of people.

I also wanted Rav Asher's name on the book. I sent one of my *talmidim* over to ask him if he would be willing to sign.

"I don't read English," he protested. "How can I sign if I can't understand what it says? Besides, it says in the letter" — the letter was written in Hebrew as well — "that I am agreeing with the material in the book. How can I agree if I don't understand it?"

"We can change the letter," my *talmid* suggested.

"But then what about all the *rabbanim* who already signed?" he replied.

In the end he wouldn't sign.

◆ ◆ ◆

When my son was finishing the eighth grade, it was time to figure out where to send him for yeshivah the following year. As an American, I didn't know the yeshivah system in Eretz Yisrael and needed guidance to choose the place that would help my son grow and was best suited to his personality. His eighth-grade rebbi recommended a specific institution, but the yeshivah wouldn't give us an answer as to whether or not he was accepted.

It turned out to be a matter of politics: the yeshivah didn't want to accept boys from the elementary school he attended, but they wouldn't give me an answer or say yes or no. This meant that we were floating in limbo for a while, which for a boy on the cusp of *yeshivah ketanah* is a terrible place to be. I asked many of the *gedolim* whom I knew to put on the pressure, but despite quite a few phone calls that were made on our behalf, nothing helped and we still hadn't been given an answer.

It was *erev Shavuos* when the yeshivah called to let us know that the answer was negative.

"But it's too late for me to get him in anywhere else," I protested. "Why did you wait so long before giving us an answer?"

"We're sorry," they said, not sounding sorry at all, "but this is the way it is."

I was utterly devastated by the turn of events. Now what? All the yeshivos had already accepted their quota of *bachurim* for the coming year. What would be with my beautiful and brilliant son?

In desperation, I turned to someone I knew who had a connection with one of the leading *gedolim* in Eretz Yisrael. I had been told that if the *gadol* banged on the table and said someone should be accepted into a certain place, then that boy was accepted and that was that. But when we met and I explained what we were trying to do, the man with the right connections said to me, "What are you talking about? Why are you trying to get your son into that yeshivah? That is not the right place for him at all! Sending him there would be disastrous!"

"So where should we send him?"

"Send him to Mishkan Yisrael."

We went to Mishkan Yisrael, and they had one or two spaces that hadn't been filled. Five minutes later my son had been accepted into the yeshivah, and there was no question in my mind that they were a perfect fit for each other.

That was how the story ended, but in the middle of the whole mess, when I hadn't known which direction to turn or who to speak with, I happened to bump into Rav Asher. I filled him in on what was going on, and he was with me one hundred percent — with complete empathy, as always.

It so happened to be that we had met while he was on the way to give *shiur* to his customary thousand *talmidim* and was walking fairly quickly to get there on time. I presume that were I not there at the time he would have used the ten minutes of walking to review the upcoming *shiur* that he was about to give — but we *had* met and we were talking and he was there for me in every way possible. To the point where he apologized to me for walking so rapidly not once but five times throughout the course of our conversation.

"I'm so sorry that I'm in a rush, but I'm on the way to *shiur*..."

A thousand people were sitting and waiting for the legendary Rav Asher Arieli to enter the *shiur* room and give one of his epic *shiurim*, while Rav Asher was busy apologizing to me for not giving me more of his precious time and remaining extraordinarily calm the entire time! It was a case of a classic *ba'al middos* and his modest approach in life, which is why I always say there are two types of people in the world: those who know Rav Asher and those who don't. Seeing Rav Asher means seeing what being a Jew is all about.

Encounters With

Rav
Tzvi Kushelevsky
שליט"א

A Bridge to the Rishonim

I'll tell you a line I heard from Rav Tzvi that I feel sums up his philosophy: "Emes is very pashut. The difficult thing is to get to the emes."

Chapter Sixteen

I learned at Toras Moshe for close to five years. When I left the yeshivah, I spent a short time in the Mir and eventually moved on to Heichal HaTorah, the yeshivah of Rav Tzvi Kushelevsky. If you want to know what direction to take in life, study the path of someone else, and then you'll have a good idea of what awaits you as well. I knew some of Rav Tzvi's *talmidim*, and I knew that ultimately the way they learned was the way that I wanted to learn and the way they acted was the way that I wanted to act. The obvious conclusion was that if I myself followed the trajectory that they had taken, I might end up at a similar stage in life.

That was the hope.

I'll tell you a line I heard from Rav Tzvi that I feel sums up his philosophy: "*Emes* is very *pashut*. The difficult thing is to get to the *emes*."

He taught his *talmidim* how to learn the Gemara and *Rishonim* and understand what they are saying, so that when you actually looked at the words inside, you truly grasped what they were coming to point out. But it wasn't easy to master his *derech*. The success of being able to honestly appreciate what a *Rishon* is saying only came to the *talmidim* after years of familiarizing themselves with his unique *derech*.

"The difficult thing is to get to the *emes*."

This is true. On the other hand, it's more difficult to be content with not finding the *emes*. There is no real alternative but to work and work until the picture clears and you are able to recognize the *emes* for yourself. It's all about learning how to read what the *Rishon* is actually saying.

"I believe that if you learn the Gemara properly," Rav Tzvi would say, "all the questions fall to the side."

Rav Tzvi balanced the entire *Shas* on his fingertips. When he offered a *sevara*, it was based on a broad array of *gemaras* and everything the *Rishonim* had to offer on the topic. He was able to say with complete clarity and assurance, "This is the *pshat* in the *Rashba*" — because he knew that it was.

I found myself connecting to the simplicity he espoused.

"How does a person learn to do what you do?" I asked him once.

"I read the *Rishon* over and over," he told me. "I'll read the *Rishon* twenty times, forty times — even a hundred times — until I see it."

So simple. Just learn it a hundred times.

Eventually I realized that the Vilna Gaon says the same thing in his commentary on *Mishlei*.

"*Im l'binah tikra*" — you acquire *binah*, understanding, by reading the words. (Over and over if that's what it takes.)

Just reading words of Torah offers a certain intangible *segulah* that allows a person to break through the walls of previously inaccessible ideas to get to the truth within.

The *pshatim* he was telling us in *shiur* were simply mind-boggling, and I was blown away by what he was doing. No matter what he said, it resonated beautifully in the words of the Gemara and commentary — clearly what he said was the truth and had always been the truth but just needed to be uncovered by Rav Tzvi.

The *talmidim* had learned the *sugya* just like he had. But only after hearing what he had to say in *shiur* did they realize they had missed the truth of the *sugya*, because his words provided an entirely different level of understanding. That was when you asked yourself how you had missed the real *pshat* when you learned it in preparation for *shiur*.

He also stressed time and again how people should make sure to finish *masechtos*. Many people learn bits and pieces, but Rav Tzvi believes that if a person wants to become a true *talmid chacham*, the only way to do that is by making sure to learn through as much Torah as possible and not just be content with knowing the "*reid*" on the more well-known *sugya*s.

◆ ◆ ◆

Rav Tzvi is of the opinion that the deepest of all the *Rishonim* is Rashi.

"There are some places where people sit on Gemara and *Rashi*," he'd say. "That's not the right way. A person cannot possibly comprehend *Rashi* just by learning Gemara and *Rashi*. Only after you have gone through the other *Rishonim* on the *sugya* and see the questions they ask will you be able to return to *Rashi* and recognize that he is coming to answer all their questions in his typically concise format."

At times he would do this in *shiur*, showing the *talmidim* how Rashi deals with every possible question that is raised by his contemporaries.

He also likes quoting Rabbeinu Gershom, who writes that a person's first takeaway of a *sugya* is almost always incorrect, and even if it is correct, it is almost never completely correct, because, he said, "you need to learn something over and over until you get through the wall and reach the truth."

Or, as Rav Moshe Shapiro used to say all the time, "*Klippah kodemes l'pri*" — the peel comes between you and the fruit.

◆ ◆ ◆

Like any educator, Rav Tzvi had a number of stories he'd repeat from time to time. One such story happened to be about kreplach.

There was once a man, he'd relate, who wanted to learn how to make kreplach. After sharing this dream with a friend, the friend reassured him that he knew how to prepare the traditional culinary delicacy that is normally served *erev Yom Kippur,* Hoshanah Rabbah and Purim and would be happy to impart his wisdom.

"But making kreplach is so difficult," worried the first man.

"No, it's not," replied his friend. "I'm going to show you how to do it. It's not as hard as it looks. Here, you just have to follow the steps."

He proceeded to take his friend through the process. "You get a bowl and put some flour in the bowl. That's easy, right? After the flour, you pour some water into the bowl and mix everything together. Then you remove the mixture and begin rolling out the dough. When the dough is rolled out, you cut out pieces, put the meat on, and fold over the corners and then — voila! — kreplach!"

When uttering the word *kreplach,* Rav Tzvi would throw his arms up in the air, as if emphasizing how the initial difficulty of preparing kreplach disappeared when a person was shown the science behind it.

"What's the *yesod*?" he'd say. "Sometimes you come across a giant *Tosafos* or a big *sugya,* and you get scared because you look at the entire picture and it seems so large that it intimidates you. The key to success in learning is to break things down into small, simple steps — and that's the idea of kreplach."

If he saw that people were getting confused because they hadn't broken things down into steps, he would sometimes repeat the entire story, and at other times just say, "*Oy,* kreplach." If he saw that there were a lot of new *talmidim,* and they had a confused look on their faces when he uttered the word *kreplach,* he'd take the time to share the story with them, so that they too could appreciate the depth of the "Kreplach Analogy."

◆ ◆ ◆

Rav Tzvi was sharp. If he had to repeat an idea more than three times, he'd comment, "I've already surpassed Rav Preidah. Rav Preidah taught his *talmid* four hundred times. Since there are over one hundred and fifty of you sitting here, I've taught the same thing many more times than he did!"

It took guts to speak up in *shiur*, because Rav Tzvi expected a *talmid's* comments to be on point. There were a number of *talmidim* who had been there for several years and were able to speak up or even argue with the *rosh yeshivah*, but the majority of the student body knew better than to interject.

I recall one particular interchange between a *talmid* named Gamliel and Rav Tzvi. Rav Tzvi said something, and Gamliel made a comment. Rav Tzvi responded, and so did Gamliel. It was like watching a verbal Ping-Pong game, as comment followed comment and rebuttal followed rebuttal.

Finally Gamliel fired his parting shot, pointing out that his position was supported by a leading *Acharon*.

Rav Tzvi banged his hand on the table and yelled, "The *yesod* of this yeshivah is *emes. Emes!*"

Rav Tzvi was saying in not so many words that every person has to work on the *sugya* until he reaches the inherent truth within — and that it isn't sufficient to simply accept a *pshat* just because someone *chashuv* holds that way.

I'll never forget that day and the way their voices rose and the caliber of their arguments and how Rav Tzvi slammed his hand on the table and ended the argument once and for all.

It was a great *shiur*.

◆ ◆ ◆

The *talmidim* of Heichal HaTorah were truly a top-level group of people. Many of them were brilliant, yet they didn't act superior; rather than becoming *ba'alei ga'avah*, they worked on their *middos* as much as they worked on their *lomdus*. I felt like a small person surrounded by giants. I had come a long way in Toras Moshe, but some of the *avreichim* at Heichal HaTorah had been learning for many years, and they were light-years ahead of me, so in a way I felt like I was starting all over again from the beginning.

Rav Tzvi used to call a few *bachurim* or a pair of *chavrusos* into his office and learn with them privately. One *zeman* I had a *chavrusa*, Reb Mattis Rosenblum, who was a genuine *ilui*. When the two of us were summoned to the office for a private learning session, I sat on the sidelines completely bowled over by the level of conversation between my *chavrusa* and the *rosh yeshivah*. In all honesty, I had no idea what they were talking about. It was a truly humbling experience, yet at the same time it showed me what I could become if I applied myself with my trademark stubbornness.

My daughter was born just before Shavuos, which meant that my wife and I spent Yom Tov in the convalescent home in nearby Telz-Stone. It was an exhausting time for us, and I wasn't sure that I'd be able to stay awake all night learning since I was lacking so much sleep. Still, I resolved to try.

Reb Mattis lived in Telz-Stone, and the two of us got together after the *seudah* and began to learn. It was incredibly difficult for me to keep my eyes open, but I persevered and the learning went extra well that night. I remember that we were learning a very deep *sugya* in *Kesubos*, and the two of us arrived at an extraordinary level of clarity within the *sugya*. By the time the sky was beginning to change color, I was feeling immensely happy that I had fought with myself to stay awake, especially since we had come up with a real "bombe *kasha*" on the *sugya*.

That particular Shavuos-night *kasha* would come to have real bearing on my life thirteen days later when I needed it most.

◆ ◆ ◆

It took me a while until I managed to work my way into Rav Tzvi's inner circle, and the truth is that it only really happened after the car accident that might have ended my life — the accident that happened right outside the yeshivah on an *erev Shabbos*, thirteen days after I stayed up all night learning that Shavuos.

As I was being rolled into the hospital, I was drifting in and out of consciousness and feeling like I was being cut into pieces from sheer agony. I felt like I needed to speak to someone to divert my mind from the excruciating pain. Both Rav Meiselman and Rav Elchanan Fishman from Toras Moshe were there, and I asked Rav Fishman a question through the haze of pain. Meanwhile, Rav Meiselman had called my wife and told her that I had been in a "little" accident and that he was coming to pick her up to bring her to the hospital.

"Please talk to me in Torah," I begged Rav Fishman. "I feel like I'm in so much pain that I am going to die!"

He agreed (what don't you do for a patient) and replied, "Ask me a question," and I found myself asking the first question that came to mind.

"What are we doing quoting the *malachim* in the middle of *Birchos Krias Shema*?" I asked him, referring to the middle of *Yotzer Ohr*, where we say "*Kadosh, Kadosh, Kadosh* — Holy, Holy, Holy," which is a quote from the angels.

I have no idea how or why that particular question suddenly showed up in my mind or if I had ever thought about it before. Perhaps that specific question came to me because I myself was kind of close to the angels at that point in time...

I don't recall the answer, but I do remember that our conversation really helped me stay composed through the pain.

Suddenly I looked up and saw one of the *rebbeim* in the yeshivah, and I remembered the question Reb Mattis and I had come up with that Shavuos night on the *sugya* in *Kesubos*. Amazingly enough, the *kasha* was still in my head (despite the fact that my head was barely in my head, if you get what I mean...), and I asked my rebbi for an answer. I had just been run over, there was blood on my clothing and body — the fact is, nobody even thought I'd make it to the hospital alive — and I was a half-dead person asking his rebbi a question on *Kesubos*. It was surreal.

In retrospect, when I remember the scene and the moment I asked him the question, I'm pretty sure that my rebbi was a little taken aback. After all, it's not every day that you are asked an *iyun she'eilah* by a guy lying on a stretcher covered in blood.

Later I was wheeled out of the room where they had taken me for a CAT scan and was thinking a little more clearly. I saw Rav

Tzvi Kushelevsky — it was *erev Shabbos*, but he was still there waiting to hear the prognosis — and I raised the question on *Kesubos* yet again. But as much as I wanted to discuss the matter, I found that my brain was not up to talking in a complex *sugya* in the Gemara right then. The pain was way too great for me to be able to concentrate, and I let the matter rest for a future opportunity.

Rav Tzvi, appreciating my pain and the fact that I was in such terrible shape, maneuvered the conversation into Torah matters that were easier to grasp, and I was able to follow the conversation without undue strain. (My wife told me that Rav Tzvi gave her a lot of *chizuk* and was very thoughtful during those difficult moments in the emergency room.)

Throughout the time I was in the hospital and during the recovery period as well, Rav Tzvi remained in close contact with me and was kept informed of everything that was happening, always wanting to know how I was doing and whether there was anything he could do for me.

I don't know this for a fact, but part of me feels that our conversation on the stretcher was one of the moments that came to define our future relationship. Later on I would come across a halachah in the *Mishnah Berurah* where the Arizal is quoted: "If someone stays awake learning all Shavuos night, *muvtach lo* — he is promised — that he will not die during the coming year." I attributed my miraculous survival to those words of the Arizal.

The day after my accident someone was killed in almost the same place where I was hit, and a month earlier someone else was hit by a car and thrown a vast distance, only to stand up on the spot and walk away of his own volition. There is no question in my mind that every single thing that happens to a person is scripted down to the last detail. Nothing is random. Everything is precise.

◆　◆　◆

After the accident and the mandate handed to me by Rav Shlomo Zalman — that "you have to discover your *tafkid* in life;

Hashem saved you, there must be a reason" — I began working on my *sefer* during *bein hazemanim*. All in all, it took me three years to finish writing *Mizmor L'Sodah*.

I couldn't discuss the *sefer* with Rav Tzvi while we were in yeshivah, because there were always a hundred *talmidim* waiting to speak to him, but I used to ride the Har Nof–bound bus with him, accompanying him home. After delivering *shiur*, Rav Tzvi would dart out of the building, rushing home to eat lunch with his *rebbetzin*, and I'd dart right out of the building after him, determined to catch the same bus and have some uninterrupted time with him, when we could discuss any subject I was learning *b'iyun*. During those fifteen- to twenty-minute conversations, the two of us really began to develop a connection.

Rav Tzvi wrote a *haskamah* for my first *sefer*. There he asked what the connection is between thanking Hashem and halachah.

Quoting the Arizal, Rav Tzvi answered his question with the words "*Mizmor l'sodah hariu laShem kol ha'aretz*," pointing out that the first letters of the words "*hariu laShem kol ha'aretz* — call out to Hashem, everyone on earth," spell *halachah*.

"The right way for a person to thank Hashem," he concluded, "is by learning halachah, because then you know how to live your life as a Jew."

He also liked to say that it used to be that the *rosh yeshivah* and the *posek* were the same person, which, he felt, is the way it should be. For some reason, it has become rare these days to find one person who does both. Rav Tzvi, however, would like to bring us back to the way things have been in the past, when the rabbi knew both *lomdus* and halachah, because he feels that matters of halachah should be culled from a deep understanding of the Gemara.

◆   ◆   ◆

Rav Tzvi used to deliver a halachah *shiur* in the yeshivah on Friday nights, and if I was staying with my brother in Har Nof for Shabbos, I'd daven in the yeshivah and walk home with him after the *shiur*, thereby having another opportunity to talk with him.

I loved the way he learned halachah, how he would go through the *Rishonim* and *pasken*, brilliance contained in every word. My own approach in halachah was forged through his *shiurim*, especially when I heard him say things like "If you understand the *Rishonim* well, then the *Shulchan Aruch* is just review."

When it comes to giving *piskei halachah*, what people find most challenging is bridging the gap between the Gemara and *Rishonim* and the *Shulchan Aruch*. There's a gaping hole between the two, and people don't understand how to cross the bridge between the *Rishon's* opinion and the actual *psak* brought by Rav Yosef Karo.

In my opinion, that's where the *Acharonim* come in. They are the ones who guide a future *posek* from point A to point B. After studying a *sugya*, a person should have come to certain conclusions as to what the Gemara means to say, and the *Acharonim* should be used as signposts to see whether his conclusions are correct. If at least some of the major *Acharonim* agree with him, he is moving along the right path. If nobody seems to have arrived at his conclusions, he might have taken a wrong detour along the way and should probably rethink his approach.

Watching Rav Tzvi in action was breathtaking in the sense that instead of using the *Acharonim* as signposts, he was able to apply the words of the *Rishonim* with unerring ease — but, like I said, he has the entire *Shas* at his fingertips. The average *talmid chacham* is not as adept at what he does.

On the other hand, he serves as a living example of the heights a person can aspire to reach.

I have come to the conclusion that even if a posek *can* do what Rav Tzvi does and *is* able to *pasken* from the Gemara and *Rishonim*, there is still an additional matter to consider and that is the question of *minhag*. Something might be completely permissible according to halachah — think silkscreen *sifrei Torah* — yet was never accepted by *Klal Yisrael*, which would make it forbidden.

This is another area where consulting the *Acharonim* is extremely important, because they are the ones who give clear indications as to what *Klal Yisrael* has accepted as the overall *minhag* and what it has not. In other words, *Klal Yisrael* is the determining factor in many cases, and the *Acharonim* are the ones who let us know decisively what *minhagim Klal Yisrael* has accepted upon itself.

◆ ◆ ◆

If you asked Rav Tzvi on whose approach to learning does he model himself, he'd tell you that his approach mirrors that of the Vilna Gaon. He's told me that he once considered writing a *sefer* on the commentary of the Gra, but eventually decided against it. "Anyone who would be able to understand such a *sefer* (which would be almost nobody)," he explained, "wouldn't need it since he'd be able to write it himself."

Rav Tzvi has since stopped giving the halachah *shiur* in the yeshivah on Friday nights, explaining that "I am getting older and need to focus on learning *Shas*," and at some point I was asked to take over. In one of my first *shiurim*, I referred to the kreplach analogy. Seeing the confused looks on the faces of the *bachurim*, I asked them, "Haven't you heard the kreplach *mashal* from the Rosh Yeshivah?"

"No," they replied. "He never told us that story."

I then told them the kreplach story that I'd heard so many times from Rav Tzvi, transmitting the chain of *mesorah* down to future generations.

◆ ◆ ◆

One of the first major terrorist attacks that took place in the nineties happened at the Central Bus Station of Jerusalem, less than a mile from the yeshivah, which was then situated in the Pressburg building in Givat Shaul. In the aftermath of the attack, Rav Tzvi delivered an earth-shattering *shiur* in the *beis midrash,* basically saying that we were all responsible for what had happened. He quoted a *gemara* where Eliyahu HaNavi didn't visit a person because someone had been killed within a *mil* (about a mile) from where the person lived.

"We're within a *mil* from the Central Bus Station," he screamed. "If we would have been learning better, we would have been able to provide protection! They are willing to be *moser nefesh* for what they believe. They are willing to kill themselves! We have to be willing to be *moser nefesh* for what we believe in as well!"

It was one of the most powerful *shmuessen* I have ever heard, before or after, and it shaped the way I'd relate to terrorist attacks for the rest of my life.

Though Rav Tzvi was very tough on the *talmidim* — "giving it" to those who spoke up in *shiur* without really knowing what they were talking about — he has since changed his approach, explaining that the generation is no longer equipped to deal with the tough love that previous generations were capable of handling.

In retrospect, I was hardly ever on the receiving end of the stick, since I knew better than to speak up in *shiur* unless I had something to say that was really on point, and I'm glad that I was there to see a rebbi demanding from his *talmidim* and pushing them to the limit of their endurance, because the tough approach when used correctly can build a student in a much stronger way than that of just using love.

I was part of the cut-off generation — the one that was still able to take the tough *chinuch* of the Telzer *derech* without falling apart. And while it was not always fun at the time, there is no question in my mind that the approach worked and built great people.

Times, however, change and so do we. Today *rebbeim* must work with gentleness and love. No longer will you hear Rav Tzvi comparing himself to Rav Preida in *shiur*. Things are different now. But if you hang around long enough, you might still hear him make a reference to kreplach.

Chapter Seventeen

One of the most vital lessons I learned from Rav Tzvi happened during a flight we shared. While I had been assigned a seat in the middle of the cabin, Rav Tzvi's seat was at the very back of the plane. I had heard that he was going to be on my flight and had spent three days preparing so that we'd be able to talk in learning.

I remember that Rav Tzvi finished the entire *Maseches Kreisos* on that flight. From cover to cover. *Kreisos* is one of the most difficult *masechtos* in *Shas*, but he covered it from start to finish by learning whenever he had a free moment. His *hasmadah* is not to be believed.

This was not news to me. During my first year at the yeshivah, Rav Tzvi's father passed away, and he made a *kabbalah* to learn the entire *Shas Bavli* in his memory. In the final week before the *yahrtzeit*, Rav Tzvi commented that he still had to finish the entire *Kodshim* and *Taharos* and was therefore going to have to take time from his normal schedule to discharge his obligation.

My rebbis approach to traveling was fascinating. He'd make sure to arrive three hours before the flight, check in, and then sit and learn in peace until the flight was boarding, when he would run through the gate at the last possible moment. He used to say that some of his best learning happened while he was traveling.

Most people find it extremely difficult to learn when they are away from their normal routine. Rav Tzvi, on the other hand, appreciated travel, because this afforded him the opportunity to learn for many uninterrupted hours at a time. Usually when he traveled he was alone, surrounded by strangers, and this meant that he was able to learn for twenty hours straight if he wanted. Rav Tzvi cherished his traveling time as a precious gift, and even though many of the trips were for fundraising purposes, for him it was like going on vacation.

Three hours of learning in the airport, then on to the plane, where he would find his seat and continue where he'd left off.

"When I go to *chutz la'aretz*," he'd say, "I'm like a *baalebos*. The Rambam writes that a *baalebos* learns nine hours and works three hours. When I'm collecting money for the yeshivah, I try to act like a *baalebos* and learn for at least nine hours a day."

To him the fundraising was something he had to do, but it was almost like an afterthought, with the learning remaining his focus throughout the time he was away. It was almost as if he hadn't even gone anywhere. He never lost his connection to what was happening with his *talmidim* and the *sugya* they were learning. I can recall him coming to the yeshivah directly from the airport and delivering a *shiur klali* in depth. I've always found that one of the most difficult things about traveling is the *hesach hada'as* — the million things that make it hard for a person to concentrate. For Rav Tzvi, that was not an issue at all.

Getting back to that flight, I had put in a few days of preparation for our time together, and I went to speak with him in learning soon after we'd taken off.

"Reb Daniel Yaakov," he said to me, "I need to learn a little first. Please come back to me later on."

I returned to Rav Tzvi toward the end of the flight. We were discussing the halachic issue of cooking on Shabbos when all of a sudden he said to me, "These trips are very hard for me! These trips to *chutz la'aretz* are very hard for me!"

"Is it because of the *bizyonos*?" I asked him.

Everyone knows that fundraisers, even *roshei yeshivah* of great stature, are subjected to all manner of embarrassment while on the road, and I wanted to know if this was the source of what bothered him so.

He looked back at me with an intense expression on his face and replied, "*Bizyonos*, Reb Daniel Yaakov? *Bizyonos*? *Bizyonos* are great!"

He uttered this line with an intensity and animation that shook me to the core with its sincerity and authenticity. It was hard to believe, but Rav Tzvi clearly considered *bizyonos* to be a privilege!

"So what does the Rosh Yeshivah find so difficult about his trips?"

"The *gashmiyus* and luxury that surrounds me everywhere. It bothers me very much."

Rav Tzvi was bothered by *gashmiyus* and not by *bizyonos*. I was fascinated by what I had just heard, and I knew that I would never forget his reaction to my question on that flight.

◆ ◆ ◆

Three years later, a few days before Pesach, I was on another fundraising trip to the States, and I found myself giving a mini *shiur* to a group of businessmen in an office building in Manhattan. As a rule, I usually bring some of my *sefarim* with me when I travel since I find that once I get into a conversation with a person, there is a good chance he will be interested in purchasing a *sefer* or two on whichever topic speaks to him. I have written a wide range of *sefarim*, and there is something for everyone.

I had sold quite a few *sefarim* by that point of the trip, but I had plenty more with me and it was no easy feat transporting them from place to place. Since I was carrying a heavy load of *sefarim*, I caught the elevator for a short ride to the ground floor, one floor down. Under normal circumstances I might have taken the stairs, but with the *sefarim* weighing me down, I opted for the more comfortable means of transport. I entered the elevator and found myself looking into the face of a man who had been at one of my *shiurim* half a year earlier during the Aseres Yemei Teshuvah.

The moment he caught sight of me, the man started yelling at me. "It's three days before Pesach and you stop an elevator to go down one flight? Don't you care about wasting other people's time?!"

My face turned red with embarrassment as he continued screaming at me in the crowded elevator. You really couldn't miss hearing what he said. It would have been bad enough if I didn't know the man, but this was a person who had attended one of my *shiurim* — a person who had learned Torah from me — and here he was shaming me in public. I was mortified, but I didn't reply and merely exited the elevator when the doors opened a few seconds later.

Standing there in the hallway of that bustling Manhattan building, my face still flaming red from the uncomfortable encounter, I said to myself, *Wow, I was just on the receiving end of a serious plateful of bizyonos!*

Suddenly Rav Tzvi's memorable words from three years earlier flashed through my mind, and I remembered him saying enthusiastically, "Reb Daniel Yaakov, *bizyonos* are great!"

Trying to get a handle on my emotions, I began repeating his words to myself over and over.

"*Bizyonos* are great, *bizyonos* are great, *bizyonos* are great!"

I must have said it a hundred times.

I had no time, however, to sit and reflect on what had just happened. I had arranged to meet with someone I knew who had promised to drive me from Manhattan to Lawrence for a meeting I had scheduled for later that evening. I gave him a call and asked him where he was and whether there was any way he could come and pick me up when he left his office.

"I'm very sorry," he said, "but I'm in the middle of a meeting and can't leave the office now, and I won't have time to drive over to where you are after the meeting is over."

"So what should I do?"

"You're going to have to make your way across town to my office building and meet me here."

I exited the building and began walking down the Manhattan avenue, thousands of people streaming past me on every side. As I walked, I suddenly heard an unfamiliar noise, the sound of someone being physically assaulted. Soon enough, I saw a policeman on the sidewalk beating someone up. I didn't know the background of what had happened; I had no idea what the person had done wrong. All I knew was that I was very uncomfortable watching a human being getting a beating. I was in the minority, however, since a huge crowd was standing around and watching, obviously enjoying the spectacle. This was brought home to me when one of the people standing and watching exclaimed with pleasure, "Wow, this is better than television!"

I couldn't believe that a person would even think such a thing, let alone say it. Far from enjoying what I was seeing, I felt a terrible sense of shame at having found myself standing in such a place and being a party (however slight) to the misfortune of the man being beaten up in front of a huge group of people on a busy street corner.

I can't believe that I'm seeing this, I said to myself. *What am I even doing here in the middle of such an impure place, being exposed to such a sight? Just having to stand here is bizyonos!*

Once again, in a very short amount of time, I found myself repeating my newfound mantra: "*Bizyonos* are great, *bizyonos* are great, *bizyonos* are great!"

It was an extremely hot day, and, like I said, I was carrying a bag of heavy *sefarim* in my hand. After passing the policeman beating the living daylights out of some hapless individual, I picked up my pace and almost ran the next twenty blocks to the building where I had agreed to meet the man who had offered to drive me to my destination.

◆ ◆ ◆

Sweating profusely, I finally arrived at the address and walked through the rotating glass door at the entrance. The building was air-conditioned, and I caught my breath as I waited for the elevator to arrive. The doors opened, and about a dozen people streamed past me in the direction of the street. When the elevator was empty, I went inside and pressed the button for the floor that I needed. Four minutes later I was heading down the hallway toward the office of my gracious driver. I was right on time and looking forward to getting into my host's clean, cool car for the ride out of the city and over to the Five Towns.

My host greeted me with a warm "*shalom aleichem*," but I could tell from his demeanor that he had something to tell me and that I probably wasn't going to like whatever it was.

I was right.

"Rabbi Travis," he said to me, "here's the thing. I know that I agreed to drive you from Manhattan to the Five Towns, but something came up and I need to meet a friend of mine in Queens. If you don't mind, I'm going to have to go there first."

"But that's going to take me two hours out of my way," I said.

"I'm really sorry, but something came up and I have to go meet this person. I'll pay for you to go out for dinner while you're waiting, so at least it won't all be wasted time."

Dinner is well and good, I thought to myself, *but I have a number of homes I want to visit in Lawrence. I don't have time to sit around and wait for them to broil me a steak!*

In the space of an hour I had been accosted in an elevator filled with people and shamed publicly, had been subjected to seeing a man being beaten up on a street corner while people watching commented loudly how enjoyable a sight it was, and had had no choice but to shlep my *sefarim* twenty blocks in sweltering Manhattan so as to get to my ride, only to be informed, after all that, that the driver wasn't taking me where I needed to go!

It was *bizyonos, mamesh bizyonos*.

"*Bizyonos* are great," I said to myself. "*Bizyonos* are great!"

Rav Tzvi had said it, Rav Tzvi had meant it, and there was no doubt in my mind that he knew what he was talking about.

I joined my host for a ride to Queens, utilized the unexpected detour to make a quick stop at my parents' home, and then called a cab for the ride to Lawrence. I had many houses to visit and I was already late.

♦ ♦ ♦

I knocked on the door of the first Lawrence house on the list. I hadn't been to this address in close to two years, and I was hoping that the person I had come to see would remember me and be happy to see me.

The door swung open in response to my knock, and I saw the familiar face smiling in welcome.

"I can't believe it," he said to me.

"Can't believe what?" I asked him.

"I just said to myself that I am going to give all my *ma'aser* for the entire month to the next person who knocks on my door for a donation — and here you are!"

Considering that the man happened to be extremely wealthy, I knew that the number on the check would be significant. We sat down at his dining-room table, enjoyed a short conversation, he gave me a drink, and then he took out his checkbook and wrote me the promised check, which he handed me with a flourish.

I wasn't wrong. It was a serious check. Thanking my host from the bottom of my heart, we shook hands and he escorted me to the door. As I made my way in the direction of the next address on my list, I couldn't help thinking, *Rav Tzvi was right — bizyonos are great!*

♦ ♦ ♦

Ten minutes later I found myself standing at the front door of another Lawrence home. It was a beautiful and imposing house, and it was also the residence of a man with whom I had been trying to develop a relationship for quite some time. I rang the bell, and someone answered the door and asked me what I wanted. I told the person why I was there and asked if the *ba'al habayis* was home.

He was.

He welcomed me into his study a few minutes later and began questioning me about the *kollel* — what we learned, how the day was structured, what *sefarim* I had written, and what I was currently in the process of writing.

Finally we got down to business.

"What do you have in mind?" he asked me.

"I was hoping that you would be willing to make a donation of five hundred dollars a month for the next year."

He considered my request for a few seconds and then agreed without any negotiation or preconditions. It was unbelievable. I had been trying to gain a connection with this individual for such a long time with no luck, and suddenly everything had fallen into place with the greatest of ease, and I had raised well over ten thousand dollars in the space of twenty minutes from two visits!

I left the man's house, Rav Tzvi's words dancing in my mind: *Bizyonos are great! Bizyonos are great!*

◆ ◆ ◆

I couldn't do anything wrong that day. Every house I visited, every person I met, every request I made — they were all answered with a smile and with a positive response, and I knew that I would never forget the message I had been taught by Rav Tzvi Kushelevsky on that flight three years earlier and that had been reinforced that very day.

While it's true that no one enjoys *bizyonos*, and they are a very difficult form of *avodah*, they are part of our lives, and, as my rebbi said, "they are great!"

I hadn't been searching for *bizyonos* that day, but in retrospect it seems to me that the reward that came my way that evening was in direct proportion to what I had gone through a few hours earlier. Once again, my rebbi showed me a new perspective and another way of looking at life.

While many of us are lucky enough to find a rebbi who teaches us Torah and shows us how to dissect a piece of Gemara, it is significantly more rare to find a rebbi who can impart his *da'as Torah* to his *talmidim* in such a way that they can then go on to adopt his approach for themselves.

I was fortunate to have such a rebbi. I wish the same for you.

One more thing. Never forget: "*Bizyonos* are great! *Bizyonos* are great!"

Chapter Eighteen

Sometimes your rebbi will do something relatively minor that has a major impact on you. One Friday night I walked him home from the yeshivah. Rav Tzvi lived on a high floor of his Har Nof building. He was already older, and it was difficult for him to climb up all the stairs. Suddenly he turned around to a person who was walking behind us and asked, "Are we holding you up?"

I hadn't even realized that there was someone behind us, but Rav Tzvi did and he was concerned that he was being a burden on that individual. A real *adam gadol* has a cognizance of his actions and their ramifications.

Shifra and Puah were called by these names because of the gentle manner with which they took care of the babies in their care. Rav Yerucham Levovitz, *zt"l*, comments that while cooing for a baby may have been a small thing, doing the *small* things in life correctly is an indication of how *big* a person is.

◆ ◆ ◆

This story occurred during my second fundraising trip to the United States. Someone offered to allow me to give a five-minute *shiur* at their Manhattan office before Minchah. I arrived at the building at the appointed time and found the room I was looking for. This was where the religious people in the building davened Minchah every afternoon. My contact had graciously invited me to speak for a few minutes before Minchah, and I was hoping that something good would come of it. Many of the people I'd be speaking to were financially successful and would be able to help support my *kollel* if I could only find the right key to their hearts.

Slowly but surely the room began filling up with men dressed in business suits, and I stood up and began giving a *dvar Torah*, before telling them about my *kollel* in the Ramat Eshkol neighborhood of Yerushalayim.

Ask anyone who gives speeches on a regular basis, and he will tell you that sometimes it goes and sometimes it doesn't. Sometimes you open your mouth, and every word that emerges is lapped up with relish. Other times, however, nothing you say makes any difference whatsoever.

Unfortunately, this was one of those times. I might have been speaking in front of a room filled with people, but I could have been standing on the moon for all the attention they were paying me. There was no question in my mind that every single person there was just waiting for me to finish so he could begin davening Minchah. Everyone just went about his business and ignored me. They checked their emails, kept their eyes glued to their phones, and studiously avoided meeting my gaze. If you have ever spoken in public, you will know that being ignored like that is a mortifying experience.

At some point I just gave up, finished my speech, and joined the assembled for Minchah.

Needless to say, it was quite a disappointing experience.

Two hours later I boarded a Monsey-bound bus for the next leg of my trip. I was pleasantly surprised to find that Rav Tzvi was on his way to Monsey as well and that we would be sharing the journey together. Seeing him sitting there, I told Rav Tzvi about my experience in the office that day, and that it had reminded me of something he'd said in a *shiur* that he gave on the Maharal.

"One version of Gehinnom," he'd said in that *shiur*, "is when a person feels like he doesn't exist."

"Today I had a good taste of what it feels like not to exist," I told him.

Rav Tzvi looked at me and replied, "That's exactly what the Maharal meant!"

◆ ◆ ◆

I wrote my second book on the subject of honesty, calling it *Priceless Integrity*. One Friday night, while learning with my *chavrusa*, I came across a *Maharal* on the topic of *nevuah ketanah*, a small measure of prophecy. The Gemara stated that if a person goes to sleep and wakes up with a *pasuk* on their lips, this is called "*nevuah ketanah*."

"I would really like to experience such a thing," I said to my *chavrusa*.

"So daven to Hashem and ask Him to send you a *nevuah ketanah*," he replied in a reasonable voice.

I followed my *chavrusa's* advice and woke up the next morning with a *pasuk* on my lips. It was the *pasuk* of "*Vayehi viShurun melech b'hisasef roshei am* — He became King over Yeshurun when the heads of the nation gathered" (*Devarim* 33:5).

This had never happened to me before, and it never happened again.

Okay, so my wish had come true. I had been granted a small measure of prophecy. Now what? What was I supposed to do with this *pasuk*?

I decided to look up what Rav Shamshon Rafael Hirsch had to say about the *pasuk* of this *nevuah ketanah*.

"*Klal Yisrael* is referred to as Yeshurun," Rav Hirsch writes, "when they act with integrity."

On the spot I decided that my next book would be about integrity. In the book I provide the sources for the halachos of integrity from stories of the *Avos* and the Torah.

I gave a lot of thought to the cover. I wanted to find the perfect picture, one that would encapsulate the concept of something priceless. In the end, I asked my graphics designer to find an image of the most expensive and flawlessly cut diamond in the world. After much research, we settled on what the publisher felt was the perfect diamond to convey the idea of something priceless.

A short while later, I left Eretz Yisrael on a fundraising trip to the States. At some point during the trip, I found myself speaking about my new book at a very wealthy shul in New York. After I finished, a kid in blue jeans approached me and said, "Rabbi, I'd like to purchase twenty copies of your book."

I was slightly taken aback at the size of his order but was obviously happy to oblige.

The kid removed a hundred-dollar bill from his wallet, handed it to me, and said, "This is a down payment."

Then he handed me his business card.

Since he was a young-looking guy, I didn't take the whole thing too seriously, but a little later I had a chance to take a better look at his card and realized that the "kid in the blue jeans" was the president of one of the largest and most successful diamond companies in New York.

When we spoke again, I just had to ask him why he liked the book so much and had decided to order so many copies.

"Rabbi Travis," the young man replied, "you won't believe this, but the diamond on the cover of your book is the exact cut of diamond that my company specializes in. When I saw the cover of your book, I had to purchase as many as I could!"

The two of us would go on to develop a very close relationship, with this young man supporting the *kollel* generously for years to come.

◆ ◆ ◆

The *avodah* of fundraising was something I have found difficult for many reasons.

"When someone gives me a significant amount of money," I told Rav Tzvi as we were standing in front of the door to his apartment, "I can't help feeling that now I have a lot of money for the *kollel* because of that person. I know that Hashem is the One deciding how much money every person receives, but I always feel a tremendous amount of *hakaras hatov* to the person giving me the donation because he made the choice to give me the donation."

"I don't feel that way," Rav Tzvi replied and entered his home.

It wasn't a lack a *hakaras hatov*, but for Rav Tzvi there was no question where the money was coming from and who was sending it.

He doesn't even ask for money. He might come to a person's home and meet with him and sit with him, but he won't make a request for financial assistance. He will just wait for the person to offer the money on his own.

◆ ◆ ◆

While writing *Takanas HaShavim*, a *sefer* that deals with questions and answers for *ba'alei teshuvah* and *kiruv* professionals, I discussed almost every question with Rav Tzvi. There were many interesting *she'eilos* that arose. There was one question regarding the mother of a *ba'al teshuvah* who wanted to invite her grandchildren to her house for Shabbos. Her son was not comfortable with this and didn't allow his children to go.

His mother's response: "If you don't allow your children to come to me, I will swear an oath that I will never come to your house!"

The son refused to back down, and the mother informed her son that she had sworn to never step foot in his house again. The next day, however, the man's mother showed up on his doorstep and knocked on his door wanting to come into the house. The son was now faced with yet another question.

How could he allow her entrance to his house if she had sworn never to come inside?

I discussed the question with Rav Tzvi, who made the following suggestion: "The son should walk out of his house to talk to his mother, and if she then enters the house, that's her business."

He also said that the oath would have to be annulled since this was a question of *issurim d'Oraisa*, and that the son should do his best to convince his mother to accompany him to a *rav* for that purpose, but he also said, "The son should tell his mother that he really cares about her and loves her. She doesn't feel loved, and he needs to show her that he loves her!"

He repeated this line over and over, saying, "He should just tell his mother how much he loves her, and everything will work out!"

It was moments like these that showed me how very much he cared.

◆　◆　◆

Rav Tzvi was a son-in-law of Rav Leib Gurwicz of Gateshead. He told me how his wife had come home crying one day when she was a little girl. The *rosh yeshivah* saw his daughter crying and asked her what happened.

"Someone told me that you are a *meikel posek*," she said through her tears.

The Gateshead *rosh yeshivah* smiled and replied, "I'm very happy they are saying that about me. *Ko'ach d'heteirah adif* — it's much better for a *rav* to be a *meikel* than a *machmir*. It's much better for a *posek* to look long and hard to find ways to make life easier for *Klal Yisrael*, not more difficult. Being called a *meikel* is a real compliment."

Bottom line: empathy for people is what creates the greatest rabbis and *roshei yeshivah*.

◆　◆　◆

Rav Tzvi's *rebbetzin* passed away a few years ago. When she became ill, they had moved into an apartment in the yeshivah. After she passed away, a group of the older *talmidim* would accompany him to his apartment on Shabbos morning after davening. He has since begun slowing down and has made the decision to stop traveling around the world as much as he did in the past. A number of *bachurim* join him for his *seudah* on Friday night, and he usually eats by himself Shabbos morning. Sometimes I join him for the *seudah* before going home to eat with my family.

Sitting with my rebbi, whom I have known for so many years, I sometimes reflect on the fact that Rav Tzvi was the one who gave me my connection to *Torah SheBe'al Peh*, and I feel infinitely grateful to him for the spiritual gifts he bestowed upon me.

Encounters With

Rav
Dovid Cohen
שליט"א

Chesed and Torah in One

"Acts of kindness refers to the type of chesed that only you can do and not anyone else," Rav Dovid said. "But there's another act of chesed that doesn't take any time at all."

"What?"

"Caring about people," he replied. "Having empathy for one another. People don't care enough. A person has to...care about every single Jew as if he were his brother! To greet them, to relate to each one as if he is a lofty being — that's what's missing from Klal Yisrael today, and that's why the geulah has still not arrived."

Chapter Nineteen

I met Rav Dovid Cohen, today *rosh yeshivah* of Chevron, soon after my arrival in Yerushalayim. A grandson of Rav Tzvi Pesach Frank, *zt"l*, the legendary *rav* of Yerushalayim, Rav Dovid Cohen possessed all the qualities necessary to become a leader in the Torah world. When you read stories about Rav Tzvi Pesach Frank, it's obvious that he knew how to connect with people, and Rav Dovid clearly inherited this talent.

Rav Dovid's father was one of the most prominent *dayanim* in the field of *gittin*, and when we learned *Maseches Gittin* my first year in Toras Moshe, his father came and gave a practical *shiur* in *hilchos gittin* to help us understand what we were learning.

Rav Dovid was accepted into the highest *shiur* in Chevron when he was very young. Rav Shach commented at the time that the young *bachur* was the future *gadol hador*. When I met him for the first time, he was still a *maggid shiur* at Ateres in Bayit Vegan, before he was eventually brought to Chevron.

I arrived in Yerushalayim at a very young age, and if I am being honest, I was trying to escape American society. I saw the world I had grown up in as shallow and empty, and my arrival in Eretz

Yisrael heralded a period in my life when I tried my very best to go in the opposite direction of everything I had known before.

Toras Moshe was located right near Rav Dovid's house, and he used to learn in our *beis midrash*, where he saw an American kid who hadn't grown up religious yet sat and learned from morning till night with barely a breather. I would eventually find my way back to the middle of the road, but at the time we met, Rav Dovid saw a teenager who was completely devoted to his Torah learning. Rav Dovid would later tell me how impressed he was by the fact that I had chosen to swim so aggressively against the tide.

Since he was such a frequent visitor to our *beis midrash*, I ended up eating many a Shabbos *seudah* at his home. His wife was American, I was able to express myself in English, and I felt at home and accepted for who I was.

◆ ◆ ◆

It was Rav Dovid Cohen who made my *shidduch*.

How the Cohen family came to know my future wife was an interesting turn of events. The Cohen daughters needed to learn how to act, dress, and talk like a Brazilian for a Purim play, and somehow they were introduced to my wife, who hailed from Rio de Janeiro and was happy to assist them.

The *shidduch* didn't work out at the time. She returned to Brazil, and I was *redt* other *shidduchim*. For various reasons, none of them worked out, many due in part to the fact that the Gulf War broke out right around then and lots of people were opting to leave the country.

Making matters even worse was the fact that I had just left Toras Moshe after having learned there for five years and moved to the Mir, and since it was *erev Pesach* and right after the Gulf War, the yeshivah had emptied out, leaving me feeling like I was the only American *bachur* left in the Beis Yisrael neighborhood of Yerushalayim. All my friends were gone, I had nobody to talk to, and the feeling of loneliness was acute.

The phone in my apartment rang early one morning. A relative was on the line. We talked. I told her how yet another *shidduch* hadn't worked out. Instead of offering me sympathy, she began admonishing me that I should leave yeshivah and stop wasting my time.

"It's time to leave the bubble and return to the real world," she shouted at me from across the ocean.

Needless to say, I got off the phone as soon as I could.

It was six forty-five in the morning when I left my *dirah* to go daven Shacharis, and I felt like the weight of the entire world was perched squarely on my shoulders. I placed my tefillin bag on one of the *shtender*s in the nearly empty room. I removed my siddur from inside the plastic tefillin holder and tried to open it. But I couldn't do it. My fingers were trembling too much. I wanted to put on my tefillin, but something was holding me back.

Finally I managed to don my tefillin and begin the opening words of davening. But then, all of a sudden, right in the middle of *Pesukei D'Zimrah*, it was as if a dam broke and the tears came gushing out of my eyes. There and then I put my head down on the *shtender*, my body rocking with silent sobs.

A minute passed, then another, then five.

Daniel Yaakov, I said to myself, *you can't do this right now. You're in the middle of davening. Pick your head up from the shtender and daven Shacharis!*

I forced myself to lift my tearstained face off the *shtender*. I had kept my finger on the place while I cried, and after I finished wiping my eyes I looked down at the *pasuk* where I had left off:

"*Harofei lishvurei lev u'mechabeish l'atzvosam* — He Who heals the brokenhearted and Who bandages their wounds" (*Tehillim* 147:3)."

I looked at the words. Then I looked again. I rubbed my eyes. Seeing those words was a sign that Hashem was looking out for me. It was a clear sign from *Shamayim* that I had nothing to worry about and that everything was going to work out.

My future wife returned from Brazil in the middle of Pesach. We began dating again on *Isru Chag* and got engaged soon afterward.

Since Rav Dovid had been the one to suggest the *shidduch*, I wanted to give him *shadchanus*.

Rav Dovid refused the money.

"I really want to pay you," I said to him.

He was equally as adamant as I was. "I cannot accept the money!"

"Why not?"

"The halachah is that you don't take *shadchanus* from a member of your *mishpachah*."

I continued trying, but he wouldn't accept a dime no matter what I said.

"Daniel Yaakov," he said to me with a warm smile, "you are a true member of my family, and there is no way in the world that I will accept money from you for making the *shidduch*."

A few years later, after we'd experienced so many challenges, I returned to his home with the money and gave it to him saying, "I heard that not paying *shadchanus* can bring *yissurim* to a person. Please take the money!"

Rav Dovid accepted the money from me and then returned it to me immediately.

◆ ◆ ◆

There is an incredible feeling of humanity and approachability to Rav Dovid Cohen. Recently I went to visit him. While there, we began discussing the security situation in Eretz Yisrael, and I asked him what we were supposed to be doing about the situation.

Rav Dovid put his arm around me.

"It's a *mefurishe gemara* in *Sanhedrin*," he replied. "In a time of danger, *yisasek b'Torah u'gemilas chasadim* — a person should busy himself with Torah learning and acts of kindness."

"What does the Gemara mean by acts of kindness?" I asked him.

He explained. "Acts of kindness refers to the type of *chesed* that only you can do and not anyone else. But there's another act of *chesed* that doesn't take any time at all."

"What?"

"Caring about people," he replied. "Having empathy for one another. People don't care enough. A person has to change his entire outlook on life and has to care about every single Jew as if he were his brother! To greet them, to relate to each one as if he is a lofty being — that's what's missing from *Klal Yisrael* today, and that's why the *geulah* has still not arrived."

I stood there listening to him speak, and I felt touched to my innermost being.

"Rav Chaim of Volozhin writes," he went on, "in the introduction to his *sefer Nefesh HaChaim*, that the *tachlis* of a person is to think about other people. Live life to think about other people and not about yourself."

The fact is, this is the way I have always felt Rav Dovid lives his life: thinking about others and caring about them with every fiber of his being. If you see his daily schedule in Chevron, how much time he spends helping *talmidim* and how he is always available to every member of *Klal Yisrael*…he is truly a unique individual.

◆ ◆ ◆

I asked Rav Dovid whether I should write *hashkafah sefarim* in addition to those I had written on halachah, or should I stick solely to halachah?

"It's very important that you write halachah, *hashkafah*, and *mussar*," was his answer. Then he told me a personal anecdote.

"When I first published my *sefer Zeman Simchaseinu* (a Succos, *hashkafah*-themed *sefer*), people mocked me for it. Some jokingly began referring to me as 'Dudi Cohen.'"

My jaw dropped.

It didn't matter at all," he said. "Not even a little bit."

Rav Dovid looked me in the eye.

"Never, ever make any decisions in life because of what this one or that one will think or say! If you do that, you will never get anywhere in life!"

◆ ◆ ◆

One Friday night my son and I walked from Har Nof to Shmuel HaNavi Street for a *shalom zachar*. On the way home we stopped off at the Cohen home in the Bukharim neighborhood for a short visit.

It was very enjoyable being with the Cohen family, and the conversation around the table turned to the topic of people having different *hashkafos* from one another — some go to the army, some are horrified by the idea.

"They are all good people," Rav Dovid said. "Every Jew is a good person. That doesn't mean that everyone's *hashkafos* are necessarily the right ones. But they are good people."

It was so refreshing to see a man of Rav Dovid's stature expressing the idea that he was able to accept all of *Klal Yisrael's* different camps.

◆ ◆ ◆

On one occasion I asked Rav Dovid what he thought of *bizyonos*.

"*Bizyonos* don't bother me at all," he replied. "*Kavod, kavod*" — and I'll never forget the way he said the word, as if it were utterly contaminated and repulsive — "that's what I'm scared of!"

◆ ◆ ◆

While describing a certain situation to him, I said that it looked to me like I needed to do such and such a thing, because events had conspired to come together in a particular way and it was *min haShamayim* that I react accordingly.

Rav Dovid clearly did not agree with my assessment.

Laughing a little, he said, "Maybe you'll call me an *apikorus*, but I don't believe in using the *min haShamayim* barometer as a decision maker."

"What do you mean?"

"I mean that I believe that a person should analyze a situation according to what the Torah has to say and make his decision based on those factors. Don't tell me about fate or circumstances. Tell me what the Torah says based on Torah knowledge and common sense."

◆ ◆ ◆

I asked Rav Dovid for a *haskamah* on different *sefarim* a number of times throughout the years. Rav Dovid explained to me that although he doesn't give *haskamos* to people, he would be happy to give me a "*michtav yedidus*" — a letter of friendship.

The way that he pens these letters is heartwarming. He will write, "My good friend, *yedid nafshi*...," the beautiful words of approbation for another human being flowing from his pen like artwork.

Rav Dovid knows the extent of his influence and prestige. He knows that as the *rosh yeshivah* of Chevron his name can open any door. He knows that he is a member of the Moetzes Gedolei Torah though he is fifteen years younger than the rest of its members. He knows all this. And knowing all this, Rav Dovid *loves* helping people, even just by making a phone call for them. There is no way to underestimate the impact that he can make with the simplest gesture.

"This is Dovid Cohen," he'll say when the person he's calling picks up.

"Rosh Yeshivah, how can I help you?"

"I am calling on behalf of a friend of mine..."

He wields incredible power in the *chareidi* world — and he wields it for *Klal Yisrael*.

On one occasion, I approached him for help in getting my son into a yeshivah. We wanted him to get accepted into a certain yeshivah where Rav Dovid was *nasi*. At the time I desperately needed to speak with him. I called him on the phone, silently begging him to pick up, but the phone rang and rang, and nothing. Obviously he wasn't home.

Clearly the matter was out of my hands. There was nothing more I could do. Besides, I had broken my ankle a short while before and had to go to physical therapy. I walked into the therapist's office, and to my disbelief and intense joy, there was Rav Dovid sitting and learning.

I told him everything that was going on, and after we discussed the situation from every angle he gave me an *eitzah*, which we implemented and which led to my son's being accepted into the yeshivah. After he had done everything he could, and I was finally able to relax, Rav Dovid turned to me and said with a smile, "*Nu*, Reb Daniel Yaakov, and what would you have done if you hadn't run into me?"

Then he answered his own question.

"That wasn't possible," he said, "because I know the way things work with you!"

While we were sitting there in the office, another person recognized Rav Dovid and took the opportunity to ask him a question.

Rabbosai, I have to say it. His response wasn't normal. The way he treated the man — not normal. The way he listened to him — as if that person was the most important person in the entire world. I distinctly heard him say, "If there is anything I can ever do to help you, please do not hesitate to get in touch."

Rav Dovid's *hakaras hatov* and his *bein adam lachaveiro* are simply beyond belief.

I have a *minhag* of taking my family every year to visit the Cohen family during Succos. Rav Dovid's succah is extremely large, and there are usually around seventy to eighty people visiting him at any given time. He knows the name of every single person who walks in, addressing him by his first name and inevitably getting updated on the minutest details of the person's life. If you saw this, you'd be amazed.

The group of visitors is fluid — the seventy or eighty people are always changing — but Rav Dovid is on top of the situation and has one eye on the people there and the second on the door, ready to greet the newest arrivals with a warm "*shalom aleichem*" and a question about their lives that shows them that he honestly remembers their issues and challenges and keeps them close to his heart.

On one of my more recent succah visits, I actually had something I wanted to discuss with him. At first my family and I took seats at the back of the succah, moving up as people left. It took a while, but eventually I found myself sitting right next to him. I laid out the question, an apparent contradiction in the *Magen Avraham*, and he gave me his full attention. I suggested one possible explanation, which he wasn't thrilled about, and then another one, to which he replied, "That's very good."

The entire time part of me was focused on our Torah discussion, while another part of me couldn't get over the fact that Rav Dovid just knows how to make a person feel so, so good.

◆ ◆ ◆

Certain lines he said made a deep impression. Here is a good example:

"There's a reason we don't have the *geulah* today. It's not because of a general lack of Torah learning. So many people have devoted themselves completely to Torah learning. That's not our problem.

"The problem," he continued, "is that it's supposed to be the same thing when it comes to doing *chesed*. We are supposed to relate to *chesed* with the same *mesirus nefesh* as we relate to Torah. We are supposed to immerse ourselves in *chesed* the same way we immerse ourselves in Torah! To look at an act of *chesed* with the same *geshmak* I'd use if I were about to dissect a *Ketzos* or a complicated '*Rav Chaim*.' To ask ourselves, 'How can I do this *chesed* in the best way, where the person I am doing this for won't feel like he's on the receiving end?'

"That is what we are missing."

◆ ◆ ◆

After a visit with Rav Dovid one afternoon, I was standing and waiting for a bus when I realized that I had no money to get me from the Bukharim neighborhood of Yerushalayim to Ramot, where I needed to go.

It shouldn't be a big deal, I told myself. *I'll just borrow some money from one of the passersby. This is a fairly central area, and I'm sure that someone I know will pass by any second.*

I waited a few minutes, before it became clear to me that I was surrounded by strangers.

I have no money, I said to myself, *and I don't know anyone here. What am I going to do?*

Then a realization hit me.

Wait a second. Is it money that gets a person from point A to point B? Hashem is the One Who helps us get to where we need to go!

Ten seconds later a car pulled up, and the driver asked me, "Excuse me, do you by any chance need a ride to Ramot?"

I didn't know the driver, and I hadn't asked him for a lift. But Hashem is the One Who gets us from place to place, and it was time for me to be on my way, money or no money.

As I got into the car, I couldn't help but remember a similar story that happened to me many years earlier, on Queens Boulevard. At the time I was still a *bachur* learning in Toras Moshe and had returned home for a visit. Wanting to spend my time productively, I had arranged to learn every day with a friend who lived in Kew Gardens Hills, which was two bus rides away from my house in Forest Hills.

One morning I left the house, *sefarim* in hand, for the relatively short ride through Queens. As the bus made its ponderous way through the city streets, I couldn't help but notice that the leaden skies above had opened up and that it was starting to snow.

The bus driver dropped me off on Queens Boulevard, and I stood at the bus stop hoping that the bus I needed would arrive shortly and that the city wouldn't halt all public transportation now, when I needed it most. A few minutes went by, the time for my bus's arrival came and went, and I realized that my fears had come true and that bus service had been temporarily halted until the weather cleared.

Now what?

It was snowing heavily, freezing cold, and too far for me to walk.

As I stood there, I remembered something I had just learned from Rav Chatzkel Levenstein in the name of the Ramban, who writes that a person's *yeshuah* usually arrives just when it seems there is no hope and nothing left for him to do.

"Ribbono shel Olam," I prayed, looking up at the sky from which drifted down an endless blanket of snow, "I have nothing left to do. There are no buses, it's too far for me to walk in this weather, and the snow is really coming down. I am all out of options. It's only You!"

A few seconds passed, and then a car suddenly materialized from out of the storm.

Coming to a halt at the bus stop, the religious driver looked at me and said, "Do you need a ride to Kew Garden Hills?"

Gratefully, I slid into the warm interior and put on my seat belt, as the driver carefully eased his vehicle away from the bus stop and back into the road.

I had barely been in the car for two minutes when the driver said, "It's so difficult to have *emunah* today..."

Of course I had to respond to that, and I told him about Rav Chatzkel's words and my saga in the snow.

To that he had no response.

◆   ◆   ◆

I went to see Rav Dovid shortly after Rav Brevda passed away. He wasn't home, so I left. As I was walking down the street, I ran into him. Catching sight of my face, he said to me, "What's wrong?"

"Rav Brevda was *niftar*."

His response was spontaneous and touched a chord deep within my soul.

"From now on I'm taking care of you," he replied immediately.

And he kept his word.

But then, I always knew that he would.

Encounters With

Rav Shlomo Zalman Auerbach
זצ"ל

Heart of the Nation

Simply speaking, Rav Shlomo Zalman was the lev ha'am — the heart of the nation. Seeing his reaction to another Yid's problems taught me how a Yid should behave and what it means to empathize with someone else's troubles.

Chapter Twenty

Rav Shlomo Zalman Auerbach told me many years ago that there are four ways to learn Torah: "You can learn halachah *b'iyun*, halachah *bekius*, Gemara *b'iyun*, and Gemara *bekius*."

In other words, one can learn halachah and Gemara in depth, or on a more superficial level, covering more ground.

"The Torah is very large," he went on, "and it's difficult to get a grasp of everything, which is why a person should focus on one of the four ways and become proficient in that area, with the idea that he will get to the rest of the Torah via his *derech*."

He felt most drawn to the halachah *b'iyun* approach, of learning halachah in depth, and I too focused on that path. In retrospect, I've seen that the people who followed Rav Shlomo Zalman's approach and focused on excelling in one area of their learning are the people who have traveled far in the world of Torah. They are the *roshei yeshivah*, the *roshei kollel*, and the *poskim*. Like in the field of medicine today, where there are heart specialists, lung specialists, and brain specialists (when it comes to the brain, there are even specialists in specific areas), so too there are those who specialize in delivering a top-notch *iyun shiur* and those who spent years covering *masechtos* and can give a *shiur* on any topic in *Shas*.

Rav Shlomo Zalman's advice to pick one area, make it your own, and develop your expertise proved to be extremely good advice, which made a massive impact on my entire life and future as the head of a *kollel* that studies halachah in depth.

◆ ◆ ◆

I decided that I wanted to study halachah seriously after learning at Rav Tzvi Kushelevsky's yeshivah for a number of years. On the day I reached my decision I discussed how best to do this with a number of my *rebbeim*, including Rav Tzvi, Rav Moshe Shapiro, and Rav Chaim Pinchas Scheinberg.

When I asked Rav Chaim Pinchas for advice, he didn't make it easy for me. "If you want to learn halachah," he cautioned, "it has to be in the same *iyun* style as you were learning Gemara until now."

He said this very firmly. Then he asked, "Do you know how many years it takes to reach a *sevara yesharah*?"

His body was shaking with intensity as he answered his own question.

"Years and years," he said, shaking his hands at me. "You think you can just sit down with a *Mishnah Berurah* and you'll be able to *pasken*?!"

I have been learning halachah *b'iyun* for over twenty years now, and the more I learn the more I realize how right he was. It does take a very long time for a person to develop the knowledge and mind-set needed to arrive at a genuine *sevara yesharah* and make a proper halachic ruling.

There's another very important point to consider, one which I've mentioned before. It's called the "fifth section of the *Shulchan Aruch*." In order to become a successful *rav* or *posek*, one needs to become as proficient in section 5 as one is in the other four. The problem is that the fifth section isn't written down anywhere. It's comprised of the innate understanding and comprehension of people that a *rav* needs to possess. It's common sense, it's being taught how to analyze properly, it's knowing people in a real way. And the only way to master the fifth section of the *Shulchan Aruch* is by observing another more experienced *rav* in action and up close — what is called "*shimush.*"

Learning how to learn is something any serious *ben Torah* can do. You sit in the *beis midrash* for a few years, you attend a *shiur*, you review — and inevitably you will learn how to learn. But how does a person learn about life? Many people are very bright. They possess a vast quantity of knowledge. They're sharp and grasp information quickly. Yet they know next to nothing about real life.

If a person remains in the realm of theoretical knowledge for his entire life without straying into the realm of practical halachah, the fact that he doesn't truly "get" life might not make that much of a difference. However, if our learned individual decides that he is ready to move on and learn halachah and that he not only wants to learn but also wants to *pasken*, then, as an old friend of mine who is a *chashuve posek* pointed out, "*Psak halachah* is ten percent information and ninety percent knowing people and how they operate."

A *she'eilah* came to me involving a person with suicidal tendencies. After weighing all the sides of the *she'eilah*, I came to the conclusion that it would be proper to be *machmir* in this case. That was back at the start of my *paskening* days and, not feeling completely comfortable about the conclusion that I reached, I called a respected *posek* to discuss the matter and hear his opinion. He, too, told me that he would rule *l'chumrah*. Still instinctively feeling that this was not the right path to take with this person, I called Rav Dovid Feinstein and asked his opinion.

Rav Dovid listened to the *she'eilah*, asked me questions regarding the person's personality, and then *paskened l'kula* without any hesitation whatsoever.

"For a person like that, there's no question at all that you *pasken l'kula*," he said, and in those few words I learned a lesson for life.

Rav Brevda told me in the name of Rav Chatzkel that a true *talmid* is someone who can take what he learns from his rebbi and transmit it to the next generation. As a *posek*, it's my job to take everything I have been fortunate to receive from my *rebbeim* and make sure that the next generation of *poskim* knows what to do as well. If I am *zocheh* to do that, if I succeed in teaching my *talmidim* what it really means to give a *psak halachah* and how it's not about the *she'eilah* but about the person, then I will be able to call myself a real *talmid* of my *rebbeim*.

◆ ◆ ◆

It was Rav Shlomo Zalman who gave me the idea to write a *sefer* by telling me that I needed to decide what to do with the gift of life that I'd been granted from Above. It was through the word of the *tzaddik* from Shaarei Chesed that I started to appreciate my own special *kochos* when it came to the study of halachah and realized that they had been lying dormant until that time. In truth, every single person in the world has his own brand of talents and strengths, and it is up to him to try to decipher what they may be — and then use them to glorify the Name of Hashem.

I soon came to understand that my *sefer Mizmor L'Sodah* was far from the first work that had come about in the wake of an accident. Both the Chayei Adam and the Pnei Yehoshua had written their monumental Torah works as a response to their own trials and tribulations. In my case, it was as if the *sefarim* I was writing were wrapped up in the *tzaros* I was experiencing. This also became a theme I focused on when speaking to people, discussing the idea of *"K'shem shemevarchim al hatov kach mevarchim al hara'ah"* — that just as a person thanks Hashem for the good in his life, so too must he thank Hashem for what doesn't seem good.

There's a *vort* I have used literally thousands of times that illustrates this concept.

The Gemara (*Berachos* 7b) tells us that Leah Imeinu was the first person to thank Hashem. Why was it that she was the one to come up with this groundbreaking idea? How could it be that Avraham, Yitzchak, and Yaakov didn't thank Hashem?

The answer can be found in a question of the Seforno, who

asks, Why did Leah merit having children before Yaakov's other wives? He answers that this was due to her suffering: "*Vayar Hashem ki senuah Leah vayiftach es rachmah...* — Hashem saw that Leah was hated, and He opened her womb..." (*Bereishis* 29:31).

Of course, anyone can thank Hashem for the good. That's an obvious course to take. But thanking Hashem for the bad, and realizing that the bad is also good — that's what real thanksgiving is all about.

In our case as well, we had a tremendous amount of *tzaros*. But those challenges led to the most incredible outcomes, which we wouldn't have traded for anything!

Nobody wants *tzaros*, but in retrospect, it's clear that they help us grow as people, and as terrible as it was, the accident that almost killed me on the day before my daughter's planned *kiddush* also built me in a very real way.

◆ ◆ ◆

While working on *Mizmor L'Sodah*, I utilized the fact that I was constantly visiting different *gedolim* in reference to the *sefer* to seek their advice regarding our situation as well. Some gave *berachos*; some didn't know how to react or what to say.

One *rav* suggested that we check all our mezuzos. We did and they were all kosher.

"Check your *kesubah*," was the next suggestion.

We checked our *kesubah*, and one of the letters was slightly longer than the rest. Though we had it rewritten, our circumstances didn't change. Basically we tried every single thing we could think of with no results. The stream of *tzaros* was simply not coming to an end. It was a very frightening time for us, with another emergency issue arising almost every week.

At some point during the never-ending chain of *tzaros*, I met with Rav Shlomo Zalman and poured out my heart, describing the difficulty of my days and how every new day seemed to bring in yet another hardship. I told him how I had built a succah in my backyard and how the neighbor had ripped it down an hour before Succos began when I didn't have enough time to build another one. It was the first time I had ever built my own succah and seeing it in pieces like that kind of broke my heart.

Among other things, I told him about how we had purchased an apartment and found ourselves embroiled in a slew of legal problems, the unwitting victims of real estate fraud. It was like we were on a conveyor belt of *tzaros* that was beginning to move faster and faster until we couldn't keep up with everything that was happening to us, all culminating in the accident that almost took my life.

When I told him about all the things that had befallen us, I could see how affected he was by the condition of our lives. Rav Shlomo Zalman epitomized the word *empathy*, and I could tell from the look of devastation on his face that his heart was breaking for me and that he was with me one hundred percent and would have done anything in his power to shield me from these vicissitudes of life. He was completely focused on what I was saying — his eyes on mine, not thinking about anything else — and just the fact that he was so completely empathetic made me feel a little better.

When I finished pouring out my heart, I looked him in the eye and said, "What does the Rosh Yeshivah think I should do?"

Rav Shlomo Zalman took my hand in his and began to cry.

Finally he brought the weeping under control and said, "I don't know what to tell you, but I feel so bad for you," and I watched as a fresh round of tears rolled down his face and into that soft white beard.

It was an incredible thing, but though he hadn't given me any practical advice whatsoever, I felt so much better, like he had bestowed me with the gift of a complete *nechamah*, the gift of knowing that the *gadol hador* cared about me.

And he was like that for all of *Klal Yisrael*. Simply speaking, Rav Shlomo Zalman was the *lev ha'am* — the heart of the nation. Seeing his reaction to another Yid's problems taught me how a Yid should behave and what it means to empathize with someone else's troubles.

As Rav Don Segal said about Moshe Rabbeinu, who left

Pharaoh's palace and went out to feel the suffering of his people: "Moshe Rabbeinu went out to his people and learned firsthand what a *Yiddishe krechtz* is."

Rav Shlomo Zalman knew what a *Yiddishe krechtz* is.

◆ ◆ ◆

We found out that we were expecting our first child shortly after our wedding. The ease with which the miracle of children had occurred with our first, however, didn't seem to be replicating itself. This was how it went for the next eight years. One day I decided to ask Rav Shlomo Zalman for a *berachah*. We had already been blessed with a daughter; we were also hoping to have a son who would grow up to become a *talmid chacham*.

I went to meet him at the Gra Shul in Shaarei Chesed where he davened, which was my usual method whenever I wanted to see him. I arrived ten minutes before Minchah, knowing that I'd find him sitting and saying *Tehillim* downstairs until it was time to begin davening.

In response to my request for a *berachah*, Rav Shlomo Zalman stopped what he was doing and began reciting the entire text of *Yekum Purkan,* a special *tefillah* we recite every Shabbos that focuses on having children who are *talmidei chachamim.*

I stood there completely taken aback at the *berachah* he had just given us — at its size and his choice of *tefillah*. It was a *berachah* without boundaries, a *berachah* with genuine goodness of heart. Out of all the *berachos* that I received through the course of my life, that was one of the most memorable of all.

◆ ◆ ◆

Rav Shlomo Zalman was a very serious person who at the same time knew how to put his visitors at ease with a joke and a smile. On one occasion, my wife and I went to see him regarding a certain *she'eilah*. We arrived at his home early and were the first on line. Since we had gotten there while he was still in shul, we were able to see him return, making his way down the street and up the stairs, seemingly without a care in the world. His *gabbai* helped prepare his lunch — I remember that he ate a specific kind of bread — and we were about to enter his study when an older man, a very tall and broad older man, just walked into the study before us.

We had gotten there early and had waited for Rav Shlomo Zalman in order to be the first visitors, and now, when we were finally ready to begin, in waltzes Mr. Giant without so much as a "How you doing?"

Five minutes passed. Ten minutes passed. Fifteen minutes passed. Eventually they opened the door, and the hulking man left. It turned out that this man was a fairly famous individual and had been a first-class martial arts expert in another life.

As we walked into the study, Rav Shlomo Zalman turned to us and said in tones of mock fright, "Do you know who that man is? I was so scared! I thought he was going to beat me up!"

With those few words he completely defused any frustration we felt at having had to wait, and he made us feel one hundred percent welcome. Instead of being upset, we were suddenly laughing. It was another side to Rav Shlomo Zalman.

◆ ◆ ◆

For a number of years I grappled with the *she'eilah* of whether to recite the *berachah* a person makes when passing by a place where a miracle happened to him: *she'asah li nes bamakom hazeh* — "Who did a miracle for me in this particular place." Rav Shlomo Zalman had *paskened* that I shouldn't recite the *berachah*; according to him, what I had experienced wasn't a miracle. When I had asked Rav Shlomo Zalman to describe a miracle to me if being hit by a truck wasn't one, he'd jumped out of his chair, mimicking a wild lion attacking a person. "If you were saved from a wild lion," he said. "That's when you make a *berachah*."

When he saw that I really wasn't comfortable with his *psak*, he came up with another suggestion.

"You can recite the *berachos* of *birchos hashachar* in the spot of the accident," he told me, "since they culminate in 'hagomel chasadim tovim l'amo Yisrael,' which is *bedieved* like saying the *berachah* of *hagomel*. If you want to do something, that's the best way. And if you really feel strongly about it, you can bring ten people there to hear you make the *berachah* — nothing more than that."

But there was something inside me that still wasn't satisfied. I would have liked to raise the question with him again, but he had passed away. If there had been other *poskim* with the same opinion, it would have been easier for me to accept his answer. But every other *posek* differed with his *psak* and felt that my experience on Rechov Givat Shaul fell within the category of a bona fide miracle that deserved a *berachah*.

In addition, I had invested a tremendous amount of time learning the *sugya*, and I still felt that a *berachah* was called for. Considering all this, I found myself disturbed by the question of what to do and how to handle the situation.

Should I make the berachah or not?

One night I found myself in the Sephardic *kollel* in Neve Yaakov. There was a pile of *sefarim* lying on one of the nearby tables, and suddenly I caught sight of a *sefer* written on *Orach Chaim* that I had never seen before. This was very interesting considering the fact that when I was writing *Mizmor L'Sodah*, I had checked out virtually every single *sefer* on *Orach Chaim* from the extensive library in the Hebrew University. I had done major research, studied the most obscure texts, yet here was a *sefer* I had somehow missed.

The *sefer* was called *Chesed L'Alafim* and had been written by the grandfather of the Chida. I opened the *sefer* and read the following words:

"If a person has a *safek* about what to do in a situation where he experienced a miracle, he should go with a *Shulchan Aruch* to the place where the event happened. Upon arrival at the exact spot, he should recite the halachah [with regard to making a *berachah* in such a place, which actually includes the words of the *berachah*] using Hashem's Name, as brought down in the *Shulchan Aruch*. A person is allowed to use Hashem's Name while learning, so there is no question of taking Hashem's Name in vain.

"If the person in question is obligated to make a *berachah*, he just said Hashem's Name while reading the halachah, which quotes the text of the *berachah* that he is to recite [in other words, he just recited the *berachah*]. And if he was not supposed to make the *berachah*, it is also fine, because the words the person read are considered Torah learning, when it is also permissible for him to use the Name of Hashem."

In the end, that was what I decided to do.

Since I had printed the words of the *Shulchan Aruch* in my *sefer*, I brought it with me to the place where my miracle happened and read the words directly from my *sefer*, fulfilling my halachic obligation while simultaneously remaining within the framework of Rav Shlomo Zalman's *psak*.

Later on I discovered the same *eitzah* in the *Tzitz Eliezer* and also given by Rav Moshe Sternbuch, but this was the first place where I saw it, and it gave me a clear direction and *derech*. For that I was incredibly grateful.

At some point I related the entire sequence of events to Rav Tzvi. I told him about Rav Shlomo Zalman's *psak* and how he disagreed with everyone else and how I eventually found a way around it with the *eitzah* of the *Chesed L'Alafim*.

"I don't hold of the *eitzah* of reading the *berachah* out of a *Shulchan Aruch*," Rav Tzvi said to me. "I hold that's a *berachah l'vatalah*. But I saw you lying on the street after the accident. I saw the state you were in and how your body was covered in blood. I have no doubt that if Rav Shlomo Zalman would have seen you lying in the street, he too would have agreed that it was a miracle that you survived. Everyone who saw you thought you were dead. Nobody imagined that you would survive after being hit that way."

A few years later I asked Rav Shlomo Zalman's son Rav Ezriel Auerbach what he thought about the whole *machlokes* and whether he held that I should be making a *berachah*.

"Of course you should make a *berachah* at the spot where you were hit," he replied.

His next words threw me for a loop.

"Being hit with a car like you were, is as if a lion jumped on top of you!"

Chapter Twenty-one

I considered Rav Shlomo Zalman my *rebbi muvhak*, my primary teacher in matters of halachah, and I tried to visit him often. Unfortunately, our paths crossed only near the end of his life, but I have done my best to learn everything he has written on halachah. And yet, despite the fact that we did not spend that much time together, I still consider him my primary rebbi — in his style of learning, his ability to give a *heter*, his method of *psak*, and his power of *sevara*.

I have had the good fortune to develop relationships with many great *poskim*. Rav Shlomo Zalman not only guided me in life but he also provided me with a framework through which to approach the unique world of halachah.

After I finished writing *Mizmor L'Sodah* on the halachos of giving thanks to Hashem, I was left with ten unanswered *she'eilos*. This was a major moment for me — the culmination of three years of work. Soon enough, I was sitting across from Rav Shlomo Zalman, but when I laid out the first question on my list, he said to me, "These are very difficult *she'eilos*, and I can't answer you on the spot."

I was at a loss. The entire project had been initiated only because Rav Shlomo Zalman had told me that since I'd experienced a miracle I had to change my life. When I'd asked him what to do, he'd replied that I needed to figure that out for myself. When I started writing the *sefer*, I realized that this was what Hashem wanted from me. First, to learn halachah, and second, to write *sefarim*. It was his *psak* that convinced me to write the *sefer* in the first place, and yet here he was unwilling to answer my question, certainly without learning the *sugya* first.

In all honesty, I was asking him about obscure halachos on how to act in the aftermath of a *nes* — halachos that nobody really discusses. The lack of discussion on the issue was what convinced me to write about it in the first place. Yet I still needed answers to my questions, and I had been counting on him to give them to me.

I had been turned down on question number one.

Then I did a very silly thing.

I asked him the second question on my list. This was a very silly thing because he had just told me that he was not holding in the *sugya* and didn't want to discuss questions like this without preparation, and then I went and asked him another question just like the first.

His response was immediate.

Rav Shlomo Zalman took me to task. Wow, did he take me to task! I would have never believed that Rav Shlomo Zalman, who was usually so genial, could become so serious and deliver such a *mussar shmuess*!

Twenty seconds later the *shmuess* was over, and Rav Shlomo Zalman reverted to the smiling elderly *posek* I remembered.

"Do you have any other questions that you'd like to discuss?" he asked me gently.

To my credit, I didn't run away after being told off and did raise a number of other questions that he was more than happy to discuss, but the lesson was extremely clear. Don't push people in a direction they don't want to go. If a *rav* doesn't want to discuss a certain *sugya* or *she'eilah*, respect his wishes and don't press him. With those few words, Rav Shlomo Zalman taught me not to cross the line of *derech eretz*. As unpleasant as it was to have been on the receiving end of such a *mussar shmuess*, I am incredibly grateful for having been taught such a valuable lesson.

◆ ◆ ◆

I had a *talmid* who was one of the top *bachurim* at a yeshivah in Yerushalayim. A blond-haired, blue-eyed young man, his engagement to a dark-eyed, dark-haired girl of Yemenite persuasion caused a major stir. Not only was the girl Yemenite, but she came from a very large family with numerous siblings.

"Where are you going to live after you get married?" I asked him when we met after the *vort*. (I was his *chasan* teacher.)

"In Yerushalayim," he replied. "I'm in yeshivah here."

"That's not where you are going to live."

He looked at me.

"You're going to live in Bnei Brak near your wife's family."

"No, I'm going to live in Yerushalayim."

This went on for a few minutes until I said, "Look, this is a *machlokes* between me and you. Why don't you go to Rav Shlomo Zalman, and he'll be the one to decide between me and you — and I'm telling you right now that he is going to *pasken* like I did."

He went soon after to ask Rav Shlomo Zalman. When he returned I said, "*Nu*, whom did he side with?"

"He agreed with you."

I was not at all surprised. I had known that there was no way in the world that Rav Shlomo Zalman would allow a young bride to live in a city that was relatively far from the rest of her family, who all lived in Bnei Brak. I knew that even if the *chasan* would say, "But I'm *shteiging* at my yeshivah," Rav Shlomo Zalman would reply, "You can also learn in Bnei Brak. But your wife will not be happy if she's suddenly separated from the rest of her family," and, as he told me once, "If your wife isn't happy, then you're not learning."

This was a classic Rav Shlomo Zalman response from the *gadol* who would brush off his hat before entering the house, explaining, "The *Shechinah* is in my house" — that's what happens when there's *shalom bayis* — "and I have to prepare accordingly."

To Rav Shlomo Zalman, marriage was something akin to the *Kodesh HaKodashim* of life.

◆ ◆ ◆

There's a story I like to tell because I feel it encapsulates the way a *rav* is supposed to *pasken she'eilos*.

A widow with fifteen children went to a *rav* with a chicken. The chicken was problematic according to many opinions — the Bach, the Shach, the Taz, Rav Akiva Eiger. Lots of problems for one chicken. The *rav's talmidim* who were present when the widow arrived took one look at the chicken and said to them-selves, "There's no way the Rav is going to permit her eating this chicken. That would mean disregarding too many important halachic opinions."

However, the *rav* examined the chicken and ruled that it was kosher.

The *talmidim* couldn't believe what their ears were hearing. Unable to control themselves, they burst out, "What about the Bach and the Shach and the Taz? What about Rav Akiva Eiger?!"

"The problem here," their rebbi replied, "is that you are look-ing at the chicken instead of looking at the person bringing the chicken."

A *rav* has to know the person who is asking the *she'eilah*. He has to really know that person and his situation in order to *pasken* correctly. Rav Shlomo Zalman was that kind of *rav* and that kind of *posek*.

This is why I always tell my own *talmidim*, "If you don't feel the person's pain, then you are not truly capable of *paskening* his *she'eilah*. More than that, you don't even know what the *she'eilah* is! If you don't know what he is going through, if you don't know his financial issues and challenges, then your *psak* is not a real *psak*! You can know the entire Torah backward and forward — you can have it all in your head — but you won't have *paskened* until you know the people. Really know them. It's the difference between knowing the chicken and knowing the person holding the chicken. And that difference is what separates the *talmid chacham* (who may know a lot) and the *posek*. Rav Shlomo Zalman was a *gaon* in *hilchos bein adam lachaveiro*, in interpersonal relationships.

For two years I read my son a book about Rav Shlomo Zalman as a bedtime story. But we didn't just read the stories — we learned them. Because his life was a *Shulchan Aruch* replete with the requisite *mefarshim* for learning how to do *chesed*, and as his *talmid*, I had an obligation to study his ways.

Encounters With

Rav
Ezriel Auerbach
שליט"א

Sensitivity in Halachah

When it comes to questions involving matters of honesty, Rav Ezriel is very much on the same page as his father [Rav Shlomo Zalman], which means that he feels a person has to grab onto the truth with every bit of strength he possesses.

Chapter Twenty-two

A friend of mine, who davened in Rav Rubin's shul in Har Nof where five of my friends were murdered, went to ask Rav Ezriel a *she'eilah* two months before the Har Nof massacre.

"I have a *chavrusa* every morning," he said, "and I want to know if I can skip part of *Pesukei D'Zimrah*, which will give me more time with my *chavrusa*. I'll make it up afterward, of course, but this way I'll have a better learning *seder*."

Rav Ezriel was taken aback by the question. "Skip *Pesukei D'Zimrah*? But that's such an integral part of davening!"

Based on Rav Ezriel's strong reaction to his *she'eilah*, my friend decided that he would try his best to never miss any part of *Pesukei D'Zimrah* from then on.

On the morning of the massacre, my friend woke up a few minutes late. He was about to walk into his usual minyan (he used to sit right next to Rav Mosheh Twersky), but remembered Rav Ezriel's *psak* and decided to wait for the next minyan.

And his life was saved.

My friend returned to Rav Ezriel to thank him for the *psak* that saved his life, and Rav Ezriel was filled with such *simchah* and thankfulness that another Yid's life had been saved through him.

Later on someone showed my friend a *psak* written by Rav Shlomo Zalman in his *sefer Halichos Shlomo* in which he writes that if a person has a minyan in which he always davens and he sees that he will be a little late, he can daven there anyway. Here we had a seeming difference of opinion between Rav Shlomo Zalman, who said a person could go into the minyan even if he will miss the beginning of *Pesukei D'Zimrah*, and Rav Ezriel, who had insisted that he not miss any part of *Pesukei D'Zimrah* at all!

I presented the whole sequence before Rav Ezriel and asked him what my friend should do and whether he could rely on Rav Shlomo Zalman if he ever saw that he was running late.

"He shouldn't ever miss even a small part of *Pesukei D'Zimrah*," Rav Ezriel said emphatically. "For him, saying *Pesukei D'Zimrah* is like offering a *korban todah!*"

One of the fundamental concepts of halachah is that of *machlokes*, or disagreement between *poskim*. There is even *machlokes* between fathers and sons; the Rosh and his son the Tur are an example, and there are grandsons disputing their grand-fathers, like Rashi and Rabbeinu Tam. Here, too, my interactions with Rav Ezriel introduced me to the concept of *machlokes* in halachah and how right this was.

In the wake of this discussion, someone sent me a letter point-ing out that it didn't seem that the *Mishnah Berurah* viewed that section of davening with the same level of severity as Rav Ezriel did.

Rav Ezriel responded forcefully. "*Pesukei D'Zimrah* is part of *tefil-lah*, and whoever doesn't say the entire thing is not treating the davening that Chazal set up for us with respect."

There was no question where Rav Ezriel stood on the question of *Pesukei D'Zimrah*.

Even though this meant that he and his father held different positions on the subject.

◆　◆　◆

The fact that I even met Rav Ezriel Auerbach in the first place happened by accident. There is a *beis din* located on Tzefania Street, and I'd sometimes go there to confer with some of the *dayanim*, who had been *paskening* complex *she'eilos* for years and were regarded as tops in their field. The room where the *beis din* met was spare and austere furniture-wise, with only a few wooden tables and benches. It was the kind of place I would have described if I were trying to picture a typical shtetl *shtiebel*, down to the piles of discarded pamphlets lying on the table.

I hadn't known that Rav Ezriel served as a *dayan* there as well. When I encountered him at the *beis din* one day and the two of us began to converse, I felt as if I were talking to his father, Rav Shlomo Zalman. I met him at least ten years after his father passed away, and despite the fact that so many years had passed since Rav Shlomo Zalman had been taken to the *Olam HaEmes,* I still missed him very much. Talking to his son was, for me, a *nechamah*, a consolation.

While I sat there talking with Rav Ezriel, I almost pinched myself, trying to figure out if I were dreaming. *He looks like Rav Shlomo Zalman, he acts like him, he speaks like him...*

The fact that I was speaking to someone who seemed to be a copy of Rav Shlomo Zalman excited me to no end, and I found myself discussing an interesting *she'eilah* with him regarding whether it was permitted to lock the door of an apartment building on Shabbos if a cat was in the building. This actually happened in a building near where I lived, and the person involved hadn't taken the time to shoo out the cat and wanted to know if by locking the door he'd transgressed the prohibition of *tze'diah*, trapping, and did he have to worry about making sure all cats were out of the building before locking the door on Shabbos in the future.

The Rema rules that cats are a species that a person would consider trapping *mid'Oraisa*: cats are part of the lion family, which a hunter might trap for its mane. After examining the question, I had reached the conclusion that locking a cat into a building on Shabbos falls under the category of trapping and is prohibited.

Though I normally try my best to *pasken l'kula*, I didn't see any way of being *meikel* in this particular scenario. Though closing the door wasn't exactly trapping the cat since it could still run away and evade any would-be trappers, which meant it might not be forbidden from the Torah, it was still rabbinically prohibited.

I had discussed the question with a number of *talmidei chachamim*, who laughed and told me I was making a big deal out of nothing, since who in their right mind would want to trap a cat in the first place? I replied that they were disregarding the fact that in countries like China cats are considered fit for consumption and would be trapped by the populace. Since the Chayei Adam writes that if an animal would be trapped anywhere in the world, it's enough to place it within the category of *tze'diah*, I refused to back down from what I felt was the correct halachah in this case.

Now, having run into Rav Ezriel, I decided that he would be the perfect person to consult with regarding this *she'eilah*, and so I asked whether I could raise a question in *hilchos Shabbos*.

He responded by saying in modest tones, "*Hilchos Shabbos* is very complex," but he allowed me to ask.

Rav Ezriel treated the question with extreme seriousness.

"I hear everything you're saying," he said at last, "but I think that today times have changed and people don't really trap cats anymore."

I responded by telling him how I'd read that many toys are actually made from cat fur and that there is a big demand for cats, which means they are trapped on a regular basis.

"Even so," he replied, unfazed, "I still feel that trapping cats doesn't enter into the category of *tze'diah* because it is so rare to find anyone interested in trapping a cat."

Later I would go on to write a *sefer* on *hilchos Shabbos* where I included this *she'eilah* along with a picture of a cat lurking in a building; although I still felt there was place to be *machmir*, after my conversation with Rav Ezriel, I was able to appreciate the opinions who *paskened l'kula* a whole lot more.

Bottom line: A *rav* could decide either way in this case. For me, the main point was how incredibly sensitive Rav Ezriel was in the way he replied to me. He was so humble, so unassuming, so easy to reach. He was a man who radiated light and *simchah*, dignity and thoughtfulness, and I knew that I would return to talk to this lofty *posek* in the future.

◆ ◆ ◆

Rav Ezriel married the daughter of Rav Elyashiv (when he married, Rav Shlomo Zalman told his son that from then on Rav Elyashiv would be his *rav*), and Rav Elyashiv commented that Rav Ezriel was the person closest to his approach in halachic rulings.

I have always felt that Rav Ezriel was an expert at synthesizing his father's approach to *psak* with his father-in-law's way of *paskening*, combining both into a completely unique way of looking at a *she'eilah* — one that I connected with on a very deep level. Interestingly enough, both Rav Shlomo Zalman and Rav Elyashiv felt that Rav Ezriel was the continuation of their *derech* of *psak halachah*.

One time I went to Rav Ezriel with a kitchen utensil called a salad spinner. Using this utensil to remove water from wet vegetables is a *she'eilah* of *borer*. A renowned *posek* in America told me that using such a device is unquestionably *borer*, and forbidden, but I disagreed and told Rav Ezriel my reasoning. He agreed with me and gave me another reason it should be permitted. (Rav Shlomo Zalman held this is considered *borer*.)

"However," he went on, "I still don't feel you should use such a utensil since this is a clear case of *uvda d'chol*, weekly work."

Leaving it at that, we parted ways, but I returned a while later, salad spinner in hand, pointing out that the *Rishonim* rule leniently in matters of *uvda d'chol*...

Rav Ezriel let me know in no uncertain terms that I was wrong.

"You don't understand," he said. "Such a device is not for Shabbos! Take this, put it in the closet, and do not use it on Shabbos!"

I understood that I had overstepped the line on that one. In all the time that I have known Rav Ezriel Auerbach, I have never seen him get upset, and true to his nature, Rav Ezriel had not gotten upset with me for pushing the issue, but he wouldn't let me go until there was no question at all where he stood on the matter and why.

He is a *posek* who has discussed certain interesting *kulos* in *hilchos Shabbos* with me, but his sensitivity for the *kedushah* of Shabbos is peerless. When it comes to a person's understanding of what Shabbos is really about, Rav Ezriel will not bend or give in. If something is "not for Shabbos," then it's *not* for Shabbos, and Rav Ezriel expected me to grasp that the question had ceased being one of halachah and moved over into another realm altogether — one no less important than the other.

◆ ◆ ◆

Rav Ezriel is a sensitive person. It's a beautiful thing to meet a person like that. In certain Jerusalem neighborhoods, when people want to criticize another person or call attention to things he has done that they feel are wrong, they will put up signs on the building walls for passersby to read. Many times those signs are pasted on the billboards and walls immediately before Shabbos because then they cannot be taken down right away. Rav Ezriel asked his father if he could remove such signs from the walls during *bein hashemashos* or did he have to leave them up? The Chazon Ish is *machmir*, but there were definitely arguments for leniency, so what to do?

Rav Shlomo Zalman replied that according to the halachah it's permissible, but we don't remove posters from buildings when Shabbos has begun, even if it has only begun technically.

This *she'eilah* reminded me of another fascinating question that arose when a swastika was painted on the *mikveh* in a Yerushalayim neighborhood one Shabbos. The question was whether there was any way to allow it to be erased on Shabbos. It wasn't applicable for that Shabbos since Shabbos was almost over by that point, but what to do if this ever occurred again in the future?

Some *rabbanim* with whom I discussed the question made light of it, but since there were Holocaust survivors living in the neighborhood who used the *mikveh*, and since seeing such a sight would cause them tremendous pain and might even possibly lead to *pikuach nefesh* (they were elderly and who knew what might happen?), I felt there was clearly a good reason to erase the swastika, even on Shabbos.

Rav Ezriel was not among the scoffers and agreed with me that it was a serious question that needed a serious answer. He immediately began discussing how a Holocaust survivor would feel upon seeing such a thing and how terrible that would be. In the end, he told me that a non-Jew should be asked to remove it, but that it shouldn't be done openly — either at night or when passersby weren't around — for the same reason as before: *kedushas Shabbos*.

These types of questions all fell into Rav Shlomo Zalman's fifth section of *Shulchan Aruch*, where halachah and "getting" the person asking the question all come together. *Kedushas Shabbos* unquestionably falls within that fifth section.

◆ ◆ ◆

Recently I brought Rav Ezriel a copy of a newly published *sefer* of mine for which he had given me a *haskamah*. He held the *sefer* lovingly in his hands and commented on how beautiful it was.

"I need a bag to carry it home," he said.

Rav Brevda, too, had made it very clear to me that a person should never walk through the streets with his personal items on public display. "Keep your belongings in a bag," he had told me.

As an aside, this way of looking at the world is the antithesis of social media, where people feel the need to post every single detail of their lives for friends and so-called friends to see. There is nothing healthy about turning our lives inside out for every person we know and don't know to comment on.

Anyway, I went to get Rav Ezriel a bag, and one of the secretaries in the Ahavas Shalom office gave me one with the words "*Aliba D'Hilchesa*" printed on it (a halachic term that means "according to halachah," which was also the name of their *kollel*). I knew Rav Ezriel would enjoy that — a bag about halachah for a *sefer* of halachah...

When I handed him the bag, his face lit up with a radiant smile, and his enjoyment was obvious, which made my day, which he no doubt was trying to do.

Bidding him farewell, I turned and left, satisfied that I had been able to predict his reaction at seeing the message on that particular bag. It meant that I had come to know his thought processes, and for me that was very important.

I had been able to think like a *posek* and predict the way a *posek* would react — and I considered that a success.

Chapter Twenty-three

I once asked Rav Ezriel the frequently-asked *she'eilah* regarding davening with a minyan on a plane. Rav Shlomo Zalman ruled that a person should daven in his seat since the arrangements required to make a minyan cause disturbances for the flight crew, but Rav Ezriel told me that he felt I should daven with a minyan.

"You should definitely try to arrange it with the crew first, asking them for a particular time that would be most convenient for them. Usually they'll be happy to comply."

"What if they aren't willing to comply?"

"Tell them that it's good for the plane," he replied with enthusiasm. "Tell them that the plane will fly much better this way!"

Admittedly this isn't the kind of answer that would get the cabin crew to change their minds for you or me, but I am fairly sure that it would work for Rav Ezriel, whose sincerity and natural charisma could melt a frozen heart. Of course, if by davening with a minyan you will cause disruption and hardship to your fellow passengers, Rav Ezriel ruled that you should remain in your seat. However, that is only in a case where your minyan gets in the way. In all other cases, the right thing to do is to get up and make a minyan.

◆ ◆ ◆

Rav Ezriel's first wife passed away at a fairly young age, after which he married his widowed niece. During his first marriage Rav Ezriel and his wife were not blessed with children. His second wife, however, had a whole bunch of children from her first marriage, and now he has become the father of a large family.

When I went to be *menachem avel* after his first wife passed away, the house was filled with people, and I could tell that even though he was the one sitting *shivah*, he was going out of his way to make everyone feel good in his trademark masterful manner.

◆ ◆ ◆

These days Rav Ezriel hears *she'eilos* at Ahavas Shalom, Rav Yaakov Hillel's yeshivah, along with many other *chashuve rabbanim* and *poskim*, as well as in a few other places.

During one visit I stood just outside the door of the room in which he was sitting, and I thought that he'd seen me. Half an hour passed, and Rav Ezriel was still busy with the one *talmid* sitting with him getting *shimush* while I waited outside. An hour passed, and still he had given me no indication that he wanted me to enter the inner room. I couldn't understand why he was ignoring me like this, especially since he had never acted this way before and the two of us had such a close relationship.

When he eventually realized I was there (it turned out that he had not seen me, after all), he became very upset and did his best to make it up to me, remaining in the *beis midrash* to answer all my questions, despite the fact that he would usually have left at that time.

In truth, he had done nothing wrong; he hadn't seen me and he had nothing to apologize for. But that didn't matter to him. The second he saw me there he grasped that I had been waiting for a long time, and he understood how I felt — and he immediately made it up to me.

◆ ◆ ◆

I've been writing a halachah column for the *Yated Ne'eman* for some time now, and I usually confer with Rav Ezriel at least once a week (almost always on Tuesdays), because the column contains his *piskei halachah* along with those of Rav Zalman Nechemia Goldberg and Rav Yaakov Hillel. People send in *she'eilos*. I study the *sugya*s and, after coming to my own conclusions, go and discuss the *she'eilos* with some or all of them. At times I will discuss the same *she'eilah* two or even three times to make sure that I have conveyed it accurately and that we are all on the same page. It's a fascinating process, one that I enjoy immensely, and that inevitably means that we all share a special relationship based on the exploration of halachah.

When I first began writing my halachah column in the *Yated*, Rav Ezriel was the sole *posek* with whom I conferred. One time I had a question that was slightly kabbalistic in nature, dealing with a stamp that had the Name of Hashem written on it, and since Rav Yaakov Hillel was passing by at the time I asked him for his *psak*, which led to his participating in the column alongside Rav Ezriel. Of course, from time to time people sent in *Choshen Mishpat she'eilos* as well, which is when I asked Rav Zalman Nechemia Goldberg to become the third member of the halachic triumvirate.

Thus our panel was created. Rav Ezriel handles *Orach Chaim* and *Yoreh De'ah*, Rav Zalman Nechemia handles *Choshen Mishpat* and *Even HaEzer*, and Rav Yaakov Hillel takes questions that veer toward the area of Kabbalah.

Originally when I asked Rav Ezriel to join me in the newspaper, he was skeptical. "You want me to be a *posek* for the American community?!"

Whereas many people wouldn't have thought twice about doing a halachic column in the paper, Rav Ezriel foresaw how seriously people would take it, with an incredible amount of feedback coming our way from our readers. But the main reason he agreed to be a part of the panel was because, as he told me, "You'll get benefit from this, right?" and since I do get paid for moderating the *poskim* roundtable, Rav Ezriel was able to justify his role as an "American *posek*," and bring benefit to the thousands of people who avidly read the column every week.

On another occasion I asked him to serve as the *nasi* of the *kollel*. His response was staggering.

"Me? A *nasi*?" he asked me, as if he just could not wrap his mind around the idea of his name being on the *kollel's* letterhead. He thought about my request for a few seconds, then asked me, "Will this help the *kollel* financially?"

"Probably it will."

"Then I'll do it."

For personal *kavod* — no way. But if it's good for someone else, no problem.

◆ ◆ ◆

When it comes to questions involving matters of honesty, Rav Ezriel is very much on the same page as his father, which means that he feels a person has to grab onto the truth with every bit of strength he possesses. This approach can challenge a person when, for example, he is in the airport and, having agreed to bring a package for a friend back home, is asked by security if all the bags are his.

"You must tell them the truth," Rav Ezriel says.

"But then they'll open up your suitcases and go through all your belongings!"

"Doesn't matter. You cannot tell a lie. Bring a *sefer* and learn while they check the bags."

◆ ◆ ◆

Rav Ezriel seldom leaves Eretz Yisrael, but a number of years ago a certain *kiruv* organization flew him into the States, where he spoke to record crowds in many locations. When he returned and we met, I found him to be incredibly positive about *bnei Torah* in America.

"Seeing sincere American *bnei Torah* gave me such *chizuk*," he said. "Lakewood is like Yerushalayim!"

"What impressed you most?"

"The *baalebatim*," he replied. "They get up at four or five in the morning to learn! They learn for three hours, go to *shiurim*! It's simply unbelievable! That's the way a Yid is supposed to be! Many people have to work, and not everyone can spend his entire life in yeshivah, but this is the way a working man is supposed to live."

I once asked him whether a Jew living in Lakewood should light his menorah outside the house the same way a Jew does if he lives in Yerushalayim.

"Lakewood is like Yerushalayim," he stated emphatically. "They should light outside."

This statement, which I made famous, caused a tumult — but was overruled in the end by a number of American *poskim*, who felt that lighting menorahs outside in the street would cause a rise in anti-Semitism.

◆ ◆ ◆

Rav Elyashiv held that going to the seashore during *bein haze-manim* is important.

"When my father-in-law went to the ocean," Rav Ezriel told me, "he'd take along *sefer Mishlei* with *Peirush HaGra*. That was his *sefer* of choice."

When asked why he felt it was so important to go to the seashore, Rav Elyashiv is said to have replied, "If I didn't go, I wouldn't be able to be Rav Elyashiv the rest of the year."

"My *shver* made an *avodah* out of going," testified Rav Ezriel, who was Rav Elyashiv's partner in this holy endeavor.

◆ ◆ ◆

I once asked Rav Ezriel whether it is permissible to chew gum on Shabbos.

"Why wouldn't it be?"

"Flattening out the gum is very similar to *memacheik*, erasing, which is an *issur d'Oraisa*."

In retrospect, chewing gum is not that similar to *memacheik* because the gum is not meant to remain flattened, but Rav Ezriel did accept the *she'eilah*, eventually *paskening* that for children it certainly would be allowed, since it soothes them.

"Gum, toys, and candy are all very important for children," he said to me. The fact that a *rav* would speak that way was not surprising in and of itself. But Rav Ezriel himself was never blessed with children and yet is extremely sensitive to the needs of children.

"What about adults? Can they chew gum on Shabbos?"

He looked at me as if he couldn't understand what I was talking about.

"Adults chewing gum?" he asked me incredulously. He couldn't seem to comprehend the idea.

To sum up, children are allowed to chew gum as it soothes them. As for adults, it was clear that Rav Ezriel didn't think it was proper for them to chew gum at all, even during the week and certainly not on Shabbos.

◆ ◆ ◆

A woman once wrote me about her child, who was not religious and dating a non-Jew. I answered all her questions to the best of my abilities. When she visited Eretz Yisrael, she told me that she wanted to meet with Rav Ezriel.

Rav Ezriel treated her with incredible sensitivity. When she asked him how she should handle her situation, he replied that the only thing to do was to show that child a world of love.

"Show him love," he said. "Show him that you care about him. And you should take a *kabbalah* on yourself."

"What type of *kabbalah* should I take on myself?"

This was a good question. Rav Ezriel suggested, "Why don't you sponsor an Arachim Shabbaton?"

She liked the idea and agreed. It was a beautiful solution all around. But what I remember most from that visit is how caring he was and how much he wanted to help her and how he really, really felt for her and the challenges she was experiencing.

In another letter, the writer, a single girl, asked if Rav Ezriel could give her a *berachah* for a *shidduch*.

This was consistent with what I always told him — how people in America felt that he was an *adam gadol* and that he had a lot of chassidim in the States.

"Chassidim in America," he'd reply with good humor. "Does that mean I should put on a *shtreimel?*"

In response to the girl's letter, Rav Ezriel gave a *berachah* brimming with sincerity and heart. If I hadn't known better, I would have thought he was giving a *berachah* to the daughter of his best friend!

◆ ◆ ◆

Another day, another email.

Rav Ezriel is of the opinion that Ashkenazic women should wear *sheitlach*. For Sephardic women he *paskens* differently, based on what is accepted by the Sephardic *poskim*. (Obviously we are talking about modest *sheitlach* and not those that are overly long or flamboyant. You know what I'm talking about.)

One day someone emailed me from the States, explaining that if women would stop wearing *sheitlach*, this would help bring Mashiach — and would Rav Ezriel give them a *psak* to that effect?

I relayed the question to him. He heard me out and said, "How can I give such a *psak*? I hold that women should wear *sheitels*. There's an advantage to wearing a *sheitel* because the *tichelach* and snoods often slide back and can lead to their hair showing. Besides," he went on, "many kerchiefs and snoods come in loud colors and aren't *tzniusdik*."

I sat there just listening, fascinated by his breakdown of the question.

"If all that is not enough," he concluded, "the Chazon Ish was in favor of *sheitels*, and so am I if they are short and modest and don't draw attention to the wearer!"

He then finished with the following line.

"Tell the lady who wrote you the email that if she wants to bring the *geulah*, she should cut out all *lashon hara* and controversy from her life, and that will help more than anything else. That's what's holding up the *geulah*, not *sheitels*!"

On the other hand, Rav Ezriel did feel that if a woman really wants to just wear a simple snood and feels that for her wearing a *sheitel* would be a lack of *tznius*, there's no question that this is praiseworthy, special, and worthy of emulation.

◆ ◆ ◆

One year, just before Pesach, I had hurt my leg and found it difficult to get around. I decided to visit the famous hot springs of Teveria, which are even mentioned in the Gemara (the *Tannaim* used to go), hoping this would bring me some relief from the pain in my leg.

We arrived at the hot springs at around twelve o'clock in the evening and had the place all to ourselves. After immersing myself in the iconic springs for a while, I pictured myself getting up the next morning with a spring in my step and fully cured. To my great surprise, however, upon rising the next morning I felt ten times worse than I'd felt the night before, to the point that I had a difficult time just getting out of bed.

Luckily this occurred before the last day of Pesach and not at the beginning, but my joy in the Yom Tov was pretty much destroyed over the next twenty-four hours, especially since I had been hoping for a reprieve and felt so much worse.

When Yom Tov was over and we were finally back in Yerushalayim, I went to see Rav Ezriel. Right away, after a handshake, he said to me, "Reb Daniel Yaakov, I haven't seen you for such a long time!" The fact that he had commented on my absence made me feel very good, and I shared with him what had happened at the hot springs and how my body had reacted exactly the opposite of the way I had imagined it would, especially considering the fact that the great *Tannaim* of the past testified that immersion in Teveria's hot springs was a miracle cure.

"Of course that's what happened," he responded. "Haven't you ever taken medicine before? Your body always feels worse before it feels better!"

I had walked into the room feeling terrible, yet by the time I left his presence I was feeling much, much better. With his heartfelt words, empathy, and cheerful disposition, Rav Ezriel had lifted me up in a few short minutes. Within a few days I began feeling better physically as well, and I couldn't help but remember his emphatic words: "Haven't you ever taken medicine before? Your body always feels worse before it feels better!"

At the end of the day, true empathy is the best medicine of all.

Chapter Twenty-four

On Rosh Chodesh Cheshvan 5776 (2015), I was on an Egged bus that was driving through the center of religious Jerusalem when I found myself in the middle of a terrorist attack, as an Arab murderer went on a rampage on Malchei Yisrael Street.

I had been on my way to a *levayah* and could have easily taken a bus straight up Bar Ilan Street, but decided at the last second to take another bus through Geulah, wanting to purchase something or other. Which meant that I was standing on the bus when a car purposely drove into a bus stop, hitting pedestrians with intent to kill.

There was the sound of shattering glass and people screaming. Then the shooting began.

It felt like a war zone. The next few minutes were very intense, especially since it took us time to figure out whether they were shooting at us or somewhere else.

Everyone was looking out the windows of the bus with morbid fascination — you don't want to look but you can't look away — the terrible scene of the carnage engraving itself on their brains for all eternity. I banged on the bus window with all my strength and yelled out, "Now is not the time to look out the window! Now is the time to daven!!!"

Seconds later, the entire bus was reciting *Tehillim* together.

Eventually the driver opened the doors, and everyone ran off the bus. I returned to the *kollel* shaky from witnessing the brutal murder of my fellow Jews.

Since it was a Tuesday, I visited Rav Ezriel soon after. He listened to everything that had occurred and uttered one word: *tze'akah*. Screaming.

"Both the Rambam and Ramban write," he went on, "that when a person experiences a *tzarah*, the proper response is *tze'akah* — that you have to scream in your *tefillos*. After a day like today, a person's *tefillos* cannot be the way they were before. When you walk into a shul, it should be a different experience now."

He wasn't referring only to my personal davening. He meant that since this had been a terrorist attack aimed at the wider *frum* community, it was incumbent on all of us to change the way we daven.

"*Tze'akah* doesn't have to be a scream that everyone hears," he explained. "It can also be inside you, in your heart."

◆ ◆ ◆

As the situation across the country intensified, with every day seeming to bring another terrorist attack, someone asked me if it was now incumbent on every person to do his *hishtadlus* and carry a gun. I asked Rav Ezriel the question.

"A person should carry three guns," he replied without skipping a beat. "*Tehillim kuf chaf alef, kuf lamed*, and *kuf mem beis*!" Psalms 121, 130, and 142.

When things grew even worse, Rav Ezriel *paskened* that carrying a gun had become *the proper thing to do*. Rav Zalman Nechemia Goldberg told me the same thing, taking it a step further when he commented, "What's the difference between carrying a gun and locking your door at night — both are considered *hishtadlus* for a person to be safe!"

◆ ◆ ◆

The concept of *tze'akah* reminds me of another incident involving Rav Nachman Bulman. It happened on Yom Kippur at the end of his life, when he was already very sick and not allowed to fast. When it was time for *Ne'ilah*, I watched as Rav Bulman pulled together every last vestige of his strength and got up to daven with the rest of the *kehillah*. I watched him rise and scream the words of davening from the depths of his heart.

Here was another version of *tze'akah* — this one not contained within, but very much on the outside where it flew around the shul and smashed into everyone standing there, entering their hearts and penetrating their souls.

I was so inspired at seeing how, although he had no *kochos*, he somehow managed to rally his strength (whatever was left) and influence other people, even when the tank was virtually empty!

Everyone in the room was crying as they watched him, it was so profoundly moving. The words *"Al tashlicheinu l'eis ziknah —* Do not cast us aside at a time of old age" had come alive before our eyes in the most authentic and incredible way, and we were smart enough to comprehend it.

Rabbi Simcha Groffman was there when this story happened. The author of "Kinder Torah," a weekly *parashah*-based Torah sheet that was distributed every Shabbos to numerous shuls around the globe, Reb Simcha recorded the story, which was read by thousands throughout the world. I myself read the story in his *parashah* sheet and kept it. I still review it every Yom Kippur before *Ne'ilah* (I keep it tucked inside my Yom Kippur *machzor*), remembering the story of what happened on that final Yom Kippur of Rav Bulman's life. Reading about the incident never fails to bring me to tears and motivate me to rise up at the end of the day and daven the way I should.

Even now, after so many years.

That was an example of a real *tze'akah*. Not the same as the *tze'akah* that Rav Ezriel is talking about, but still, so authentic and intense.

Rav Bulman possessed a true heart. As did Rav Brevda. As does Rav Ezriel and Rav Zalman Nechemia Goldberg. But it's rare to find people like this— people who really care.

Rav Brevda attributed the general apathy of our times to the tremendous degree of exposure we have to the outside world. We don't have to say hello anymore. We don't even have to talk to one another. WhatsApp and texting have replaced the old-fashioned methods of communication. We have reached the point where your doctor will say, "Just text me the information."

The human emotion has been replaced. Is it any wonder that our *lev* factor has disappeared? I feel very privileged to have been blessed with a connection to *gedolim* who really had a *Yiddishe* heart. *Chas v'shalom* that we should lose our collective "*hartz*"!

Just recently I was working on a *shiur* when a person called me from America with a *she'eilah* in *pikuach nefesh*. Before I realized, I had been on the phone with him for quite a while, trying to get a handle on the illness he was describing, after which I went to confer with Rav Sternbuch and hear his *psak*. By the time I was finished with the whole thing, it was already past two in the morning and I still hadn't finished preparing my *shiur*.

I sat down at my desk intent on trying to find an answer to the questions I had been working on before the phone rang a few hours earlier, and suddenly an idea flew into my mind that answered all my questions and I had *pshat* — just like that! I felt as if Hashem were telling me, "If you take care of My children, I will make sure to take care of you!"

◆ ◆ ◆

Being a *posek* means that you hear the most interesting *she'eilos*.

Once, a chaplain in a hospital (who was also a *rosh yeshivah*) got in touch with me. It seemed that one of the patients he was working with owned an ancient statue of Buddha worth a few million dollars. The two of them had come to develop a close relationship, and the patient decided that he wanted to donate his precious statue to the chaplain's yeshivah. The question was whether he was allowed to accept such a gift, which was literally *avodah zarah*.

I took the *rosh yeshivah* to Rav Ezriel, and he asked his question. Rav Ezriel was very taken aback.

"You want to accept an idol as a gift to a yeshivah?" Rav Ezriel asked him like he couldn't even believe the words coming out of the man's mouth, or that he had even entertained such a thought for even a second.

"Even if it's permissible according to the halachah (there is a way to render *avodah zarah* into a mundane item), you shouldn't consider receiving benefit for a yeshivah from such a direction."

"So the Rav is saying that I shouldn't even accept it in the first place?"

"Only if you are prepared to make a ceremony where you smash it on a rock into tiny pieces!"

◆　◆　◆

When there was a mass gathering of upward of 600,000 Yidden for a peaceful protest against drafting all yeshivah *bachurim* into the Israeli army, someone asked Rav Ezriel whether it was permitted to recite the special *berachah* that is recited upon seeing such a large group of people.

"I cannot give an answer," he replied.

"Why not?"

"Because I never had *shimush* on this question."

From his refusal to answer that question, I understood that Rav Ezriel *did* have *shimush* for every other question he was asked, and answered; either with his father, Rav Shlomo Zalman, or his father-in-law, Rav Elyashiv.

That's a *posek*!

Encounters With

Rav Zalman
Nechemia Goldberg
שליט"א

The Humble Authority

He is beloved by everyone, from the most chareidi of Jews living in the heart of Meah Shearim to the hesder yeshivah bachur learning in the far reaches of Eretz Yisrael. He himself is Chabad, which brings yet another color to his outlook. He doesn't look down on anyone because of hashkafah or politics; in fact, he doesn't get involved in any of that and he simply doesn't care to.

Chapter Twenty-five

As I wrote earlier, I met Rav Zalman Nechemia through the halachah column that I write for the *Yated*. People were sending in questions regarding *Choshen Mishpat* issues, Rav Ezriel recommended that I ask his brother-in-law Rav Zalman Nechemia Goldberg to respond, and the rest is history.

Rav Ezriel told me how someone once asked him a *Choshen Mishpat she'eilah*, and Rav Ezriel suggested that they confer with his brother-in-law Rav Zalman Nechemia instead.

"Can we rely on him?" the person had the temerity to ask.

"My father, Rav Shlomo Zalman, said that he's the biggest authority in the world on both *Choshen Mishpat* and *Even HaEzer*," came the response.

That was thirty years ago.

One of the character traits that jumped out at me immediately was his humility. Here was a man about whom Rav Shlomo Zalman, the *posek hador*, personally testified that he was the biggest authority in the world, yet not only would you never know it from speaking with him, it seems as if he himself doesn't know it! He acts in a completely unassuming fashion, as if he is a regular person from Yerushalayim, no airs at all. Meeting such a person is a beautiful thing, especially since it is so rare.

One time we happened to meet, and he turned to me and said, "You know, there's a *she'eilah* that I wanted to ask you," as if we were equals and he was seeking my advice like I sought his.

I used to take the bus a lot, often running into him traveling from here to there like anybody else, no driver or special treatment of any kind. In fact, such an idea would be completely foreign to him.

When my son was born, we named him Yitzchok after my father-in-law. Once we were naming him Yitzchok, I wanted to add the name Elchonon after Rav Yitzchak Elchanan Spector, the Kovno Rav. My wife was not particularly enamored with the name Elchonon, and in the end we called our son Chaim Yitzchok. When I shared all this with Rav Zalman Nechemia, he commented, "The most important thing is that your wife should be happy with the name of her son, and Rav Yitzchak Elchanan would have told you the same thing."

I agreed with him, having come to know something about Rav Yitzchak Elchanan Spector. The thing that impressed me most about the famous Kovno Rav was that every single hashkafic camp saw him as one of theirs; each group held him in esteem and related to him. Even the *maskilim* felt that the Kovno Rav wasn't completely opposed to their *derech*. Of course, this wasn't true, but just the fact that he was such a master of diplomacy and interpersonal relationships made me look at him as the true definition of a *gadol*. And his connection to all the camps meant that his influence was enormous, allowing him to set guidelines for European Jewry at a time when true leadership was critically needed.

The way I see it, Rav Zalman Nechemia fills the same role today.

He is beloved by everyone, from the most *chareidi* of Jews living in the heart of Meah Shearim to the *hesder yeshivah bachur* learning in the far reaches of Eretz Yisrael. He himself is Chabad, which brings yet another color to his outlook. He doesn't look down on anyone because of *hashkafah* or politics; in fact, he doesn't get involved in any of that and he simply doesn't care to.

The way I see it, Rav Zalman Nechemia's approach is really a continuation of that of his father-in-law, Rav Shlomo Zalman. Anyone who attended Rav Shlomo Zalman's *levayah* could attest to the wide range of Jews who were present (more than half a million people came to Yerushalayim to pay their final respects); every type of Jew was represented. It was the same thing at the *levayah* of Rav Ovadia Yosef. Both of these *gedolim* remained a person whom every kind of Jew, no matter his level of observance or political affiliation, was able to feel connected with. It's no wonder that so many people felt the need to say farewell when these *gedolim* were summoned back to the Ribbono shel Olam.

Back to Rav Zalman Nechemia's approach. When I questioned him about the proper way to learn halachah, he said something that I found very interesting.

"There's a short way to learn halachah and a long way to learn halachah. In the short way, students study key information that they need so that they can be tested. Personally I feel that a person who wants to study halachah should take the long route, because that will save him a lot more time."

When I asked him what he meant, he replied, "Look, if you put in the time you really need from the beginning, you'll have a much deeper understanding of halachah, which will save you a lot of time in the long run, when you eventually need to actually *pasken* and want to get it right."

◆ ◆ ◆

There was a woman in the process of getting divorced who used to call me with a lot of *she'eilos*. When she celebrated the bar mitzvah of her son, I attended the *simchah*, which was held at the Beis Yisrael hall, five minutes from Rav Zalman Nechemia's house. It was a small bar mitzvah, with what felt like five people on the men's side and another five on the ladies'. Looking around me, I felt incredibly saddened by the whole picture. Here she'd just gone through a terrible divorce, and instead of being able to immerse herself in a major *simchah*, we were basically sitting in an empty hall! I felt like I had to do something to turn the whole bar mitzvah around.

I left the hall and made my way to Rav Zalman Nechemia's house, where I found him home and available. After explaining the situation to him, I asked him if he would be able to come back with me to the hall, since I felt that his presence would turn a "not very successful" party into a bar mitzvah celebration that would be remembered for life.

He rose, donned his hat and jacket, and prepared to leave.

"Where are you going?" his wife asked him, seeing her husband about to leave for places unknown.

"We're going to do a mitzvah," he replied.

He had been asked to do something for someone else, and he didn't hesitate — very much an outcome of his *middah* of humility. You asked me to do a mitzvah? If I can make it work, of course I will do it.

We returned to the hall together. The moment Rav Zalman Nechemia entered that hall everything changed. You cannot imagine the happiness on the faces of the *ba'alei simchah* when they saw who had come to join them. He joined the family at the head table, stayed for about fifteen minutes talking to the bar mitzvah boy, and left a room one hundred percent different from the way it had been before he showed up.

In retrospect, I was most impressed by the fact that he didn't hesitate for even a second before agreeing to come. There were no excuses — "I'm too busy… I have to do this or that…" I asked, it was a mitzvah, and he came.

◆ ◆ ◆

I wrote a halachic responsum about how and when to give *mussar* to *ba'alei teshuvah*. When I showed it to Rav Zalman Nechemia, he said to me, "I want to tell you something about giving *mussar*."

He went on to relate how the Chafetz Chaim was once speaking to a soldier who wasn't doing well spiritually. The Chafetz Chaim needed to give the man *tochachah*.

This is how it went.

"My dear son, you're in the army surrounded by a thousand temptations, yet you haven't ceased keeping the Torah…"

He praised him and praised him and praised him — and then the Chafetz Chaim said what he had to say.

"That," concluded Rav Zalman Nechemia, "is the way to give *tochachah*. Not by putting people down but by building them up. This is especially true for *ba'alei teshuvah*, who are changing their entire lives around and need to be treated with real sincerity and appreciation for their *mesirus nefesh*."

It was clear to me that Rav Zalman Nechemia felt that the only way to give *tochachah* was with a positive attitude and tone.

"You don't scream when you're doing the mitzvah of buying an *esrog*," he pointed out. "So why do you have to scream when you're doing the mitzvah of giving someone *mussar*?!"

◆ ◆ ◆

A *ba'al teshuvah* came to me with the following *she'eilah*.

"My parents want us to come to them for Shabbos," he said. "They are not religious, but they still want a warm and close connection with their children and grandchildren. What should I do?"

I discussed the question with Rav Zalman Nechemia, who told me that I should work closely with the man to help him iron out any halachic problems that were in the way of the family getting together with their grandparents.

"I cannot stress how important this is," he kept on saying over and over. "*Ba'alei teshuvah* need to know that becoming religious does not need to mean a break with the rest of the family."

His reaction reminded me of a story I'd heard from Rav Mendel Kaplan about two mothers who were discussing their sons in the army. One mother said, "I can't wait for my son to come home! His three years are almost done and soon he'll be back with us!"

"My son isn't coming home," the second mother rejoined.

"Why not?" asked the first.

"Because he's a *ba'al teshuvah*," the other mother said before erupting in a torrent of tears.

When I wrote my *sefer Takanas HaShavim*, which presents

she'eilos encountered by *ba'alei teshuvah*, I was hoping that the *sefer* would help make it easier for people to become *frum* and maintain a good relationship with their families. Speaking with Rav Zalman Nechemia, one got the feeling that with the right intentions, painful wounds can always be healed and families torn apart by discord can be put back together. So much, it was obvious, had to do with the attitude of everyone involved.

◆ ◆ ◆

A girl who was studying at a *ba'al teshuvah* seminary in Yerushalayim found herself at a loss around Pesach time when the school wasn't serving meals. Not being financially independent, she wasn't sure how to handle the next few weeks.

It so happened that she had developed a close relationship with a Sephardic family in her neighborhood who welcomed her into their lives, but since their *minhag* was to eat *kitniyos* on Pesach and she was Ashkenazi, she wanted to know what she was allowed to do.

Rav Zalman Nechemia thought about the *she'eilah* for a few minutes. I saw his answer as an incredible *chiddush*.

"If she's really a *bas bayis* in their home, then there's an argument to be made that she should be allowed to eat *kitniyos* herself. Being a *bas bayis* means that in a sense she has become part of the household, and she should be allowed to take on their *minhagim* and use their dishes and eat their food, *kitniyos* included."

"But she has a family of her own," I said.

"Yes, but she's not really connected to her family. She's on her own. For all practical purposes, this Sephardic family is her family. Certainly they are closer to her than her biological relatives right now."

"So the Rav is giving her a *heter* to eat *kitniyos* this Pesach?"

"Not yet. I need to know exactly how close they are first. But if they are *mamesh* like her family, then I would definitely say there's a valid argument to permit her to eat *kitniyos*."

Whenever I've discussed *she'eilos* with Rav Zalman Nechemia, I always walk away with the feeling that here is a *rav* who possesses the ability to put himself into the mind and heart of the person asking the *she'eilah* — to feel what he feels and to *pasken* according to his needs.

◆ ◆ ◆

The parents of a *ba'al teshuvah* wanted him to eat a certain type of healthy bread that was imported from outside Eretz Yisrael and baked by non-Jews.

Many follow the opinion that *pas palter*, the bread of a non-Jewish baker, is only permissible to eat if it's better-quality bread, which the person really desires. In this case, the person asking the *she'eilah* didn't want the bread; he would have been happy to eat regular bread baked in a Jewish bakery. The only reason he even considered eating the bread was because it was important to his parents.

When I discussed the *she'eilah* with Rav Zalman Nechemia, he commented decisively, "Just the fact that eating this bread is *kibbud av va'eim* turns it into a better bread!"

This is a classic case of the type of *chiddushim* that Rav Zalman Nechemia comes up with. This is not to say that he could or would be able to permit every *she'eilah* that comes his way. *Pas palter* is not a very stringent type of *issur*, and there is plenty of room to maneuver. Even so, Rav Zalman Nechemia's *chiddushim* are beautiful in their breadth and scope, and for the obvious concern he has for every Jew.

◆ ◆ ◆

At my daughter's *chuppah*, one of the guests who had been honored with a *berachah* made a mistake and began reciting the wrong one. Realizing his mistake in the middle of the *berachah*, he immediately went back and fixed it.

My son-in-law, who had been immersed in his davening up until that point, suddenly spoke up and commented, "He didn't fix the mistake *toch kedei dibbur*." In other words, it wasn't fast enough to constitute a valid *berachah*.

Of course, this series of events precipitated an entire halachic debate under the *chuppah*. It went on and on until Rav Zalman Nechemia settled the question by saying, "It's fine. The mistake happened in the middle of a *berachah*, he fixed it, and it's not a problem."

He was totally clear. He had no doubts, and we were able to continue with the *chuppah*.

We can be certain that Rav Zalman Nechemia had halachic reasoning to back up his *psak*. But in my mind it was a classic "Rav Zalman Nechemia" moment. Someone made a mistake and everyone was discussing it. This must have been extremely embarrassing for the person who made the mistake. For Rav Zalman Nechemia, the priority was to make everyone realize that it was fine and have us move on so that the focus would shift back to the wedding (where it belonged) and away from the mistake.

In this he succeeded admirably, as in everything that he did.

◆ ◆ ◆

Rav Yitzchak Berkovits, the esteemed *rav* of Sanhedria Murchevet and one of the leading *poskim* of Yerushalayim in general and for *she'eilos* concerning *ba'alei teshuvah* in particular, told me that there's no question that *ba'alei teshuvah* do not have to take on everything right away.

There was a man in the process of becoming religious who still hadn't managed to wean himself off of eating in *tereifah* restaurants. His question was whether he should take off his yarmulke when he frequented those non-kosher establishments.

Intrigued, I discussed the *she'eilah* with Rav Zalman Nechemia, telling him that on the surface it appeared that Rav Moshe Feinstein would be *machmir* in such a case. I recalled a response Rav Moshe had given to the *she'eilah* of an on-the-way-to-becoming-religious person intent on visiting a disco: "Should he add insult to injury and take off his yarmulke in addition to visiting such a place?"

Rav Zalman Nechemia heard and appreciated the question.

"If he's not holding at being completely kosher in his life," he said, "that's one thing. But he cannot enter a *tereifah* restaurant wearing a yarmulke! That would be a clear *chillul Hashem!*"

Rav Zalman Nechemia understood where the man was coming from, that he hadn't yet reached the level of being willing to abstain from everything he had enjoyed throughout his life. On the other hand, that didn't mean he was allowed to make a *chillul Hashem*. While it was true that he was in the process of making a life change of great magnitude and couldn't do everything at once, that didn't give him the right to do something detrimental to *Klal Yisrael*. Walking into a *tereifah* restaurant with a yarmulke on one's head would do no good for anyone and only cause damage. Rav Zalman Nechemia weighed the situation of the *yachid*, the individual, against the outcome for the *rabim*, the majority, and, keeping everyone's best interests in mind, gave his *psak*.

At no time did he forget his honed level of sensitivity for people, yet neither did he forget his sensitivity for Hashem.

◆ ◆ ◆

While I was working on my *sefer Takanas HaShavim*, I asked Rav Zalman Nechemia which *sefarim* a *ba'al teshuvah* should focus on learning.

"The main thing for a *ba'al teshuvah* is to know what to do, and that means spending significant amounts of time studying *Kitzur Shulchan Aruch*. This way he will know what he's allowed to do and what is forbidden."

He didn't feel this way only regarding *ba'alei teshuvah*.

"I feel that everyone should be learning *Kitzur*," he said to me. "There are many important matters in the realm of *Choshen Mishpat* and *Even HaEzer* where people, even those who have been *frum* their entire lives, do not know basic halachos. It is therefore imperative for *Klal Yisrael* to learn *Kitzur Shulchan Aruch* until they know it. And for *ba'alei teshuvah* it is crucial."

"How many times should a person review the *sefer*?" I asked him.

"Once, twice, three times, four times," he replied, smiling. "Until he knows everything that's written inside."

◆ ◆ ◆

As I mentioned previously, I used to learn with a professional boxer named Yuri Foreman, who was in the process of becoming totally *frum*. While some may have been very impressed by how he made his money, there were quite a few *rabbanim* who felt that boxing was against halachah and that he should be told to quit. I discussed the *she'eilah* with Rav Zalman Nechemia, who said that he could continue doing what he had been training for since he was eight years old. Not only was boxing his *parnassah*; it was his life.

Bringing a proof from the *Shulchan Aruch HaRav*, Rav Zalman Nechemia pointed out that since boxing is something people do for *parnassah*, the boxers are *mochel* one another for any potential damage and consider any injuries that happen during a fight par for the course.

In this particular case, Rav Zalman Nechemia *paskened* that a *rav* couldn't just say, "Well, boxing isn't within the spirit of Torah, so he has to stop." No, it was incumbent on the *rav* to take all factors into consideration — the man's *parnassah*, his years of training, the fact that he was becoming religious, the fact that the boxers understood that they might get hurt inside the ring — and give a *psak* tailored for the individual and not for the *klal*.

Once again Rav Zalman Nechemia surprised many with his *heter* for Yuri Foreman, who ended up winning a major fight at Yankee Stadium. But that was a specific *psak* for Yuri, not for anyone else, and it showed Rav Zalman Nechemia's keen and broad grasp of halachah and its applications, which he viewed through the prism of genuine sensitivity and understanding of the person asking the *she'eilah*.

As always, Rav Zalman Nechemia never ceased to amaze me.

Encounters With

Rav
Moshe Sternbuch
שליט"א

Defender of Truth

On the one hand, he is constantly talking about ahavas Yisrael and ending controversy and how we need to get along. On the other hand, there's no question in his mind that Klal Yisrael needs to reach a certain level of kedushah, and when it comes to that, he will not budge or give an inch, because he feels that this is what we need in order to end the galus.

He loves everyone, and he is demanding of everyone at the same time. That, I feel, is the essence of his "kana'us."

Chapter Twenty-six

When talking about Rav Moshe Sternbuch, the only way to begin is with words of praise for his mother. As a young child in school, the boy's math teacher told his mother that her child was going to become the greatest math professor in the world.

In response, Mrs. Sternbuch pulled her son out of the school, commenting, "I want my son to grow up to become a *gadol b'Torah*, not a math professor."

Rav Sternbuch's father passed away at a young age, leaving a house full of children for his *chashuve rebbetzin* to raise. There was no question of her fulfilling the mission; the only question was how. One thing that helped a lot: whenever Rav Elchanan Wasserman traveled to England, he stayed at the Sternbuch home. Observing Rav Elchanan up close is not something that's very easy to forget, and his visits had a tremendous impact on the entire family. It also afforded Mrs. Sternbuch the opportunity to seek his counsel.

"I have ten children," she told Rav Elchanan. "I have to work. Otherwise I won't have the money we need."

Rav Elchanan's answer went down in the annals of Sternbuch family history.

"Your first priority is taking care of your family. If there's any time left, you can make *hishtadlus* for *parnassah*."

Apparently, Mrs. Sternbuch was quite an amazing woman because her son speaks of his mother often. At a *yahrtzeit* gathering for the Har Nof *kedoshim*, Rav Sternbuch spoke.

"My mother used to go to my father's grave once a year," he told the assembled, "where she cried out to Hashem in an incredibly dramatic scene.

"'There are three partners in the creation of a person,' she would shout. 'The father, mother, and You, Hashem. One of the partners is missing from this home, and I am requesting that You, Hashem, take on two-thirds of this partnership instead of one-third!'"

Her *tefillos* paid off, and her children grew up to become incredible assets to *Klal Yisrael*. One of Rav Sternbuch's sisters is the mother of Rav Asher Arieli, another is married to Rav Dovid Soloveitchik, *rosh yeshivah* of Brisk, and another to Dayan Chanoch Ehrentrau, a prominent *rav* in England. These are just a few of Mrs. Sternbuch's children, because each one grew up to be a special person — all from one mother who had to do everything on her own. And she succeeded.

◆ ◆ ◆

On one occasion I asked Rav Sternbuch if women should count *sefiras ha'omer*.

"Telling them to count the *omer* makes them feel pressured," I explained, "especially since they have so many other things to do inside their homes. Besides," I continued, "Rav Shlomo Zalman Auerbach also *paskened* that women do not need to count *sefiras ha'omer* if having to remember to count makes them feel overly pressured."

"My mother used to put up signs in every corner of the house," he replied, "reminding herself and the rest of us to count *sefiras ha'omer*."

I did not belabor the issue any more after that. Clearly his mother had been a *tzaddeikes* and someone who loved to serve Hashem. For her, counting *sefiras ha'omer* was not a burden, and she wanted nothing more than to be reminded of the mitzvah.

◆ ◆ ◆

The more I heard about Rav Sternbuch's mother, the more I realized that the way the Sternbuch children turned out was no coincidence.

A woman came to Mrs. Sternbuch and asked her to get involved in a certain project around Elul time.

"I am unable to take part at this time," was her answer.

"Why not?" the woman wanted to know.

"Because I have a big court case coming up, and I have to prepare myself for it. I would be happy to help you out after the case is over."

"Maybe I can assist you with the case," the visitor suggested.

When she realized that the court case Mrs. Sternbuch was referring to was actually the *Yom HaDin*, the woman resolved to return after the *Yamim Nora'im*.

◆ ◆ ◆

For close to eight years I davened in Rav Sternbuch's minyan every Friday night. I sat a few seats away from him and was thus in the unique position to witness the way he recited *Krias Shema*, which was other-worldly. Halachah dictates that one is supposed to recite *Shema* each day like it is brand new to you and you never said it before, like it's a letter from the king that just arrived and you're excited to see what the king has to say.

Sitting in such close proximity, I was able to see how Rav Sternbuch put his entire heart and soul into saying every single word. It was *kabbalas ol malchus Shamayim* in the truest sense of the word.

◆ ◆ ◆

Rav Sternbuch was very close to the Brisker Rav and would learn with him every day. The two of them also went for walks together. Much of Rav Sternbuch's conduct toward the *klal* stems from his deep connection to the Rav.

"People think that the Brisker Rav's greatness was in his Torah," Rav Sternbuch likes to say. "Of course, he was an *adam gadol ad me'od* (a very great man), and his father, Rav Chaim, said that he was an extension of his *derech* of learning. But I feel that his real *gadlus* lay in his *emunah* and *bitachon*: the Brisker Rav would not even move his little finger without first considering how that action was going to affect his relationship with Hashem! He was completely in tune with Hashem during every second of every day, and even the smallest movement he made reflected his incredibly deep *emunah* in the *Borei Olam*.

"Not only that," Rav Sternbuch would say, "but the Brisker Rav testified about his grandfather the Beis HaLevi that his hands were black because he used to stick them into the fire every single day to remind himself of what it must feel like in Gehinnom."

While writing that story in an article, my laser printer wasn't working properly, and I had to stick my hand inside, forgetting how hot such machines tend to get. Of course, I touched something that not only burned my hands, but turned them black as well — an interesting coincidence considering that I was writing about the Beis HaLevi's blackened hands...

When I showed my hands to Rav Sternbuch, he commented, "It's much better to be given black hands in this world than in the next."

When war broke out in summertime between Gaza and Israel, thousands of missiles were shot by Hamas and other terrorist groups across the border, with several reaching Yerushalayim and its outlying suburbs. During those days a siren could go off at any second, and people would have only a few minutes to make their way to the nearest shelters before the rockets landed. Needless to say, it was a very stressful few weeks.

One Friday night a siren went off in the middle of davening. While everyone around him began to panic, Rav Sternbuch didn't so much as move. He was completely at peace with the situation and was not worried even a tiny bit.

The Brisker Rav would have been proud.

◆ ◆ ◆

Rav Sternbuch likes to reminisce about his days standing at the side of the Brisker Rav. Clearly he considers that time to be among the best days of his life.

"One time I missed our *seder*," he told me. "When I came to the Rav the next day, he asked me where I had been the day before. I told him that something small had come up, and I had to deal with it."

The Rav wanted to know what that small thing was.

"The milkman in our neighborhood passed away, and I had to attend the *levayah*."

The Brisker Rav reacted very strongly to his younger *chavrusa's* words.

"A Yid passed away and you call that something small?" he admonished, his tone of voice clearly indicating his displeasure at the remark. "Do you realize how important every single Yid is to *Klal Yisrael*?!"

The Brisker Rav was on fire, and Rav Sternbuch never forgot his words.

◆ ◆ ◆

It was the Chazon Ish who suggested Rav Sternbuch as a *shidduch* prospect to his future father-in-law, Rav Schechter. He did this at the end of his life when he was already very old and frail.

"In the last year of his life," Rav Sternbuch said, "the Chazon Ish made a record three hundred *shidduchim*! In fact, at that time nobody made a *shidduch* in Bnei Brak without first conferring with the Chazon Ish.

"Even though the Chazon Ish passed away before the *shidduch* was finalized, my in-laws followed his advice, and I was introduced to my future *kallah*."

It did not take long for his wife to recognize whom she had

married. Later she went so far as to make the following statement: "My husband is going to be one of the *gedolei hador*, and I accept any *yissurim* he will ever have on myself!"

Toward the end of her life Rebbetzin Sternbuch suffered from difficult *yissurim*. When people suggested that maybe it was time for her to retract her decision to take his *yissurim* on herself, she quieted them, explaining that this was what she wanted.

It was the Rebbetzin who typed all his *chiddushei Torah*, and it was the Rebbetzin more than anyone else who was responsible for the publication of all her husband's *sefarim*. This made sense, considering that his learning was the most important thing in her life.

When the Sternbuch family finally acquired an air conditioner to combat the unbearable Bnei Brak heat, the Rebbetzin insisted that it should not be installed in their bedroom or dining room but in her husband's study, so that he would be able to learn in comfort.

After their youngest child married, the Sternbuchs packed their bags and moved to South Africa, where Rav Sternbuch accepted a job as the spiritual leader of a large *kehillah*. For the Rebbetzin, South Africa was a brand-new world — and a far cry from her simple Bnei Brak life — but if this was where their life was taking them, she accepted her new role with typical aplomb.

Rav Sternbuch would comment later in life that when searching for a wife, a major attribute to look for is flexibility. There is no question that he was talking from the experience of having lived with a person who considered her husband's Torah learning paramount and was willing to do anything to help him further his goals.

And there is no doubt Rebbetzin Sternbuch was one woman in a million, and if Rav Sternbuch was the king of their home, there was no question that she was very much its queen.

◆ ◆ ◆

On Rebbetzin Sternbuch's *yahrtzeit*, the Rav was being driven to her *kever* on Har HaZeisim when the GPS sent the driver in the wrong direction. Within minutes they found themselves driving through a hostile Arab village. As soon as the natives realized they had visitors, about fifteen Arabs began running after their car armed with sticks and rocks, which they had no compunction using. One of the Arabs managed to score a direct hit on the car's front window, sending slivers of glass on the driver. Although bleeding from his wounds, he had the presence of mind to press down on the gas pedal and drive away from the scene of their attempted lynching. *B'chasdei Hashem*, they managed to escape with minimal damage.

The real point of this story, however, is not that one cannot trust his GPS (or Waze, for that matter), but that Rav Sternbuch had been learning while the entire wrong-turn-chase-attack had been going on, never once lifting his head from the *sefer*. He only realized something was amiss after it was all over, when he paused for a second, took a look outside the window, and asked, "Where are we?" having been completely oblivious to everything happening around him, so deeply immersed was he.

But the story didn't even end there. In his rush to get away from the attackers, the driver had driven toward the first clear opening he'd seen, not bothering to keep track of where they were going. When they eventually came to a stop, none of the people in the car had any idea where they were. They called the army and asked to be rescued, but the army couldn't help them out since they needed a location and nobody could give them one.

Eventually an Arab approached from one of the local homes. Seeing the stranded vehicle with the shattered front window and the venerable-looking rabbi, he offered his assistance. Handing the Arab their phone, they asked him to give the army staff directions so that they could send a rescue jeep. The army showed up an hour later and escorted them back to friendly territory.

Rav Sternbuch made a *kiddush* that Shabbos, in *hakaras hatov* that everyone had gotten out of the car alive and in one piece. I looked at him closely as he spoke, trying to determine if he was in any way shaken by his close brush with death, but it seemed to me that he was not affected by what had occurred in one of the Arab villages surrounding Yerushalayim.

Rocks were flying, the window shattered, Arab youths were chasing the vehicle baying for their blood, the driver was racing the car in any direction just to escape the carnage, an Arab had to direct the army where to find them — and Rav Sternbuch took it all in stride. As long as he had his *sefer*, everything was right with the world. No matter what happened, his *emunah* was unshakable, steady as a rock. The fact that they were stranded in the middle of a hostile Arab town was not something that worried him at all. He was completely at peace with his surroundings and situation.

As I sat and watched him as he recounted the events, I was filled with admiration and amazement, thinking, *Here sits an adam gadol!*

Chapter Twenty-seven

Since I write a halachic column for the *Yated*, every time I hear about another groundbreaking *psak* from Rav Sternbuch, I make sure to visit him, discuss the issue with him, and then write about it, presenting the *she'eilah* in a clear format for my readers. I do this with his blessing, and the way this came about — that I have merited being his "voice," so to speak, for the American public — happened in an interesting way.

Operation Cast Lead broke out not long after we had moved from Neve Yaakov to Har Nof. At the time I was davening in different shuls, trying to get a feel for which minyan spoke to me. One Friday night, at the start of the war, I found myself davening in Rav Sternbuch's minyan. When he rose to speak, he began talking about the war, and although he usually spoke in a fairly quiet voice, when he mentioned the hostilities that had broken out, he grew animated and his voice rose to a roar. I sat there spellbound, feeling like I was in the presence of a prophet of old exhorting his nation to better themselves in the Name of Hashem.

He listed a number of reasons he felt the war had broken out and what we needed to learn from it. I was so impressed by what he said and the way in which he said it that as soon as Shabbos ended I sat down and wrote a series of articles on the subject, which were printed by both *Yated* and *Hamodia*.

One of his main themes was the idea that Hashem is constantly doing miracles for us, and since miracles are being done for us on such a regular basis, this is something that obligates us.

"There's no such thing as receiving miracles for free," he stressed. "Miracles happen in order to raise our level of consciousness and should be applied to help us see things differently, since miracles are a clear manifestation of Hashem's hand.

"When you witness a miracle, there's a price to pay: that a person needs to change his life accordingly. If you don't utilize the opportunity to make changes where needed, there's a *ta'anah*, a claim, against you."

The entire Shabbos his words rang through my head, and I sat down to record them all the second I had made *Havdalah* on *motza'ei Shabbos*, finishing the first article even before Rav Sternbuch had made *Havdalah* himself. I brought the article over for him to read, and it was obvious that he enjoyed it very much. The fact is, his words had been reverberating through my mind the entire Shabbos — with my giving much thought to the structure and placement of every idea — and when I actually sat down to write, I merited *siyatta d'Shmaya*, and the words flowed with natural ease.

That was the first article.

The series of articles continued for the next five weeks, until the war came to an end, at which time Rav Sternbuch requested I continue publishing his *divrei Torah*. The fact that his Torah was accessible to people on the other side of the world, people who were reading it avidly and commenting about it and sending him questions, made him very happy. After I'd been writing the column for some time, there was enough material to turn it into a book, and I brought a copy to his home on the Purim after it was printed.

In response to my *"mishlo'ach manos,"* Rav Sternbuch basically emptied his house, probably giving me the largest *mishlo'ach manos* I had ever received in my entire life! He just kept on putting more and more items into a huge basket, which he pressed on me, his smile of pure joy accompanying me out the door and into streets bustling with Purim revelry.

◆ ◆ ◆

Whenever something major happened in Eretz Yisrael, be it the terrorist swap for Gilad Shalit or anything else of magnitude, I'd go and discuss it with Rav Sternbuch. I felt that he grasped the most subtle nuances of complicated situations and that his responses were in the category of small prophecies. Just for the record, Rav Sternbuch feels that we are currently in a period when Mashiach can arrive, but we have to make sure not to squander the opportunity.

Writing his ideas and *yesodos* was not exactly simple. Rav Sternbuch is eminently capable of delivering a sharp answer to a question, and at times, I feel the need to tone down certain responses. Rav Sternbuch, understanding my hesitations yet wanting me to write his words and messages exactly as he said them, once gave me an affectionate jab in the arm and said, "We're going to make a Sternbuch out of you yet!"

The upshot of all this is that when people read what he says, they think he is extreme, which is certainly true to some degree, especially when you consider that he had a close relationship with the Satmar Rebbe. I remember him sharing a *vort* from the Rebbe with me.

He said, "When Avraham Avinu went to daven for the people of Sedom, he didn't take Yitzchak or Yishmael with him. This is strange, especially when we know that a *chashuve* person is supposed to go out accompanied by at least two people."

The answer: "When Avraham went to daven for Sedom, he poured his heart out to Hashem, begging Him to save that terrible city of sinners, and he didn't want his children to overhear him doing so."

Rav Sternbuch explained to me that there was no question that the Satmar Rebbe loved every single Jew, even those with whom he disagreed hashkafically, and davened with all his heart for their *hatzlachah* — in private. At the same time, he felt that what was happening in Eretz Yisrael wasn't the right approach and didn't hesitate to state his opinion in public because he considered everything that was happening across the ocean an authentic danger to the fabric of the Jewish people.

This dichotomy of this "inside-outside" approach sums up Rav Sternbuch's *derech* as well. On the one hand, he is constantly talking about *ahavas Yisrael* and ending controversy and how we need to get along. On the other hand, there's no question in his mind that *Klal Yisrael* needs to reach a certain level of *kedushah*, and when it comes to that, he will not budge or give an inch, because he feels that this is what we need in order to end the *galus*.

He loves everyone, and he is demanding of everyone at the same time. That, I feel, is the essence of his "*kana'us.*"

After Rav Elyashiv passed away, Rav Chaim Kanievsky stated unequivocally that Rav Sternbuch was now the *posek hador*. To me this makes sense, since after years of conversations between the two of us, I can personally attest to the fact that he is completely conversant in every single area of Torah, whether Gemara *b'iyun*, halachah, *aggadah*, or *Zohar*. He can answer any question in depth, served up with a helping of *chiddushim*.

◆ ◆ ◆

In the aftermath of the 2014 attack, when two terrorists entered Kehillas Bnei Torah during *Shacharis* with guns and hatchets, we in Har Nof, and especially those of us living on Agasi Street where the attack occurred, were devastated by what had happened. The more we found out about the *tzaddikim* who were murdered, the more devastated we became.

Days passed, but we could not settle down. Hashem had shaken up the entire planet, and we didn't know what to do with ourselves. A neighbor of mine was lecturing at that time in various non-Jewish universities outside the country. He told me that after the attack, all the students were talking about "the holy rabbis of Jerusalem who had been killed while praying."

It was a matter of interest around the world. The question now became, "Okay, so what does Hashem want from us?"

Rav Sternbuch spoke about the idea of *machlokes* and how we have to end it in our midst. His words resonated deep within my *neshamah*, to the degree where I feel this is one of the most important points in this book!

"Why was Korach so bad?" Rav Sternbuch asked. "Korach," he explained, "represented the quintessential *machlokes* not for the sake of Heaven, and one of the things that Hashem hates most of all in this world is when people don't get along. Anytime a person has a *machlokes* with another Jew, he should remember that he is causing pain to the Creator of the world. We have to therefore do everything we can to avoid this type of behavior. A person might be completely justified in the path that he's taking, but he should not forget that he is causing Hashem tremendous pain with his actions.

"The meaning of *machlokes* that is being waged not for the sake of Heaven is when people know that they are in the middle of a *machlokes* and they don't even try to pull out. Moshe Rabbeinu tried to put a stop to the *machlokes* between him and Korach. He tried to find a middle ground, searched for a way to compromise.

"Korach did not. He stayed where he was and wouldn't even consider finding a way to end the fight. It was completely *lo l'sheim Shamayim*, not for the sake of Heaven.

"Anyone," Rav Sternbuch concluded in a groundbreaking *psak*, "who has the power to end a *machlokes* between others and doesn't is actively holding back the Final Redemption with his own hands."

Hearing those wisest of words and feeling the resounding chord of truth, I began delivering *shiurim* on the topic of *shalom* and ending controversy in our camp.

A person should live every day as if it is his last, I would say. Would you really want your final day on earth to be filled with pointless and acrimonious arguments between you and your friends or relatives? Or are you willing to put in the effort needed, to really go beyond your limitations, to end any vestiges of *machlokes* that you are involved with?

When it comes to *machlokes*, look to our *gedolim* to learn how to handle it. When one is doing the right thing in the Name of Hashem, when it is *l'sheim Shamayim*, a person should stick to what is right no matter what people say. Otherwise, do everything you can to maintain the peace.

◆ ◆ ◆

In the field of alternative medicine, there is a technique called "One Brain," which works to unify the right and left sides of a person's brain so they work together, which helps make a person much more productive and successful. In many cases, the practitioners of this stream of alternative medicine use muscle testing to access information about their patients with fascinating and, in many cases, life-changing results.

There were a number of people who felt that practicing One Brain went against halachah and tried to stop those who were using it to heal their patients. In the end, Rav Elyashiv and Rav Mordechai Gross *paskened* unequivocally that there is no problem at all with One Brain, and the commotion died down.

Rav Sternbuch was also one of the *poskim* who never had a problem with One Brain, saying that "any method of healing that can be credibly explained has no problem." He didn't become emotional over the question that had so many people in an uproar. Like many other leading *poskim*, he listened to the *she'eilah*, weighed all the sides, and made a decision — in favor. The more others screamed, the cooler and more deliberate he became. The question was about halachah, and like any other question, it would be clarified, understood, and dealt with in the calm and collected matter it deserved.

◆ ◆ ◆

Rav Sternbuch was once approached by an army general who asked him why he tells people they don't have to enlist. Rav Sternbuch feels that although a country may need an army (nobody would suggest that Israel give up the IDF), the power behind its success is the yeshivah students sitting and learning across the country. "You know what our problem is?" Rav Sternbuch says. "It's the fact that we don't believe that the IDF's strength and success stems from our learning. If we truly believed that our learning was the source of the power, the army would leave us alone."

He looked the general in the eye and told him in no uncertain terms that it was the people learning Torah who were protecting the country and that the IDF would not be successful without the *olam haTorah*!

The general had nothing to say in response — especially since he was blown away by Rav Sternbuch's obvious sincerity.

When I picture that meeting between Rav Sternbuch and the IDF general, I imagine the fire in Rav Sternbuch's eyes and the passion in his voice. And I understand completely why the general had nothing to say.

◆ ◆ ◆

Recently someone from America called me with the following question. There was a *ba'al teshuvah* who spent a great deal of time learning Gemara *b'iyun* in a certain yeshivah.

"The man knows half of *Shas*," the caller told me. "He's very smart and really knows how to learn."

"What's the problem?"

"The problem is that he still has a ponytail, and some of the people in the yeshivah want to tell him to cut his hair. What do you think we should do in this situation?"

I discussed the question with Rav Sternbuch and Rav Yitzchak Berkovits, the premier *posek* for *kiruv* questions, and both of them felt that the man should be left alone. "Such an important decision has to come from the person himself," was how they put it.

Unfortunately the people who asked the question didn't listen, and they suggested to the ponytailed *talmid chacham* that it might be a good idea if he had a haircut, something that he obviously hadn't been ready to do.

The result: the man left the yeshivah for many months.

Eventually he returned, but damage had been done, since, as Rav Sternbuch said, when it comes to real change, it has to come from the person himself.

◆ ◆ ◆

Recently a friend of mine wanted to open a *beis din* in the Five Towns and asked me to help him get a letter of approbation for this undertaking from Rav Sternbuch. I told Rav Sternbuch about his idea, and he was very excited to hear that such an important development was in the offing. But when I brought my friend in to see him, Rav Sternbuch wouldn't give him a letter, explaining that he couldn't get involved in halachic affairs of the United States and he had more than enough to deal with in Eretz Yisrael.

Since we know each other so well, I tried pressing him a few more times. In the end he said, "Look, you don't need a letter from me. When there's something that needs to be done, just do it! Don't start looking for approval or join up with too many people. When you feel that something's right and needs to be done, just do it!"

(Like Rav Sternbuch does.)

◆ ◆ ◆

Rav Sternbuch can at times throw out a quote from interesting people of the past. One of these is none other than Winston Churchill, former prime minister of England and the man who led his country during World War II. When there was a spate of terrorist attacks all over Eretz Yisrael, with Arabs attacking unsuspecting Israelis at gas stations and restaurants on an almost daily basis, Rav Sternbuch quoted one of Churchill's famous remarks from his days of roaring like a lion on the wireless.

"When the Luftwaffe was bombing England during the London Blitz, Churchill would get on the radio and rally the citizens, saying things like 'Tell Adolph Hitler that we can take it!'

"The Arabs need to understand this as well," Rav Sternbuch said. "They need to grasp the idea that we can take it too! They will not be able to close our country down, life will go on, we will fight back, and ultimately they will lose. They need to understand that we can take it and are not afraid of them, because at the end of the day, everything going on has nothing to do with the Arabs at all. It has to do with us.

"Chazal write in numerous places that the Arabs are an integral part of the *geulah* process. They are Hashem's messengers. His *shelichim*. This is not about them, it's about us and the fact that we need to fix ourselves for Mashiach to come.

"We need to strengthen ourselves, and not be afraid of them or allow them to break us. They are here for a reason and this is taking place in order to wake us up."

At the same time, when his fellow Yidden were hurt in the attacks, Rav Sternbuch empathized with the injured and their families to a degree that is difficult to accurately describe. He was with them one hundred percent — with the people who had been attacked and with their children and families. He felt that every Jew has to feel the pain of his fellow Jew in his heart and soul and to be with them mentally and emotionally.

On the one hand, what was going on was never about the enemy but always about *Klal Yisrael*, and ways they need to improve, and he never let us forget the truth of the matter. On the other hand, we had to recognize our brothers' pain and react accordingly. This may seem like a contradiction, but I assure you that there was no contradiction at all.

It takes a true *adam gadol* to see the world the way he does.

Encounters With

Rav Shlomo Yedid Yedid Zafrani

Zafrani

שליט"א

A Rare Blend

Curious as to why Rav Zafrani spreads himself so thin and travels abroad so often, I asked him how he had become an international rav.

He answered by telling me a story about Rav Yehuda Tzadka. When a fire broke out in a shul, and a sefer Torah was burned, the shul held a levayah for the sefer Torah. At the levayah, Rav Tzadka spoke and declared, "Who knows if Hashem has allowed such a thing to happen to our sefer Torah because we have abandoned our nonreligious brothers!"

"From that moment," Rav Zafrani told me, "I decided that I would be a rav for everyone!"

Chapter Twenty-eight

A t the end of Shaul HaMelech Street in Sanhedria, there's a little shul and *beis din* that is frequented by Sephardic Jews. In 2006, I had a very *chashuve* Sephardic *talmid* who told me about the *beis din* and how a certain *rav* by the name of Rav Shlomo Zafrani comes there once a week. My *talmid* suggested that we go speak with him and get to know him.

Always interested in meeting yet another *talmid chacham*, I accompanied my *talmid* to the *beis midrash* down the road, met Rav Zafrani, and proceeded to be blown away in a very short amount of time.

I found Rav Zafrani to be a *posek* very much in the mold of Rav Shlomo Zalman Auerbach, with whom he was close. This meant every question was answered with the relevant *gemaras*, *Rishonim*, and *poskim*, with an incredible sense of clarity and with the classic mastery of Rav Shlomo Zalman.

The fact that Rav Zafrani is not Ashkenazi was something that excited me. I am a person who naturally feels drawn to the davening in Sephardic minyanim. I find the decorum and *derech eretz* that pervades the minyanim to be very unique, and I feel that we

Ashkenazim have a lot to learn from how our Sephardic brothers conduct themselves when in shul. I was therefore happy to discover a mentor who was also able to give me the Sephardic take on halachah in every situation.

For the next half year, my *talmid* and I went to speak in learning with Rav Zafrani, until that particular *beis din* closed down, by which point the two of us had already developed a close relationship. Unfortunately, when the *beis din* closed its doors, and Rav Zafrani stopped coming to Sanhedria, I no longer saw him on a regular basis. I missed our relationship but wasn't sure how to rekindle it.

One winter I was supposed to fly to the States when the weather forecasters began warning the country about a major impending snowstorm heading our way. That Wednesday night I got into a taxi, and when the driver found out that I was planning to leave for America the next day (we tell our taxi drivers everything), he advised me to leave that night or risk missing my Thursday flight and not being able to get out of the country for a while.

I had a problem with following his advice.

In the eleven years since I had established the *kollel*, I had never missed even one day during the *zeman*, and would travel only during *bein hazemanim*. Recently, I have begun going during Aseres Yemei Teshuvah, but at the time of this story, that was still in the future.

"I haven't missed a trip yet," I told the taxi driver. Then I added, "If I see that the snow is really starting to come down hard, I'll go to the airport."

I went into the *kollel* that Thursday morning. By the time I had begun giving *shiur*, there was already a thick layer of snow on the ground. The snow kept coming down, and after a few hours I realized that the taxi driver had been right (how are they so smart?), and that if I didn't get to the airport soon, there was no way I was going anywhere that evening except back home.

It took many hours to reach the airport. When I finally arrived, I had about eight hours at my disposal until my flight was to leave, so I sat down in the airport shul and had a great learning *seder* interspersed with doubts about whether my decision to remain in the country another day had been correct. Maybe I should have listened to the forecasts and traveled the previous night? Why did I always think I knew better? On the other hand, I had always tried my hardest not to miss giving my *shiur*. So what if I had to wait in the airport for eight hours?

As you can see, I was not sure if I had made the right decision.

About three hours before the flight, I left the airport shul and went out to get a drink of water when I noticed Rav Zafrani sitting on one of the benches. Of course, I immediately went over to speak with him, and he explained that he had just flown in from France and was temporarily stuck at the airport until the roads had been sufficiently cleared for traffic to enter Yerushalayim.

With both of us not going anywhere for a while, we had a very productive conversation. The fact that we had met at the airport and had the opportunity to spend some quality time together was especially pleasant since we had fallen out of touch for a few years before that unexpected meeting. As we were saying goodbye, I said to the *rav*, "We really have to rebuild the *kesher* that we used to have."

He agreed.

Since that meeting, our relationship only got better. With such an outcome, I can only conclude that my decision not to skip morning *seder* that Thursday was the right one, as Hashem rewarded me with a chance encounter with a *rav* whom I sincerely respect and from whom I have learned a tremendous amount.

At the time of this writing, Rav Zafrani is the *rav* and *nasi* of some fifty shuls around Eretz Yisrael and the *rosh av beis din* in France. Since he is the *rav* for so many places, he needs to actually visit those places, which means that he is away from Har Nof, where he lives, more than he is there. Yet even with all his responsibilities, in the wake of that snowstorm we have made a concerted effort to make the relationship happen and it has flourished.

◆ ◆ ◆

Curious as to why Rav Zafrani spreads himself so thin and travels abroad so often, I asked him how he had become an international *rav*.

He answered by telling me a story about Rav Yehuda Tzadka. When a fire broke out in a shul, and a *sefer Torah* was burned, the shul held a *levayah* for the *sefer Torah*. At the *levayah*, Rav Tzadka spoke and declared, "Who knows if Hashem has allowed such a thing to happen to our *sefer Torah* because we have abandoned our nonreligious brothers!"

"From that moment," Rav Zafrani told me, "I decided that I would be a *rav* for everyone!"

◆　◆　◆

Rav Shlomo's middle name is Yedid, which means "friend," and what makes our relationship so special is that not only do I feel extremely close to him, but I intuitively understand that he feels the same way about me. My son and I used to walk him home after davening on Friday night, and we'd get such a wonderful feeling just from a few minutes of conversation. And I know that I'm not the only one who feels this way. It can be very difficult to talk to Rav Zafrani in the street, because every few steps he meets another friend and has to stop and say hello.

All this is alluded to in his name.

Shlomo: he is wise.

Yedid: he is a friend.

Zafrani: This word means "saffron," which is a golden-colored spice derived from the crocus flower and delightful, very expensive, and a beautiful addition to any dish in which it is used.

◆　◆　◆

These days I give a *shiur* at Heichal HaTorah every Friday night. But prior to that time I davened at Rav Zafrani's shul every Shabbos he was in Har Nof. Just being in his presence taught me innumerable life lessons, one more precious than the next.

I'll begin with the people in his shul. They love him! You can feel the love and adoration his *tzibbur* has for him.

I understand them completely.

When Rav Zafrani announces that one of the people in the shul is making a *simchah* that Shabbos, he's always so, so happy about the person's good fortune. For real! This might sound a little strange, but he has three different voices. There's his regular speaking voice, which he uses when he speaks to you as a friend. There's a second voice he uses when he gives *shiurim*, and a third, completely different voice for when he announces a *simchah* in the shul. When he delivers his *shiurim*, a feeling of majesty envelops the shul, as opposed to when he announces a *simchah* and one feels a tangible sense of happiness pervading the entire room.

But it's even more than that.

Whenever he can find an opportunity to show how much he appreciates and esteems another person, he grabs it. Recently I organized a gathering in the Mishkan Esther shul in Ramat Eshkol to mark a certain occasion. There were a number of speakers there, all of whom I had asked to speak. Rav Zafrani was the only one who actually began his speech with the words "*Birshus* Rav Travis, the *mara d'asra* of the *beis midrash.*"

The other speakers were all special people. They were all *chashuve* people. But Rav Zafrani possessed an extraordinary degree of sensitivity, and I realized all over again why I have such profound respect for this incredible *talmid chacham.*

When I brought a group of *talmidim* to meet with him at Rav Yaakov Hillel's yeshivah (he has joined the group of phenomenal *talmidei chachamim* who sit there and hear *she'eilos*), he stood up for me when we entered the room. He was clearly trying to convey a message to my *talmidim* with his actions because I am definitely not worthy of having Rav Zafrani stand up for me. Then he said to them, "Make sure to stick to your rebbi and never let him go!"

He treats people with genuine friendship, like a true *yedid*. The way he acts personifies his name.

When he gives a *shiur* in the shul, he speaks to those assembled with tremendous friendship, yet at the same time he is very serious about the points he is making. I know many *rabbanim*.

Some are solemn and pensive when they speak with you. Others are very down to earth. It is extremely rare to find a *rav* who knows how to combine the friendly aspect with a very serious approach to halachah. With Rav Zafrani, neither side of his personality detracts from the other even a little bit.

It's a rare blend.

◆ ◆ ◆

Rav Zafrani's words are a combination of down-to-earth practical advice and ideas that a person needs to hear. He speaks about *emunah*, and he speaks about *tefillah*, and when he tells a story, you can sense him reliving it and it never fails to make a strong impact on his listeners. I'll give you an example of what I mean.

At one point I was counseling a couple who were on the verge of divorce, and I discussed their case with Rav Zafrani. He took the case to heart, and you could see that the matter weighed on him. Rav Zafrani is the *talmid muvhak* of Rav Benzion Abba Shaul and actually wrote the second section of his rebbi's *she'eilos* and *teshuvos*. When I brought this case to him, he opened up his *sefer* and read me a letter that had been written by a child from a divorced home whose entire life had been ruined because of his parents' divorce. He read the child's letter word for word, and he was crying as he read it.

He didn't really have an answer to solving the couple's difficulties, but at the same time he wanted me to understand the severity of divorce and how it should only be the absolute last resort, after trying every conceivable solution to make things work again.

It is very possible that I would not have worked so hard to save that couple's marriage were it not for hearing Rav Shlomo Zafrani read that gut-wrenching letter and seeing the tears streaming from his eyes and down his cheeks. After that, I redoubled my efforts to help the couple, and in the end, we merited seeing a miracle.

◆ ◆ ◆

When I organized a gathering after a tragic event that had happened to a member of our community, one of the *rabbanim* who had been scheduled to speak misunderstood the time I had told him to be there and didn't show up. This was a major problem. There were two hundred people waiting inside the shul, another hundred outside, and the next speaker hadn't arrived! I sent one of my *talmidim* to go pick up the missing *rav*, and meanwhile I updated Rav Zafrani, who was the first speaker, on the situation and explained that we had a sudden unexpected gap in the program.

Normally, when you invite someone to speak at an event about a certain topic, the average length of the speech is between forty-five and fifty minutes long. Without meaning to, I had put Rav Zafrani in an uncomfortable position. No doubt he had prepared a fifty-minute speech, and here I had sent him a note in the middle of the *shiur* basically informing him that I needed him to continue speaking until the next speaker arrived. Most people in such a situation would have eventually run out of what to say.

He didn't.

Rav Zafrani spoke beautifully for an additional forty-five minutes. He spoke with incredible gracefulness and poise, and no one present had the slightest inkling that he was speaking off the cuff, biding time until the next speaker arrived, because he wasn't biding time. He just kept on getting better and better as he spoke. The *ma'amarei Chazal* rolled off his tongue with accurate fluency; he was completely at ease, and I had the feeling that he could have kept going for another hour if need be.

In the aftermath of the event, when I explained to the members of the *kollel* what had really been going on while we were waiting for the missing *rav* (he had thought he was supposed to arrive an hour later and was in the middle of a different *shiur* in front of two hundred people), everyone recognized that they had been in the presence of greatness.

◆ ◆ ◆

A year after the snowstorm that brought us back together, the forecast called for a heavy snowstorm yet again. In an interesting turn of events, however, in the end there was only a light dusting of snow and nothing more.

"What's the connection between these two snowstorms and what happened to Pharaoh the king of Egypt?" Rav Zafrani asked me.

"A year ago," he explained, "they were expecting a light storm, and we ended up with a major blizzard. This year we were warned to expect a major storm, and in the end almost nothing fell.

"If you think that the weather forecasters were wrong, think again. They use science to determine the course of the coming storms, and when they warn of a blizzard they know what they're talking about. But at the end of the day, Hashem controls everything.

"It's like the *pasuk* says," he added. "'*Asher hisallalti b'Mitzrayim*' (*Shemos* 10:2) — that I, Hashem, made a mockery of Pharaoh and the Egyptians, and showed them that no matter how great they thought they were, I am Hashem and they were mortal and would always be at My mercy."

Then he repeated the point again.

"Don't think that the weather forecasters are wrong. They know what they're talking about. But at the end of the day, Hashem is the One Who decides what will come to pass."

◆ ◆ ◆

When it comes to questions, Rav Zafrani remembers everything he learns, is intimately familiar with the Gemara, *Rishonim*, and *poskim* on every topic, and has a clear picture of the entire *sugya*.

My son once asked him a question on how to pronounce certain words in *Shema Yisrael*. My son was fourteen years old at the time, but Rav Zafrani treats every single question and questioner with the same seriousness, regardless of background or age. Before he answered the question, Rav Zafrani asked my son what yeshivah he was in, what he was learning, and how it was working out for him.

Eventually they got back to my son's question.

"It's a good question," Rav Zafrani said to him, "but as a rule you shouldn't get too caught up in these types of things. The main thing is to enjoy the *tefillah* and to feel close to Hashem."

This was critical *mussar*, delivered in a way that was guaranteed to be accepted.

◆ ◆ ◆

On one occasion I asked Rav Zafrani how a person is able to acquire the trait of *yashrus*, of uprightness.

"There is one major rule," he said, "and if you follow that, you'll become a *yashar* person."

Now I was very curious. As a rule I love rules.

"A person needs to be straight with his money. Yaakov Avinu lived with Lavan for twenty-two years, and he never cheated him, despite the fact that Lavan tried his best to take advantage of his nephew on multiple occasions.

"You have to be *yashar* with your money all the time, and inevitably that will affect the rest of your life. This is the litmus test, this is the area in life where you see what a person is really about. If you want to be a trustworthy member of society, you must first and foremost be straight with your money."

◆ ◆ ◆

I asked Rav Zafrani for a *haskamah* for my *sefer Takanas HaShavim*. He gave me his *haskamah*, and after a few months had gone by, he said, "*Nu*, where's the *sefer*?"

"It takes a while," I replied. "I wrote it in Hebrew, and it needs to be edited."

After that, he'd ask me for a report on the *sefer's* progress every time we met. We'd discuss the *sefer* and I'd share many of the *she'eilos* that would be addressed in the *sefer* with him. Once, I told him about a certain *kula*, a leniency, that I felt made sense.

"I hear where you're coming from," he replied, "but you can't write that. Not everything that's true can be written. There are certain halachos that are applicable specifically for people who are not well. In such cases, the *posek* will have to confer with the doctors who really understand their physical condition. But in many cases, such *piskei halachah* cannot be written down."

His words struck a chord.

Not everything needs to be written, even if it's halachah and even if it's true.

At some point we discussed the halachic category of *tinok shenishbah* — literally translated as a baby who was taken into captivity. This is a term used to describe a nonreligious person who has no knowledge of religion or its significance.

I told him that I considered all nonreligious people in the *tinok shenishbah* category because they do not have an accurate understanding of halachah or mitzvos.

Rav Zafrani agreed with me, telling me that he once asked a *ba'al teshuvah* about his mind-set before becoming religious. "Now you know the truth about the Torah," he had said to him. "What did you think about religion before you became *frum*?"

"Before I became religious," the man replied, "I thought that every person has the right to choose to live his life however he wants and in whichever way will make him happiest. I thought that there are twenty-five different streams of Judaism and that it's up to the individual to determine which one works for him."

After hearing this person's outlook on life, Rav Zafrani recognized that this is the way nonreligious Jews think, which is how he came to agree with me that the vast majority of nonreligious Jews would fall under the category of *tinok shenishbah*.

He then quoted me a long list of *poskim* who agree with this *psak*.

It takes a broadminded *posek* to not only appreciate what I was saying, but to bring a proof to my words and agree with me on so controversial a topic.

◆ ◆ ◆

I could tell that Rav Zafrani was beginning to be concerned about the delay in publishing the *sefer*, and the truth is I did hit a snag for a few months, leading me to think for a while that this *sefer* might end up not being published. It was not a simple process. There were one hundred *she'eilos* in the *sefer*, *she'eilos* that needed responses that provided the *halachah l'ma'aseh*, the practical halachah telling a person what he should do in each situation presented, and that was just the beginning. Many of the *she'eilos* were delicate; at one point I was even threatened by a *rav* to whom I had showed the *sefer* that he would put me in *cherem* if I printed it.

"I'm already printing the *cherem* signs now," he said. "Do not put out this *sefer*!"

But Rav Zafrani was unfazed by these reactions and advised me to pay no attention to them at all. Not only did he quiet my fears; he continually encouraged me to keep on working on the *sefer* until it was finally ready for print, constantly repeating, "This is a very important *sefer* for *ba'alei teshuvah*, and it needs to be published!"

The positive energy that Rav Zafrani exuded every time I showed him another *she'eilah* and *teshuvah* gave me the drive to see the project through to fruition.

I received my copies of the *sefer* on Zos Chanukah and, copy in hand, hurried to Rav Zafrani's house to present him with my token of appreciation for all his positive reinforcement. The moment he understood why I had come and what I was holding in my hand, Rav Zafrani broke out in a huge smile and called out to his wife, "Bring out the wine!," making it obvious that my joy was his joy. He kissed me, and the two of us danced together.

Always remember: people work extremely hard on the *sefarim* they write. They put their life into it. Your reaction to someone else's work is critical. The slightest twist of the mouth, the lifting of an eyebrow, or a mocking expression can devastate a person who spent days and nights putting his Torah thoughts in order.

Conversely, a positive response, a real smile, *simchah* for the other person, appreciation for what he has written, and an offer to buy the *sefer* will make an author's day, week, even month.

I will always remember the people who made me feel that my work was special and worthwhile.

◆　◆　◆

I quoted a story about Rav Yitzchak Greenberg, who had been a close *talmid* of the Chazon Ish, in the introduction to *Takanas HaShavim*. A *ba'alas teshuvah* told Rav Greenberg that her father turns the light on in her room every Friday night, despite repeated requests on her part not to do this.

"This is what you should do," Rav Greenberg said. "On Sunday, ask your father if you should buy pita or rolls for the house. On Monday ask him if you should buy Gila or Eshel (two types of yogurt). On Tuesday ask him if you should make shnitzel or chicken. Ask him for his advice every day until Friday, and you will see that he won't touch the light this coming Shabbos."

She followed his advice, and the story played itself out exactly as Rav Greenberg had said it would. His reasoning was simple. If you show a person that you respect him, he is able to allow you to go your own way. But he needs to feel that you still value him and his opinion.

Rav Zafrani loved that story. You could tell that its message truly resonated with him because he is a person who honestly values other people.

"This is my favorite part of the *sefer*," he told me later on.

The message was invaluable. Show respect for parents, for teachers, for people. The moment you do that, everyone wins. This is the secret of life. We live in a generation where people have really low self-esteem. When you show them respect, they begin to flourish like a flower in bloom. You can do this 24/7, with every person you come in contact with. And the more people you help feel good, the more lives you are saving.

The well-known *mechanech* and author Rabbi Dov Brezak related how he was walking down the street and saw a person who looked depressed. Knowing how important it is to greet every person with a big smile, he proceeded to do just that. He then continued on his way. He hadn't gone far when he looked back and noticed that the person still looked depressed, so he returned and greeted him again. In the end, it turned out that the person had been on his way to commit suicide and Rabbi Brezak's greeting saved the person's life! And there are so many people like this all around us. People with terrible *shalom bayis*, people with major *parnassah* troubles. Some of these people's lives are so bad that they don't want to live anymore. When you look them in the eye and give them a giant smile and greet them with warmth and show them that they have earned your respect, you are saving their lives!

Showing respect for people and making them happy is plain old good advice — and it works!

This attitude is classic Rav Zafrani — the man who knows how to show love and respect other people in an honest, authentic way — and it's why he liked that story so much.

◆ ◆ ◆

We have an annual tradition in the *kollel* that all the *yungeleit* and their families celebrate the Purim *seudah* together at one of the member's homes. A few years ago we were eating at one of the *yungeleit's* homes in Har Nof, when a group of *bachurim* entered the house to collect *tzedakah* for their yeshivah. When I questioned them as to where they learned, they replied (almost apologetically, it seemed to me) that they were *talmidim* in a certain yeshivah for *ba'alei teshuvah*.

By this time, I was already somewhat in my cups (having recited the *berachah* of *hatov v'hameitiv* more than once or twice by then), and I looked them in the eye and yelled, "You guys are making a big mistake," emphasizing my words with emphatic bangs on the table.

"What do you mean?" they asked me.

"You think that just because you happen to be *ba'alei teshuvah* you cannot possibly become *gedolei hador*. That is not true! All of you can become great Torah leaders!"

As I spoke, I could see that my words, words that emanated from my heart, were entering theirs, and I watched as smiles of hope broke out on their faces.

As I spoke to them, I recalled a conversation I'd had with Rav Noach Weinberg, *zt"l*, the *rosh yeshivah* of Aish HaTorah, many years earlier.

"Rebbi," I'd asked him, "where does your success in *kiruv* come from?"

"I look at every guy with long hair and an earring," he said, "as if he's the next *gadol hador*. That's where my success comes from."

His words pierced the walls of my heart and made an indelible impression on my soul.

Which brings me to a personal question that I asked Rav Zafrani. *Encounters With Greatness* was almost finished, and I wanted to know whether I should reveal the fact that I myself am a *ba'al teshuvah* in the book. Maybe I should tone that down or gloss over that part of my life...

"I feel that you should write your story exactly as it is," he told me.

"Why, Rebbi?"

"Because your story will be a *chizuk* for many people who will read it and understand that a person can be born into a nonreligious family and still become *frum* and still become a *talmid chacham* and still become a *rav* and a *posek* and still acquire *da'as Torah*."

"So we should write the whole story?"

"Let the people know the truth about where you came from and how far you've traveled. It will give them the knowledge that they can do it too."

My rebbi spoke and I listened.

Encounters With

Rav
Yisroel Belsky
זצ"ל

Psak and Chesed
Down to a Science

He combined the fifth section of Shulchan Aruch with an incredible understanding of human psychology and a powerful grasp of Torah issues, and he did it with gentleness and a smile. There was no rush when you spoke to him. He gave every person as much time as he needed. When you sat with him, nothing else existed in the world besides the two of you.

Chapter Twenty-nine

One of the first *sefarim* I published was called *Yoreh Binah*, an encyclopedia of *issur v'heter*. Since the *sefer* was in English, and I expected the bulk of the sales to be in the United States, I decided that I wanted to get a *haskamah* from a respected American *posek* as well. Hearing that Rav Yisroel Belsky, *zt"l*, was visiting Eretz Yisrael and staying in Kiryat Sefer, I decided to go and speak with him.

I called the contact number I was given and found out that Rav Belsky was going to be in the country for a week. I asked for a meeting and was told to call back. I called back every single day, but he was very busy and our meeting was pushed off from day to day.

The entire week passed, and suddenly it was Friday. Knowing that with Rav Belsky's busy schedule the entire visit might very easily go by without my having had the opportunity to see him, I made a snap decision.

I'm going to Kiryat Sefer to see Rav Belsky.

I caught the bus and off I went.

As I took my seat in the middle of the bus, I caught sight of an older *rav* sitting a few seats ahead. Motioning toward him, I asked another passenger who the *rav* was.

"You can see his name on his tallis bag," he replied. "That's Rav Yisroel Belsky."

I went over and introduced myself, explaining that I had been trying to reach him all week with no success. He invited me to take the seat beside him, and I ended up having him to myself for the entire bus ride. Once again I received proof that sometimes you just have to take the first step, and then Hashem will clear the road for you.

That conversation was very memorable. I don't know how many people have had Rav Belsky to themselves for an hour straight, but no doubt the list is not very long. We discussed the *sefer*, and he gave me many *eitzos* that would improve it.

People think that if you learn *issur v'heter* and take a test, then you're a rabbi. That, however, is not really the case. *Issur v'heter* is an indication of a rabbi's *paskening* abilities, in the sense that if he can deal correctly with the complex halachos of *issur v'heter*, then he can probably deal with the other halachos as well. The problem is that so many people just learn *issur v'heter* and don't know the rest of *Shulchan Aruch*. Merely taking a test on *issur v'heter* does not make a person a *rav*, because it gives no indication whether the person has what it takes to be a *rav* who *paskens she'eilos*.

Rav Belsky was a real *rav*. He knew everything and was holding everywhere. He knew *Shas*, *Rishonim*, *Shulchan Aruch*, *poskim*, and various secular subjects as well. Any time we had an interaction I saw his expertise on every part of Torah — the stars, animals, *tereifos*, everything and anything. There's no question that the vast majority of people trying to become *rabbanim* do not possess the brilliance of Rav Belsky.

So what should a person do?

Every *gadol* has told me the same thing: a prospective *rav* needs to learn the Gemara and the *Rishonim*, which leads you to the *Tur* and *Shulchan Aruch*, which leads you to the *poskim*

— and then you can *pasken*. But don't just learn *issur v'heter* and imagine that you have now become a rabbi. Don't make the mistake of thinking that you know how to *pasken* when you really know nothing.

There are no shortcuts. If you want to become a *rav* and a *posek*, you need to learn the *sugya*s — in depth. If you study the *Shulchan Aruch* with the *Shach* and *Taz*, you may think that you understand, but if they are discussing a *sugya* you didn't really learn, how can you expect to truly understand what they are talking about?

This was one of the reasons I decided to write *Yoreh Binah*. It was so that when future *poskim* are beginning to learn the *sugya*s, they would have an encyclopedia available as a reference for every one of the many, many complex terms that are used throughout *issur v'heter* — terms such as *chanan, chatichah hara'ui l'hiskabed, blios, plitos*… This will assist them, but it is not a shortcut, because there are no shortcuts if you want to become a genuine *posek*.

I told all this to Rav Belsky, about my approach and intention in putting out this *sefer*, and he gave me advice on how to perfect the *sefer* during that hour-long conversation on the bus to Kiryat Sefer.

"The only way to grasp *peratim* (minor nuances and details)," Rav Belsky said, "is *derech klalim*, through understanding the broader picture."

People write thousand-page *sefarim* today on subjects like "*Negel Vasser* by Your Bed *K'Hilchasah*," but learning a *sefer* like that will just confuse a person completely.

"You need to grasp the *klal*," Rav Belsky said, "the general idea, which happens by learning the *sugya* inside and in depth so that you have a framework for reference. Then all the *peratim* fall into place. Focusing on the details without a framework leaves a person with nothing in the end. Many *sefarim* today make that mistake. You shouldn't make that mistake."

After we finished the first part of our conversation, I asked Rav Belsky whether he'd be willing to give me a *haskamah*. He wasn't against the idea, but he told me that in order for him to do as I wished, he'd have to review the entire *sefer*.

I have published some twenty *sefarim* through the years, and not one of the many people who have graciously given me *haskamos* has felt the need to read through the entire *sefer*. But Rav Belsky did.

Every *haskamah* from Rav Belsky took between two and three years for him to write. He'd ask me to send more parts of the *sefer* and more parts ("Send them to me at the OU," he'd tell me. "Send them to me at the Agudah..."), and I'd email the pieces of the *sefer* to my contacts at the OU for them to print out for Rav Belsky to read. And he'd read them all.

Most people who give you a *haskamah* are giving it because they know you and trust that the information in the *sefer* is of value for the general public. For Rav Belsky that was not enough. It was not sufficient that he knew who I was and that I was a *rosh kollel*. He needed to read the *sefer* himself before he'd give me his *haskamah*.

That, however, was all in the future.

During our initial conversation on the Kiryat Sefer–bound bus, Rav Belsky basically agreed to furnish me with a *haskamah* after making the caveat that he would have to read the entire work before sending it to me. At the time, I didn't take that so seriously, but he was true to his word, and it ended up taking close to two years before his *haskamah* finally arrived. That *haskamah* was infinitely precious to me because it meant that an incredibly busy *gadol* had sufficiently valued my work to take the time to read through everything I had to say before giving me his seal of approval.

◆　◆　◆

After we concluded our discussion about the *sefer*, we began talking about life, and Rav Belsky told me a *yesod*, a guiding principle, that has saved my life many times.

"If you have to send an important letter (or email), never send it on the day that you first write it. Everything important in life needs *linas lailah*." A person needs to sleep on it.

In retrospect, I know that there were many times when I sat down at the computer and wrote an email that I didn't send right then because Rav Belsky told me to wait a day. And I know that if I would have sent the email, the person on the receiving end might have chosen to never talk to me again.

Anyone in the public arena knows that sometimes you receive missives from Yankel Q. Public, where the author of the letter or email castigates what you wrote or even you personally in the strongest terms possible (clearly they didn't wait a night before sending out their email...), and when that happens you want to respond — and make them feel just as good about themselves as they made you feel.

But you can't.

So, as per Rav Belsky's instructions, I will write a first draft and put it in Drafts and then return the following day to see if it can go out as is. Almost always it needs to be rewritten, which it is, and then it can be sent or not, as the case may be.

That piece of advice has saved me countless times.

I consider this the golden rule in dealing with correspondence in the modern day and age, when the possibilities of responding to people who offend you are many and varied. So many of the emails I get should not have been sent, and if the writer would have taken the time to review what he wrote, I have no doubt that the majority of those emails would not have been sent in the first place. Remember — nothing should be done in haste, or chances are you will come to regret your actions.

The same thing goes for conversation as well. It's a good idea not to give an answer right away. If someone asks you to be part of something, tell him that you need a day to consider it.

"You never see things the same the next day," Rav Belsky said. "It's the way of the world that you will always see things differently in the morning."

This conversation took place twenty years ago, when the Internet was in its infancy, yet Rav Belsky had already developed very strong opinions on the subject.

"Internet will destroy the world," Rav Belsky predicted. He told me about some of the cases that came his way and how the Internet was destroying *Klal Yisrael* from within.

As the bus turned into its destination, Rav Belsky asked me, "By the way, why were you coming to Kiryat Sefer today?"

"I just came to speak to the Rav," I replied.

This made him very happy. We parted with warm regards, and he told me to keep in touch and let him know how the writing was progressing.

And of course I did.

◆ ◆ ◆

It took me between three and four years to receive a *haskamah* from Rav Belsky for my *sefer Takanas HaShavim*. The reason it took so long was because Rav Belsky was sick throughout that time. During that period, I was told that he had stopped giving *haskamos*. Since I was targeting this *sefer* at an American demographic that would find it very worthwhile, I felt that I needed the *haskamah* of an American *posek* of Rav Belsky's stature, so I persisted anyway.

I visited him just before he gave me the *haskamah*.

"I've read enough of the *sefer* to write a *haskamah* for you," he said, "but I believe in *linas lailah*, so I'd rather wait until tomorrow morning to put pen to paper and write down my ideas."

I called him the next day and he told me, "I'm sorry, Reb Daniel Yaakov, but I feel like I need to read more of the *sefer*."

The next time I visited, he did feel ready to write the *haskamah*, but again brought up his wish to sleep on it.

"I'm *mevater*," I said.

In the end, he wrote the *haskamah* right then and there.

Rav Belsky ended up gifting me with three *haskamos* through the years. The first one took him close to two years to write. The second *haskamah* was given to me on the spot, after sitting with me for a few hours and going through the entire *sefer*. The third was for *Takanas HaShavim*.

He put a lot of thought into what he wrote in the *haskamah* of each *sefer*. There was nothing generic about his *haskamos*. In the second *haskamah* he wrote that the *sefer* was based on my *chaburah* and *shiurim*, which, in his opinion, "is really the best way to write a *sefer*."

That final *haskamah* was a major challenge for me to obtain since he was sick for four years and I almost gave up. However, I decided to try my luck the next time I was in the States. The day Rav Belsky ended up giving me the *haskamah*, I called him, told him that I was in town, and asked him if I could come over.

"I'm giving a *shiur* tonight on *Mishnah Berurah* at Torah Vodaath. You're welcome to join us."

Needless to say, I took him up on the offer.

It was such an amazing *shiur*. I sat there enthralled by everything I heard. There were *baalebatim* and noted *talmidei chachamim* sitting side by side. I saw young people and old people eagerly learning together. Rav Belsky was speaking to all of them, and every one of them loved the *shiur*. Somehow he managed to find the language that spoke to each person. That was classic Rav Belsky: he knew how to relate to every person. He had no airs about him. When you spoke with him, you felt like you were speaking to a real person.

In the middle of the *shiur*, one of the participants asked him a question about *Krias Yam Suf* based on a new archaeological discovery, and Rav Belsky was very interested in what the person had to say, immediately asking him seven questions on the topic.

After the fascinating *shiur*, I accompanied him to his modest home at 506 East Seventh Street. He was in a really good mood that night and very excited about the subject matter of my *sefer Takanas HaShavim* and how it was geared toward helping *ba'alei teshuvah* with the myriad halachic *she'eilos* they faced.

We sat together for two hours that night, Rav Belsky reading and reading.

"Now I feel like I read the entire thing and can give a *haskamah*," he said at last.

Of course, as I mentioned, at the last second he wanted to push off the writing until the next morning, as was his custom, but in the end he acquiesced and wrote the *haskamah*.

My experiences with Rav Belsky were very similar to those with Rav Brevda. Both of them pushed me off at first, yet I returned time and again, and during the process we developed a relationship.

+ ◆ ◆

Rav Belsky was extremely strong-minded. When he felt that he had arrived at the correct course of action, nothing in the world could change his mind. In many cases strong-minded people don't get along with others, but Rav Belsky possessed the unique ability to really feel strongly about the things he believed in while knowing how to connect with everyone around him at the same time.

He was also blessed with a unique writing style, which he would use when he wanted to make a point. For example, he writes in his *sefer Shulchan HaLevi*, "There's this existing myth in the world that there's something called a *mezonos* roll..."

He then went on to tackle the inherent issues point for point, explaining and dissecting the problems of the "*mezonos* roll" with his trademark clarity and detail. And he didn't have any problem when other *rabbanim* didn't agree with him. He had his halachic opinion, and they had theirs, and if you wanted to change his mind, he was open to listening to your reasoning while at the same time being very sure of his.

In today's world, being a *posek* is a very difficult prospect because the *posek* needs to have a knowledge of science and chemicals that *poskim* in previous generations never had to think about. Many people make mistakes. There are a lot of *chumros* being thrown around today, about matters related to electricity, for example, partly because many people just do not know how everything works.

A *posek* whom I know was asked whether or not using the popular toy Rubik's Cube falls under the category of *borer*. The Rubik's Cube has small squares of different colors, and parts of the toy are maneuvered into different places. On the surface, one could hear the argument of why such a toy should be considered *borer*. But there is no real mixture here, and no issue of repairing anything here, and all that is before one remembers one additional point — which is the most salient point of all — and that is that *this is a toy!*

322   ◆   ENCOUNTERS WITH GREATNESS

Borer is about fixing something that's not the way you want it. Here you are not fixing anything. It's a toy. The whole purpose of the toy is simply to move parts of it around.

That's the whole answer to the question of whether using this toy constitutes *borer* or not. The answer is no, it is not. Why? Because it's a toy. It's not something that needs to be fixed. End of discussion.

But in order to get the *psak* right, a *posek* needs to understand what he's dealing with: What's a toy? What's a game? How does it work?

In today's complicated world, many people don't really understand how things work and how to *pasken* accordingly. But Rav Belsky certainly did.

◆ ◆ ◆

Throughout the course of my writing *Takanas HaShavim*, I contacted Rav Belsky many times. Some of the questions that arose involved scientific or medical conditions that are extremely rare and that are in most cases unfamiliar to the average *posek*. Inevitably Rav Belsky knew exactly what I was talking about and was able to *pasken* accordingly.

One *she'eilah* that arose concerned a teenage *ba'al teshuvah* whose parents lived in a house without a mezuzah: did he have an obligation to do something about it or not? The Israeli *poskim* whom I discussed this question with all concurred that the son was under no obligation to do anything about the mezuzah-less situation.

Why was that?

Since the parents could throw him out if they so desired, he didn't even have the halachic status of a *sho'el*, a borrower, and putting up a mezuzah was not up to him.

When I raised the question with Rav Yitzchak Berkovits, he said, "That may be true in Eretz Yisrael, but in the United States it is much more difficult for parents to throw a teenager out of his house. The kid would go to the police."

In the end, I asked Rav Belsky for his opinion. He agreed with

Rav Berkovits that in the States a child's room is his room and good luck dislodging him, in which case he would need a mezuzah, but he did add that the teen should leave such an environment on his own, because it would be very detrimental for him to continue living in such a home.

To be a genuine *posek*, the person must be familiar not just with the halachah but also with the mentality of the people asking him the questions. Rav Belsky understood the mentality of American Jews, and he was therefore the quintessential American *posek*. He never failed to amaze me with how on target he was, whether it was a matter of science or anything else complex or technical.

He knew bits of knowledge that few in our generation know. Rav Belsky used to spend his summers at Camp Agudah. One evening he looked up at the star-studded sky over Ferndale, New York, and said, "There's a star missing from the sky! There's something wrong with the constellations!"

Knowing the way the sky over Camp Agudah was supposed to look, Rav Belsky was very upset. In the end, someone contacted NASA to verify the situation. NASA corroborated Rav Belsky's claim of a missing star and said that it had apparently been blocked from sight by something in the sky.

There's a line that the Gemara sometimes uses to describe a person who really knows what's going on: "He's as familiar with the streets of Heaven as he's familiar with the streets of Nehardei'a." This is like saying about a native New Yorker: "He's as familiar with the streets of Heaven as he's familiar with the streets of Brooklyn."

A friend of mine published a *sefer* on *Chullin* that has many detailed photos that explain everything a person needs to know about animals in order to learn and understand the *masechta*. Rav Belsky was very involved with the *piskei halachah* in the *sefer*, and the author attested to me that Rav Belsky knew every millimeter of the cow's body. Learning *tereifos* in general is very difficult; most people have no connection to cows and don't know the first thing about how their internal systems operate. But for Rav Belsky, answering a question on a cow's intestines was as simple as taking a walk down the street. He was Torah, general knowledge, and interpersonal relationships all in one.

◆ ◆ ◆

The nature of being a *rav* means that you will inevitably receive emergency queries from time to time. This happened to me one day, and after going through the list of *poskim* with whom I could address the question, I decided to call Rav Belsky.

Which I did.

The phone rang a number of times and went to the answering machine. I didn't really feel comfortable leaving Rav Belsky a message, but it was an emergency question and in the end I left him a message.

The next day my phone rang from an international number. I answered and heard the words, "This is Yisroel Belsky returning your call…"

Another time someone called me with an emergency at two in the morning. It was a very complicated *she'eilah*, and I had no idea what to tell the people on the other end of the line. I told them that I would get back to them as soon as possible, then I sat there with the phone in my hand and tried to decide who I could disturb in the middle of the night. Flipping idly through one of my *sefarim* that was lying on the table, I began going through the pages of *haskamos* that had been given to me by a wide range of *rabbanim*. Seconds later I turned a page and saw Rav Belsky's *haskamah*. There was a number on the page.

I called it.

He answered, listened to the question, and gave me a *psak* five seconds later (which was *l'kula, baruch Hashem*), and I was able to call the people back a few minutes later with a clear answer.

It's good to have people like Rav Belsky on the other side of the ocean, I said to myself before finally going to sleep for the night.

◆ ◆ ◆

There was a man working for one of Rav Belsky's *talmidim*. At some point the *talmid* overheard his employee badmouthing his rebbi. The man was angry at Rav Belsky because he had *paskened* against him in a *din Torah* and didn't hesitate to tell the world what he thought of America's preeminent *posek*.

"If you say one more word of *lashon hara* about my rebbi," the *talmid* told the employee, "I am going to fire you."

The employee, possibly erroneously thinking that his boss was joking, kept on talking badly of Rav Belsky.

"You're fired," his boss said. "Please take your stuff and leave immediately!"

The employee obeyed his boss, left the premises, and promptly made his way to see Rav Belsky.

"Your *talmid* fired me," he complained.

"Why did he do that?"

The man had no choice and told Rav Belsky the entire story. Rav Belsky promptly picked up the phone and called his *talmid*.

"Listen," he said, "it's more important to me that another Jew has *parnassah* than that you preserve my *kavod*. Please take him back."

◆ ◆ ◆

A few decades ago someone asked Rav Belsky how many times he had finished learning *Shas*.

"About fifty times," he replied.

Rav Belsky was an exceptional *masmid*, to the point that he finished *Shas* dozens of times, yet at the same time he sat with thousands of people for thousands of hours.

There was a man who suffered from OCD. It used to take him an hour just to get through *Krias Shema*. Rav Belsky sat down with the man and removed a *Shulchan Aruch* from the shelf. He gently guided the man to a new understanding of what he needed to do when reciting *Shema*, and he did it with all the patience in the world.

He was able to do this because he understood what OCD is and he understood what the *chumros* involved in saying *Shema* are. He combined the fifth section of *Shulchan Aruch* with an incredible understanding of human psychology and a powerful grasp of

Torah issues, and he did it with gentleness and a smile. There was no rush when you spoke to him. He gave every person as much time as he needed. When you sat with him, nothing else existed in the world besides the two of you. Do you realize how unique that is in today's day and age?

He was the *rosh yeshivah* of Torah Vodaath, he wrote thousands of halachic responsa, he was majorly involved in the *kollel*, had a connection with a very large percentage of the *bachurim*, gave *shiurim* to *baalebatim*, was a *dayan*, and was a major force in the OU. With all of that, he still had time for the people who came to see him. He was so busy, yet he personified a term used by the *Chovos HaLevavos*: *mei menuchos*, "calm waters." He was always *mei menuchos* when you spoke with him. You didn't get the feeling that there were a million thoughts and ideas running through his mind and that he had to leave any second and that he really didn't have the time but was doing you a major favor and shaving off some of his precious minutes for you.

He had time management down to a science. And he had *chesed* down to a science.

Afterword

As I mentioned earlier, Leah Imeinu was the first person to give thanks to the Ribbono shel Olam. Upon further examination, this is not the case — others certainly thanked Hashem before Leah did, leading one to ask what the Gemara means by telling us this. The answer is not that Leah was the first person to ever thank Hashem. It's that Leah was the first to thank Hashem for the things in her life that seemed to be negative.

Recently I realized something very important.

Rabbi Yochanan is the rabbi in the Gemara (*Berachos* 7b) who tells us this piece of information. I don't think it is a coincidence that Rabbi Yochanan is the author of this idea, considering the fact that he had a very challenging life — we are told that all his children died in his lifetime — yet clearly considered that whatever Hashem did to be for the best.

As you no doubt know from reading this book, I travel to the States very often. A few years ago I landed on Rosh Chodesh Nissan. I went to daven Shacharis at a shul in Manhattan. It was snowing outside, and when I left the shul I slipped, broke my ankle, and had to be taken to the hospital. By the time we reached St. Luke's hospital, my ankle was three times its usual size. The doctor came to examine me and give me a diagnosis.

When he finished the examination, he said, "Rabbi, can I ask you a question?"

"Certainly," I replied. "What do you want to know?"

"I'm just curious why you're smiling right now."

"Because I know this is for the best."

The doctor looked at me as if I had lost my mind.

The truth is, the fall had forced me to make a general *cheshbon hanefesh* and to rethink the way I did things all across the board. It taught me to slow down and to be more careful. To understand that a person has to take care of himself.

It's a funny thing. When I was a teenager, I trained to run in the Olympics. At one point I broke my leg, after which I shifted my interests and began learning Torah. I broke my leg again years later after I had my first child. Then, too, that accident shifted my life in a completely different direction. And this time as well, in the wake of my broken ankle on a snow-covered street of New York, I found myself rethinking many things and coming up with a whole new set of conclusions.

This reminds me of a story in *Maseches Niddah* about a man who was running to catch his ship. He broke his leg, which caused him to miss the boat. The man cursed Hashem, but later the man found out that the ship had sunk and he realized how breaking his leg had saved his life.

As it says in davening, "*Oseh nifla'os levado ki l'olam chasdo* — He does wonders by Himself, for His kindness endures forever." Hashem does wonders by Himself — *He* knows what's He's doing, but in many cases *we* don't understand how miraculous it is. But even when we don't necessarily understand what happened or is happening to us, we still have to remember that it is good, that whatever Hashem does for us is always for the best.

◆ ◆ ◆

This important concept was demonstrated to me once again

after a meeting I recently had with a wealthy businessman at his office in a skyscraper on Broadway in Manhattan. I had been trying to meet with this man for quite some time with no success. But I kept on trying and eventually it happened. The meeting lasted quite a while — we were together for about an hour — and I really needed to leave because I was scheduled to give a *shiur* in Flatbush that night, but the man I was with kept on asking me for yet another Torah idea, and I was loath to interrupt what was turning into such a productive meeting.

"One more piece of Torah, Rabbi," he said to me, and I chose to say a *shiur* on the concept of how everything that Hashem does is always for the best. As I delivered the *shiur* to my audience of one, I couldn't help but remember how, so many times after I'd spoken on the subject, seemingly "bad" things had happened shortly afterward, as if Hashem were testing me to see if I really believed what I was saying to everyone else.

I know that I'm setting myself up here to be tested, I thought to myself, *but what can I do? I feel that it needs to be said!*

I left the office a few minutes later and hailed a cab for what should have been a relatively short ride to Brooklyn.

From his accent, the driver didn't appear to have been in the country for longer than a month, and when I gave him the address, East Thirty-fourth Street and Avenue L, in Flatbush, he drove us to an entirely different section of Brooklyn, with no idea where we were and no idea how to get us where we needed to go. He didn't even know how to use a GPS, could barely speak a word of English (which made it extremely difficult for the two of us to communicate), and the doors were locked, which made it impossible for me to leave.

After I determined that there seemed to be little chance of my escaping the taxi until the driver allowed me to leave, I looked out the window and decided that this might be for the best since one glance at the neighborhood where we had ended up convinced me that I was probably better off in the cab, lost though we might be.

The minutes crawled by as we drove around in what seemed

like circles. Twenty minutes passed, then half an hour, then forty-five minutes. The meter kept ticking, raising the fare higher and higher, and things were not looking good for me or the *shiur* I was supposed to deliver. I tried to be firm with the driver, telling him to stop and get directions. He listened to me and asked someone in the street how to get where we needed to go, but either they weren't the world's clearest directions or, more likely, the driver hadn't understood them.

And so we bungled on for what seemed like an eternity, unhappy with each other, he blaming me for not being able to direct him where I needed to go, and I explaining to him in a somewhat loud tone of voice that it was the taxi driver's job to know where to go. He looked me in the eye through the mirror and gave me a cutting *mussar shmuess*. In retrospect, this was appropriate since it all happened during the Aseres Yemei Teshuvah. I don't know how a taxi driver from halfway across the world knew me well enough to zero right in on the faults I needed to correct, but suffice it to say, that *shmuess* was one of a kind and didn't endear him to me in any way.

Finally, after what seemed like forever, we got near enough to where I needed to go, and I told him that he could drop me off right where we were. He pulled over to the side of the road, I paid him, got out of the cab, and then, before I could pull my things out of the trunk, he merged with the traffic and drove off into the night with my tallis and tefillin still in his car.

Things were going from bad to worse!

I would have written down the cab's license plate number, but I was so upset by what had just happened to me that by the time my mind started working again, I had to find a pen, and by the time that occurred, my wonderful driver was long gone. I dropped everything I had been carrying with me onto the ground and began running after the cab, but he was driving too fast and I soon realized that chasing him was pointless. I returned to the spot where I had dropped my belongings, only to find that the rest of my things were now gone as well.

Things had now gone from worse to terrible!

Five minutes before I had lost my tallis and tefillin. Now I had lost my computer and clothing as well. In the space of a few minutes I had lost everything I had brought with me to America! I stood there in the middle of Brooklyn and didn't know what to do with myself.

Looking up at the sky, I said to myself, *Kol man d'avid Rachmana l'tav avid — Whatever Hashem does is for the best. No question about it!*

I didn't stop at saying it once. I stood there repeating that line over and over again. I must have said it to myself a good one hundred times.

Whatever Hashem does is for the best! Whatever Hashem does is for the best! Whatever Hashem does is for the best!!!

It took me a while, but eventually I felt that I was standing on firm ground again. Knowing that I needed to get to the *shiur* — no doubt people were waiting for me and had been for a while — I began walking down the street in the direction that I needed to go.

Suddenly I stopped in my tracks, and a smile crossed my face.

There were my belongings — the computer case and luggage — sitting near a garbage can, seemingly untouched and still in one piece. Apparently, someone had not been happy that I'd left my things in front of his house and had moved them somewhere else. They hadn't been stolen, just moved. This was very good news.

Hefting my computer bag onto my shoulder with one hand and wheeling my suitcase with the other, I strode off into the wilds of Flatbush, determined to give that *shiur*, come what may.

I found the house and apologized for arriving late, explaining how the taxi driver was a newly arrived immigrant to the States, hadn't known English or how to work a GPS, had taken us to the wrong part of Brooklyn, and had driven off with my tallis and tefillin. The people sitting in the room were shocked by the story, and one of them voiced the question that was clearly on every one of their minds.

"Rabbi Travis, how are you so calm?"

"I am so calm because I know that whatever happens is for the best."

My host filed a complaint online against the taxi company on my behalf, but I did not have high hopes that I would ever see my tallis bag again, especially considering the personal feelings of animosity that existed between the driver and me. Still, I appreciated his efforts.

I gave the *shiur*, stressing over and over that there was no question that everything that had happened that evening was for the best, and then I left the house and moved on with the next phase of my trip, after borrowing a pair of tefillin from one of the people at the *shiur*.

◆ ◆ ◆

I was in Monsey two days later when I had an idea. One of the reasons I had come to the States was to fundraise for a *bein hazemanim kollel* where about thirty *avreichim* were learning. Each *yungerman* was paid five hundred dollars for his participation. While on the phone with my *chavrusa* in Yerushalayim, I said, "Listen, do me a favor. I lost my tallis and tefillin and need to buy another set. Please ask the *avreichim* to put aside their *ma'aser* for me to use to purchase another pair of tefillin."

I felt that this was a valid idea, especially considering the fact that I had lost my tallis and tefillin while raising money for this particular *kollel.*

Soon after I hung up with Yerushalayim, my phone rang, this time with a local number. It was someone calling from the taxi company to tell me that they had found my tallis and tefillin.

New developments in hand, I called my *chavrusa* in Yerushalayim and told him that instead of using the *ma'aser* for me to purchase a new set of tefillin, he should give it instead to one of the men who learned in my *erev Yom Kippur kollel*, and who I knew had a very difficult time making *parnassah*. Some years I had been able to give him some extra money to help him buy food for Yom Tov, but so far I hadn't managed to help him out this year.

"So give him the *ma'aser*," I told the *kollel* organizer.

"Will do."

When I ran into this particular *yungerman* after Yom Tov, he told me that were it not for the money I had arranged for him, they would not have had food for Yom Tov.

◆ ◆ ◆

I learned so many lessons from this story.

Number one: Hashem moved heaven and earth so that a *yungerman* in Yerushalayim should receive the money he needed for Yom Tov.

Number two: The taxi driver I had the good fortune to take a ride with gave me a *mussar shmuess* delineating the exact elements of personality that I needed to work on, just in time for Yom Kippur. I only realized this a few days later, but there was no question that it was so.

Number three: When I stood on that Flatbush street after the taxi driver drove away from me with my tefillin in his trunk and my computer case stolen, I suddenly understood how completely powerless we are. Everything was gone from one second to the next!

Baruch Hashem, I withstood the test and recognized that "*kal man d'avid Rachmana l'tav avid*" — that everything Hashem does is for the best.

In my opinion, this is the message of our generation: the concept of "*kal man d'avid.*"

So many people are experiencing challenges in their lives. I hear their stories all the time. I am here to tell you that if you search for the good within your trials, you will find it, no question at all.

I was hit by a car. Nobody thought I would live. Yet that episode in my life brought me to a completely different place, shaping my existence in a direction I never even dreamed of!

After seeing the entire sequence of events, there is no question that everything that happens to us is all for the best!

Despite the fact that I myself have been working on this very idea for most of my life, it is still not an easy challenge to master, which is why I have begun giving a daily *shiur* on this very topic, constantly reminding myself of what I should never forget.

A few years ago I was talking to my *chavrusa*, and I told him how I had noticed an interesting phenomenon.

"What's that?"

"It seems to me that every summer I am faced with a *nisayon* that I have to overcome, and after it's all over and been dealt with, the *kollel* usually has a huge surge of *hatzlachah*."

He listened quietly to my theory, which I foolishly concluded by saying, "I wonder what is going to happen this year."

An hour later a close relative called to let me know that she had fallen and needed to go to the hospital, reinforcing what I had known even then — that I shouldn't have said such a thing.

I met her at the hospital, and when we were finally sitting in front of a doctor, we were told that she needed an emergency operation, but that there was no way it could be scheduled for at least another three weeks.

"How could that be?" I asked the doctor. "We have an emergency!"

"Right now," he explained, "the majority of the specialists who can handle this kind of complicated surgery are overseas in Nepal helping the people there who were hurt in the recent earthquake."

I was incredulous at the thought that Israel had just sent virtually all their top specialists across the world to help another country, leaving their own people with no medical staff in case of an emergency. It seemed to me that this was a clear case of misguided *chesed*, but this was not the time or place for a *mussar shmuess*.

"What can you do for us?" I implored the hospital staff.

"At this point, there's really nothing to do other than wait until the right doctor returns from the mountains of Nepal."

It was like a bad dream, but we were awake. (Bad dreams are always worse when you're awake.) I could only think of one possible move that would help change the situation: I immediately began saying and thinking, "*Ein od milvado* — There is no one but Him," over and over again. I did this for about an hour. "*Ein od milvado... Ein od milvado... Ein od Milvado...*" Over and over.

My relative needed a *yeshuah*, the doctors weren't able to help, but Hashem could do anything in the world.

Soon afterward I had the idea of calling someone I know who works with Rabbi Elimelech Firer, the legendary conduit between the medical world and the layman. Rabbi Firer listened to the whole story, then told me that he might be able to arrange for one of the only specialists who was still in the country to treat my relative. Soon enough, he got back to me with the good news that he had been able to arrange for the operation that was needed so badly.

Being a person who likes to take care of things as soon as possible, I kept asking the hospital when I could pay for the upcoming operation. Nobody would give me a clear answer, which meant that I still owed money by the day my relative was scheduled to be wheeled into the operating room.

We were all set to begin, when the surgeon who was to perform the operation approached me and said, "Rabbi Travis, I can't begin the operation until it is paid for."

My relative had already been wheeled into the operating room when he told me this bit of news — exactly the type of news I had been hoping to prevent with my continued questions about where and how to pay.

"I have been asking people over and over again how to pay," I told him, "but nobody has given me a straight answer."

"It shouldn't be a big deal," he replied. "Just go into the office here in the hospital that deals with privately paid procedures, and they should be able to help you out."

I found the office and told them the story.

Hearing the urgency in my voice, the people in the office immediately called my insurance agency to facilitate the needed paperwork, but were unable to get through to anyone there. Meanwhile, my relative was lying on the operating table. I called them again and again, but nobody picked up the phone. I tried calling the insurance company's main branch, but was told that they couldn't help me and that I had to get in touch with my local branch.

My relative had been on the operating table for an hour, nobody was answering at the insurance place, and the doctor refused to proceed until we had paid for the surgery. I felt helpless.

Suddenly I remembered that there was one thing I could do. I could say *"Ein od milvado,"* which I did for the next half an hour, at which point I thought of calling someone who lived in Har Nof and asking them to walk into the insurance office and speak to someone there directly.

The doctor was about to leave for the day when word came that the payment had been settled and he could operate.

◆　◆　◆

My relative ended up needing yet another operation. Unfortunately her *teudat zehut* (Israeli ID card) had gotten lost in the hospital during the craziness of the first operation, and she needed to get another ID card, an extremely difficult if not impossible thing to do without the presence of the owner of the card. But my relative was in the hospital and couldn't get to Israel's Interior Ministry, where the card would be issued. Which meant that it would have to be done without her.

I went down to Ministry of the Interior armed with all the many papers that I needed to sign. When I was finally seated at the desk that I needed, I was told by the formidable "Guardian of the Holy Signature" that she couldn't help me since my relative's pictures were not "new enough." We had used them for her previous ID card, but suddenly they were not new enough, and I was up against a wall. But I didn't have the luxury of leaving without the necessary documents and told them as much.

"If you don't leave," one of them threatened me, "I will call the police and have them evict you."

"Go right ahead," I replied. "While you are at it, why not tell the police that you are unwilling to give a new ID card to a woman in a life-threatening situation, all because of a technical issue with her pictures, which as you know were fit for use just a short time ago."

"She needs to come here herself," one of them yelled at me, "or make new pictures!"

"She would love to do that," I replied, "but she is currently lying in a hospital bed and cannot go anywhere!"

In the middle of all the chaos, as they threatened and blustered and raged at me, I quietly began repeating the words *"ein od milvado"* to myself over and over. I ignored them as they yelled at me to leave and made it clear that I would not be going anywhere until I had the documents in hand that would allow my relative to receive the operation she needed.

The debate continued unabated for an hour and a half, with me unwilling to leave and the staff yelling at me. And all the while I was whispering the words *"ein od milvado"* to myself.

Finally, one of the other clerks, who happened to be a religious individual, spoke up and said, "Look, this man's relative needs an emergency operation! Why don't you just give them the documents they need?"

"Okay," the Guardian of the Holy Signature said agreeably and proceeded to do exactly that, stamping the forms and facilitating the process so that I'd be able to receive my relative's ID card on the spot.

Smoke had been coming out of this woman's ears not twenty minutes before, along with bountiful threats involving the police and who knew what else, yet here she was suddenly doing exactly what she promised she wouldn't do, and she was doing it *"al mei menuchos,"* peacefully, graciously, and with a smile of goodwill on her face!

At that moment I came to an understanding.

When a person truly comprehends the power of *"ein od milvado,"* he is no longer confined by the limitations of the physical world. He has risen above it all, to a place where anything can happen. The moment a person reaches the clarity that Hashem is the only One, walls will be removed and obstacles will disappear.

This happened to me on the beach in Brazil just after my wedding, and this happened to me again just now. Grasping that everything is dependent on Hashem is the key to life. And knowing, really knowing, that whatever happens, whatever we face — *gam zu l'tovah.*

That's what I am hoping that every one of you reading this *sefer* will take out of this. To recognize that every single thing that happens to us every single day is ultimately for the good.